Quick
& Easy

Practical Cookery

Quick
& Easy

p

This is a Parragon Book
This edition published in 2002

Parragon
Queen Street House
4 Queen Street
Bath BA1 1HE, UK

Copyright © Parragon 2001

ISBN: 0-75258-313-1 (Hardback)
ISBN: 0-75258-319-0 (Paperback)

Printed in China

NOTE

Cup measurements in this book are for American cups.
Tablespoons are assumed tobe 15ml. Unless otherwise stated,
milk is assumed to be full fat, eggs are medium
and pepper is freshly ground black pepper.

Recipes using uncooked eggs should be
avoided by infants, the elderly, pregnant women and anyone
suffering from an illness.

Contents

Introduction 8

Soups

Starters & Snacks

Fish & Seafood

Meat Dishes

Chicken & Poultry

Pasta & Rice

Puddings & Desserts

Introduction

This book is designed to appeal to anyone who wants a wholesome but quick and easy diet, and includes many recipes suitable for vegetarians and vegans. Its main aim is to show people that, with a little forethought, it is possible to spend very little time in the kitchen while still enjoying

Appetizing Food

The recipes collected together come from all over the world; some of the Indian and barbeque dishes featured require marinating, often overnight, but it is worth remembering that their actual cooking time is very short once the marinade has been absorbed. The more exotic dishes on offer are balanced by some traditional dishes which are sure to firm family favourites. If you want fast food for everyday meals, or you are short on time and want to prepare a tasty dinner party treat, there is something for everybody in this book.

To save time in the kitchen, always make sure that you have the requisite basics in your cupboard. By keeping a stock of staple foodstuffs

such as rice, pasta, spices and herbs, you can easily turn your hand to any number of these recipes.

KEEPING A FULL STORE-CUPBOARD

Flour

You will need to keep a selection of flour: Self-raising and Wholemeal (Wholewheat) are the most useful. You may also like to keep some rice flour and cornflour (cornstarch) for thickening sauces and to add to cakes, biscuits and puddings. Buckwheat, chick pea (garbanzo bean) and soya flours can also be bought. These are useful for combining with other flours to add different flavours and textures.

Grains and Rice

A good variety of grains is essential. For rice, choose from long-grain, basmati, Italian arborio, short-grain, and wild rice. Look out for fragrant Thai rice, jasmine rice and combinations of different varieties to add colour and texture to your dishes.

When choosing your rice, remember that brown rice is a better source of vitamin B1 and fibre.

Other grains add variety to the diet. Try to include some barley millet, bulgur wheat, polenta, oats, semolina, sago and tapioca.

Pasta

Pasta is very popular nowadays, and there are many types and shapes to choose from. Keep a good selection, such as basic lasagne sheets, tagliatelle or fettuccine (flat ribbons) and spaghetti. for a change, sample some of the many fresh pastas now available. Better still, make your own – handrolling pasta can be very satisfying, and you can buy a special machine for rolling the dough and cutting certain shapes.

Pulses (Legumes)

Pulses (legumes) are a valuable source of protein, vitamins and minerals. Stock up on soya beans, haricot (navy) beans, red kidney beans, cannellini beans, chick peas (garbanzo beans), lentils, split peas and butter beans. Buy dried pulses (legumes) for soaking and cooking yourself, or canned varieties for speed and convenience.

Herbs

A good selection of herbs is important for adding variety to your cooking. Fresh herbs are preferable to dried, but it is essential to have dried ones in stock as a useful back-up. You should store dried basil, thyme, bay leaves, oregano, rosemary, mixed herbs and bouquet garni.

Chillies

These come both fresh and dried and in many colours. The 'hotness' varies so use with caution. The seeds are hottest and are usually discarded. Chilli powder should also be used sparingly. Check whether the powder is pure chilli or a chilli seasoning or blend, which should be milder.

Nuts and Seeds

As well as adding protein, vitamins and useful fats to the diet, nuts and seeds add important flavour and texture to vegetarian meals. Make sure that you keep a good supply of nuts such as hazelnuts, pine kernels (nuts) and walnuts. Coconut is useful too.

For your seed collection, have sesame, sunflower, pumpkin and poppy. Pumpkin seeds in particular are a good source of zinc.

Dried Fruits

Currants, raisins, sultanas (golden raisins), dates, apples, apricots, figs, pears, peaches, prunes, paw-paws (papayas), mangoes, figs, bananas and pineapples can all be purchased dried and can be used in lots of different recipes. When buying dried fruits, look for untreated varieties: for example, buy figs that have not been rolled in sugar, and choose unsulphured apricots, if they are available.

Oils and Fats

Oils are useful for adding subtle flavourings to foods, so it is a good idea to have a selection in your store-cupboard. Use a light olive oil for cooking and extra-virgin olive oil for salad dressings. Use sunflower oil as a good general-purpose oil.

Ragu Sauce

3 tbsp olive oil

45 g/1½ oz butter

2 large onions, chopped

4 celery stalks, sliced thinly

175 g/6 oz streaky bacon, chopped

2 garlic cloves, chopped

500 g/1 lb 2 oz minced (ground) lean beef

2 tbsp tomato purée (paste)

1 tbsp flour

400 g/14 oz can chopped tomatoes

150 ml/¼ pint /⅔ cup beef stock

150 ml/¼ pint /⅔ cup red wine

2 tsp dried oregano

½ tsp freshly grated nutmeg

salt and pepper

1 Heat the oil and butter in a pan over a medium heat. Add the onions, celery and bacon and fry for 5 minutes, stirring.

2 Stir in the garlic and minced (ground) beef and cook, stirring until the meat has lost its redness. Lower the heat and cook for 10 minutes, stirring.

3 Increase the heat to medium, stir in the tomato purée (paste) and the flour and cook for 1-2 minutes. Stir in the tomatoes, stock and wine and bring to the boil, stirring. Season and stir in the oregano and nutmeg. Cover and simmer for 45 minutes, stirring. The sauce is now ready to use.

Introduction

Sesame oil is wonderful in stir-fries; hazelnut and walnut oils are superb in salad dressings. Oils and fats add flavour to foods, and contain the important fat-soluble vitamins A, D, E and K. Remember all fats and oils are high in calories, and that oils are higher in calories than butter or margarine.

Vinegars

Choose three or four vinegars – red or white wine, cider, light malt, tarragon, sherry or balsamic vinegar, to name just a few. Each will add its own character to your recipes.

Mustards

Mustards are made from black, brown or white mustard seeds which are ground and mixed with spices. Meaux mustard is made from mixed mustard seeds and has a grainy texture with a warm, taste. Dijon mustard, made from husked and ground mustard seeds, has a sharp flavour. Its versatility in salads and with barbecues makes it ideal for the vegetarian. German mustard is mild and is best used in Scandinavian and German dishes.

Bottled Sauces

Soy sauce is widely used in Eastern cookery and is made from fermented yellow soya beans mixed with wheat, salt, yeast and sugar. Light soy sauce tends to be rather salty, whereas dark soy sauce tends to be sweeter. Teriyaki sauce gives an authentic Japanese flavouring to stir-fries. Black bean and yellow bean sauces add an instant authentic Chinese flavour to stir-fries.

Storing Spices

Your basic stock of spices should include fresh ginger and garlic, chilli powder, turmeric, paprika, cloves, cardamom, black pepper, ground coriander and ground cumin. The powdered spices will keep very well in airtight containers, while the fresh ginger and garlic will keep for 7-10 days in the refrigerator. Other useful items, to be acquired as your repertoire increases, are cumin seeds (black as well as white), onion seeds, mustard seeds, cloves, cinnamon, dried red chillies, fenugreek, vegetable ghee and garam masala (a mixture of spices that can either be bought ready-made or home-made in quantity for use whenever required).

Using Spices

You can use spices whole, ground, roasted, fried, or mixed with yogurt to marinate meat and poultry. One spice can alter the flavour of a dish and a combination of several can produce different colours and textures. The quantities of spices shown in the recipes are merely a guide. Increase or decrease them as you wish, especially in the cases of salt and chilli powder, which are a matter of taste.

Many of the recipes in this book call for ground spices, which are generally available in supermarkets as well as in Indian and Pakistani grocers. In India whole spices are ground at home, and there is no doubt that freshly ground spices do make a noticeable difference to the taste.

Introduction

Some recipes require roasted spices. In India, this is done on a *thawa*, but you can use a heavy, ideally cast-iron frying-pan (skillet). No water or oil is needed: the spices are simply dry-roasted whole while the pan is shaken to stop them burning on the bottom of the pan.

Remember that long cooking over a lowish heat will improve the taste of the food as it allows the spices to be absorbed. This is why re-heating dishes the following day is no problem for most Indian food.

USEFUL ORIENTAL INGREDIENTS

Bamboo Shoots

These are added for texture, as they have very little flavour. Available in cans, they are a common ingredient in Chinese cooking.

Beansprouts

These are mung bean shoots, which are very nutritious, containing many vitamins. They add crunch to a recipe and are widely available. Do not overcook them, as they wilt and do not add texture to the dish.

Black Beans

These are soy beans and are very salty. They can be bought and crushed with salt and then rinsed or used in the form of a ready-made sauce for convenience.

Chinese Beans

These long beans may be eaten whole and are very tender. French (green) beans may also be used.

Chinese Five-Spice Powder

An aromatic blend of cinnamon, cloves, star anise, fennel and brown peppercorns. It is often used in marinades.

Chinese Leaves

A light green leaf with a sweet flavour. It can be found readily in most supermarkets.

Hoisin Sauce

A dark brown, sweet, thick sauce that is widely available. It is made from spices, soy sauce, garlic and chilli and is often served as a dipping sauce.

Lychees

These are worth buying fresh, as they are easy to prepare. Inside the inedible skin is a fragrant white fruit. Lychees are available canned and are a classic ingredient.

Mango

Choose a ripe mango for its sweet, scented flesh. If a mango is under-ripe when bought, leave it in a sunny place for a few days before using.

Noodles

The Chinese use several varieties of noodle. You will probably find it easier to use the readily available dried varieties, such as egg noodles, which are yellow, rice stick noodles, which are white and very fine, or transparent noodles, which are opaque when dry and turn transparent on cooking.

However, cellophane or rice noodles may be used instead.

Oyster Sauce

Readily available, this sauce is made from oysters, salt, seasonings and cornflour (cornstarch) and is brown in colour.

Pak Choi

Also known as Chinese cabbage, this has a mild, slightly bitter flavour.

Rice Vinegar

This has a mild, sweet taste that is quite delicate. It is available in some supermarkets, but if not available use cider vinegar instead.

Rice Wine

This is similar to dry sherry in colour, alcohol content and smell, but it is worth buying rice wine for its distinctive flavour.

Sesame Oil

This is made from roasted sesame seeds and has an intense flavour. It burns easily and is therefore added at the end of cooking for flavour, and is not used for frying.

Soy Sauce

This is widely available, but it is worth buying a good grade of sauce. It is produced in both light and dark varieties – the former is used with fish and vegetables for a lighter colour and flavour, while the latter, being darker, richer, saltier and more intense, is used as a dipping sauce or with strongly flavoured meats.

Star Anise

This is an eight-pointed, star-shaped pod with a strong aniseed flavour. The spice is also available ground. If a pod is added to a dish, it should be removed before serving.

Szechuan Pepper

This is quite hot and spicy and should be used sparingly. It is red in colour and is readily available.

Tofu (Bean Curd)

This soya bean paste is available in several forms. The cake variety, which is soft and spongy and a white-grey colour, is used in this book. It is very bland, but adds texture to dishes and is perfect for absorbing all the other flavours in the dish.

Water Chestnuts

These are flat and round and can usually only be purchased in cans, already peeled. They add a delicious crunch to dishes and have a sweet flavour.

Yellow Beans

Again a soy bean and very salty. Use a variety that is chunky rather than smooth.

Basic Recipes

These recipes form the basis of several of the dishes contained throughout this book. Many of these basic recipes can be made in advance and stored in the refrigerator until required, so that cooking a dish can be even quicker!

Basic Tomato Sauce

2 tbsp olive oil

1 small onion, chopped

1 garlic clove, chopped

400 g/14 oz can chopped tomatoes

2 tbsp chopped parsley

1 tsp dried oregano

2 bay leaves

2 tbsp tomato purée (paste)

1 tsp sugar

salt and pepper

1 Heat the oil in a pan over a medium heat and fry the onion for 2-3 minutes or until translucent. Add the garlic and fry for 1 minute.

2 Stir in the chopped tomatoes, parsley, oregano, bay leaves, tomato purée (paste), sugar, and salt and pepper to taste.

3 Bring the sauce to the boil, then simmer, uncovered, for 15–20 minutes or until the sauce has reduced by half. Taste the sauce and adjust the seasoning if necessary. Discard the bay leaves just before serving.

Béchamel Sauce

300 ml/½ pint/1¼ cups milk

2 bay leaves

3 cloves

1 small onion

60 g/2 oz/¼ cup butter, plus extra for greasing

45 g/1½ oz/6 tbsp flour

300 ml/½ pint/1¼ cups single (light) cream

large pinch of freshly grated nutmeg

salt and pepper

1 Pour the milk into a small pan and add the bay leaves. Press the cloves into the onion, add to the pan and bring the milk to the boil. Remove the pan from the heat and set aside to cool.

2 Strain the milk into a jug and rinse the pan. Melt the butter in the pan and stir in the flour. Stir for 1 minute, then gradually pour on the milk, stirring constantly. Cook the sauce for 3 minutes, then pour on the cream and bring it to the boil. Remove from the heat and season with nutmeg, salt and pepper to taste.

Lamb Sauce

2 tbsp olive oil

1 large onion, sliced

2 celery stalks, thinly sliced

500 g/1 lb 2 oz lean lamb, minced (ground)

3 tbsp tomato purée (paste)

150 g/5½ oz bottled sun-dried tomatoes, drained and chopped

1 tsp dried oregano

1 tbsp red wine vinegar

150 ml/¼ pint/⅔ cup chicken stock

salt and pepper

1 Heat the oil in a frying pan (skillet) over a medium heat and fry the onion and celery until the onion is translucent, about 3 minutes. Add the lamb and fry, stirring frequently, until it browns.

2 Stir in the tomato purée (paste), sun-dried tomatoes, oregano, vinegar and stock. Season with salt and pepper to taste.

3 Bring to the boil and cook, uncovered, for 20 minutes or until the meat has absorbed the stock. Taste and adjust the seasoning if necessary.

Cheese Sauce

25 g/1 oz/2 tbsp butter

1 tbsp flour

250 ml/9 fl oz/1 cup milk

2 tbsp single (light) cream

pinch of freshly grated nutmeg

45 g/1½ oz mature (sharp) Cheddar, grated

1 tbsp freshly grated Parmesan

salt and pepper

1 Melt the butter in a pan, stir in the flour and cook for 1 minute. Gradually pour on the milk, stirring all the time. Stir in the cream and season the sauce with nutmeg, salt and pepper to taste.

2 Simmer the sauce for 5 minutes to reduce, then remove it from the heat and stir in the cheeses. Stir until the cheeses have melted and blended into the sauce.

Espagnole Sauce

2 tbsp butter

25 g/1 oz/¼ cup plain (all-purpose) flour

1 tsp tomato purée (paste)

250 ml/9 fl oz/1⅛ cups hot veal stock

1 tbsp Madeira

1½ tsp white wine vinegar

2 tbsp olive oil

25 g/1 oz bacon, diced

25 g/1 oz carrot, diced

25 g/1 oz onion, diced

15 g/½ oz celery, diced

15 g/½ oz leek, diced

15 g/½ oz fennel, diced

1 fresh thyme sprig

1 bay leaf

1 Melt the butter in a pan, add the flour and cook, stirring, until lightly coloured. Add the tomato purée (paste), then stir in the hot veal stock, Madeira and white wine vinegar and cook for 2 minutes.

2 Heat the oil in a separate pan, add the bacon, carrot, onion, celery, leek, fennel, thyme sprig and bay leaf and fry until the vegetables have softened. Remove the vegetables from the pan with a slotted spoon and drain thoroughly. Add the vegetables to the sauce and leave to simmer for 4 hours, stirring occasionally. Strain the sauce before using.

Italian Red Wine Sauce

150 ml/¼ pint /⅝ cup Brown Stock (see page 30)

150 ml/¼ pint /⅔ cup Espagnole Sauce (see left)

125 ml/4 fl oz/½ cup red wine

2 tbsp red wine vinegar

4 tbsp shallots, chopped

1 bay leaf

1 thyme sprig

pepper

1 First make a demi-glace sauce. Put the Brown Stock and Espagnole Sauce in a pan and heat for 10 minutes, stirring occasionally.

2 Meanwhile, put the red wine, red wine vinegar, shallots, bay leaf and thyme in a pan, bring to the boil and reduce by three-quarters.

3 Strain the demi-glace sauce and add to the pan containing the Red Wine Sauce and leave to simmer for 20 minutes, stirring occasionally. Season with pepper to taste and strain the sauce before using.

How to Use This Book

Each recipe contains a wealth of useful information, including a breakdown of nutritional quantities, preparation and cooking times, and level of difficulty. All of this information is explained in detail below.

This amount of time represents the actual cooking time.

The nutritional information provided for each recipe is per serving or per portion. Optional ingredients, variations or serving suggestions have not been included in the calculations.

The number of chef's hats represents the difficulty of each recipe, ranging from easy (1 chef's hat) to difficult (5 chef's hats).

This amount of time represents the preparation of ingredients, including cooling, chilling and soaking times.

The ingredients for each recipe are listed in the order that they are used.

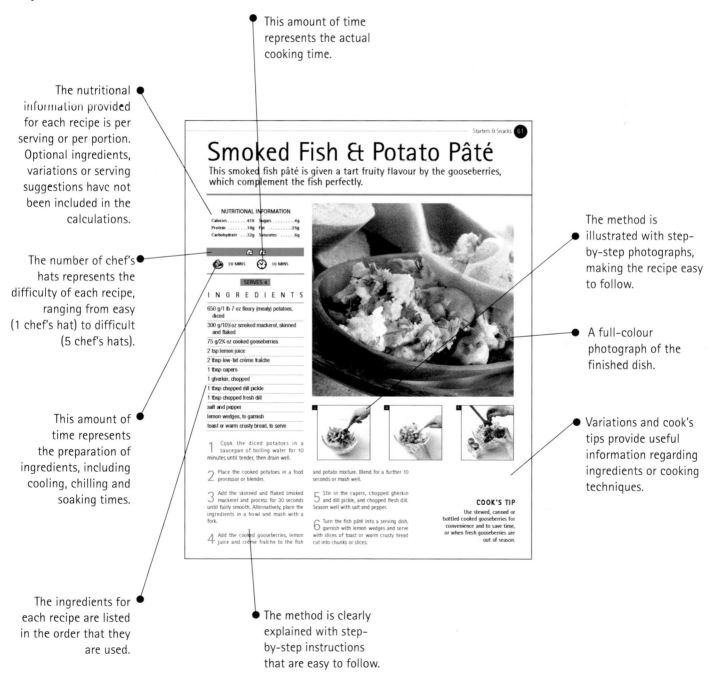

Starters & Snacks 61

Smoked Fish & Potato Pâté

This smoked fish pâté is given a tart fruity flavour by the gooseberries, which complement the fish perfectly.

NUTRITIONAL INFORMATION

Calories ....418 Sugars 4g
Protein ....18g Fat 25g
Carbohydrate ...32g Saturates 6g

20 MINS   10 MINS

SERVES 4

INGREDIENTS

650 g/1 lb 7 oz floury (mealy) potatoes, diced
300 g/10½ oz smoked mackerel, skinned and flaked
75 g/2½ oz cooked gooseberries
2 tsp lemon juice
2 tbsp low-fat crème fraîche
1 tbsp capers
1 gherkin, chopped
1 tbsp chopped dill pickle
1 tbsp chopped fresh dill
salt and pepper
lemon wedges, to garnish
toast or warm crusty bread, to serve

1 Cook the diced potatoes in a saucepan of boiling water for 10 minutes until tender, then drain well.

2 Place the cooked potatoes in a food processor or blender.

3 Add the skinned and flaked smoked mackerel and process for 30 seconds until fairly smooth. Alternatively, place the ingredients in a bowl and mash with a fork.

4 Add the cooked gooseberries, lemon juice and crème fraîche to the fish

and potato mixture. Blend for a further 10 seconds or mash well.

5 Stir in the capers, chopped gherkin and dill pickle, and chopped fresh dill. Season well with salt and pepper.

6 Turn the fish pâté into a serving dish, garnish with lemon wedges and serve with slices of toast or warm crusty bread cut into chunks or slices.

COOK'S TIP

Use stewed, canned or bottled cooked gooseberries for convenience and to save time, or when fresh gooseberries are out of season.

The method is illustrated with step-by-step photographs, making the recipe easy to follow.

A full-colour photograph of the finished dish.

Variations and cook's tips provide useful information regarding ingredients or cooking techniques.

The method is clearly explained with step-by-step instructions that are easy to follow.

Soups

The soups in this chapter combine a variety of flavours and textures from all over the world. There are thicker soups, thin clear consommés and soups to appeal to vegetarians. The range of soups include thick and creamy winter warmers and light and spicy oriental recipes. Many

have been chosen because of their nutritional content and may be eaten as part of a low-fat diet. All, however, can be eaten as starters or as a light meal with fresh bread. The recipes are taken from all over the world, with special emphasis on Mediterranean, Indian and Oriental soups – something to please everybody.

Tuscan Onion Soup

This soup is best made with white onions, which have a mild flavour. If you cannot get hold of them, try using large Spanish onions instead.

NUTRITIONAL INFORMATION

Calories 390	Sugars 0g	
Protein 9g	Fat 33g	
Carbohydrate ...15g	Saturates 14g	

 5–10 MINS 🕐 40–45 MINS

SERVES 4

INGREDIENTS

50 g/1¾ oz pancetta ham, diced

1 tbsp olive oil

4 large white onions, sliced thinly into rings

3 garlic cloves, chopped

850 ml/1½ pints/3½ cups hot chicken or
    ham stock

4 slices ciabatta or other Italian bread

50 g/1¾ oz/3 tbsp butter

75 g/2¾ oz Gruyère or Cheddar

salt and pepper

1 Dry fry the pancetta in a large saucepan for 3–4 minutes until it begins to brown. Remove the pancetta from the pan and set aside until required.

2 Add the oil to the pan and cook the onions and garlic over a high heat for 4 minutes. Reduce the heat, cover and cook for 15 minutes or until the onions are lightly caramelized.

3 Add the stock to the saucepan and bring to the boil. Reduce the heat and leave the mixture to simmer, covered, for about 10 minutes.

4 Toast the slices of ciabatta on both sides, under a preheated grill (broiler), for 2–3 minutes or until golden. Spread the ciabatta with butter and top with the Gruyère or Cheddar cheese. Cut the bread into bite-size pieces.

5 Add the reserved pancetta to the soup and season with salt and pepper to taste.

6 Pour into 4 soup bowls and top with the toasted bread.

COOK'S TIP

Pancetta is similar to bacon, but it is air- and salt-cured for about 6 months. Pancetta is available from most delicatessens and some large supermarkets. If you cannot obtain pancetta use unsmoked bacon instead.

Pumpkin Soup

This thick, creamy soup has a wonderful, warming golden colour.
It is flavoured with orange and thyme.

NUTRITIONAL INFORMATION

Calories	111	Sugars	.........4g
Protein	.........2g	Fat	...........6g
Carbohydrate	....5g	Saturates	.......2g

 10 MINS   35–40 MINS

SERVES 4

I N G R E D I E N T S

2 tbsp olive oil

2 medium onions, chopped

2 cloves garlic, chopped

900 g/2 lb pumpkin, peeled and cut into
    2.5 cm/1 inch chunks

1.5 litres /2¾ pints/6¼ cups boiling
    vegetable or chicken stock

finely grated rind and juice of 1 orange

3 tbsp fresh thyme, stalks removed

150 ml/¼ pint/⅔ cup milk

salt and pepper

crusty bread, to serve

1 Heat the olive oil in a large saucepan. Add the onions to the pan and cook for 3–4 minutes or until softened. Add the garlic and pumpkin and cook for a further 2 minutes, stirring well.

2 Add the boiling vegetable or chicken stock, orange rind and juice and 2 tablespoons of the thyme to the pan. Leave to simmer, covered, for 20 minutes or until the pumpkin is tender.

3 Place the mixture in a food processor and blend until smooth. Alternatively, mash the mixture with a potato masher until smooth. Season to taste.

4 Return the soup to the saucepan and add the milk. Reheat the soup for 3–4 minutes or until it is piping hot but not boiling.

5 Sprinkle with the remaining fresh thyme just before serving.

6 Divide the soup among 4 warm soup bowls and serve with lots of fresh crusty bread.

COOK'S TIP

Pumpkins are usually large vegetables. To make things a little easier, ask the greengrocer to cut a chunk off for you. Alternatively, make double the quantity and freeze the soup for up to 3 months.

Artichoke Soup

This refreshing chilled soup is ideal for *al fresco* dining. Bear in mind that this soup needs to be chilled for 3-4 hours, so allow plenty of time.

NUTRITIONAL INFORMATION

Calories 159	Sugars 2g
Protein 2g	Fat 15
Carbohydrate 5g	Saturates 6g

5 MINS   15 MINS

SERVES 4

INGREDIENTS

1 tbsp olive oil

1 onion, chopped

1 garlic clove, crushed

2 x 400 g/14 oz can artichoke hearts,
   drained

600 ml/1 pint/2 ½ cups hot vegetable stock

150 ml/¼ pint/⅔ cup single (light) cream

2 tbsp fresh thyme, stalks removed

2 sun-dried tomatoes, cut into strips

fresh, crusty bread, to serve

1 Heat the oil in a large saucepan and fry the chopped onion and crushed garlic, stirring, for 2-3 minutes or until just softened.

2 Using a sharp knife, roughly chop the artichoke hearts. Add the artichoke pieces to the onion and garlic mixture in the pan. Pour in the hot vegetable stock, stirring well.

3 Bring the mixture to the boil, then reduce the heat and leave to simmer, covered, for about 3 minutes.

4 Place the mixture into a food processor and blend until smooth. Alternatively, push the mixture through a sieve to remove any lumps.

5 Return the soup to the saucepan. Stir the single (light) cream and fresh thyme into the soup.

6 Transfer the soup to a large bowl, cover, and leave to chill in the refrigerator for about 3-4 hours.

7 Transfer the chilled soup to individual soup bowls and garnish with strips of sun-dried tomato. Serve with crusty bread.

VARIATION

Try adding 2 tablespoons of dry vermouth, such as Martini, to the soup in step 5, if you wish.

Vegetable & Bean Soup

This wonderful combination of cannellini beans, vegetables and vermicelli is made even richer by the addition of pesto and dried mushrooms.

NUTRITIONAL INFORMATION

Calories ....294 Sugars 2g
Protein ....11g Fat 16g
Carbohydrate ...30g Saturates 2g

30 MINS   30 MINS

SERVES 4

I N G R E D I E N T S

1 small aubergine (eggplant)

2 large tomatoes

1 potato, peeled

1 carrot, peeled

1 leek

425 g/15 oz can cannellini beans

850 ml/1½ pints/3¾ cups hot vegetable or
    chicken stock

2 tsp dried basil

15 g/½ oz dried porcini mushrooms,
    soaked for 10 minutes in enough warm
    water to cover

50 g/1¾ oz/¼ cup vermicelli

3 tbsp pesto (see page 223 or use shop
    bought)

freshly grated Parmesan cheese, to serve
    (optional)

1 Slice the aubergine (eggplant) into rings about 1 cm/½ inch thick, then cut each ring into 4.

2 Cut the tomatoes and potato into small dice. Cut the carrot into sticks, about 2.5 cm/1 inch long and cut the leek into rings.

3 Place the cannellini beans and their liquid in a large saucepan. Add the aubergine (eggplant), tomatoes, potatoes, carrot and leek, stirring to mix.

4 Add the stock to the pan and bring to the boil. Reduce the heat and leave to simmer for 15 minutes.

5 Add the basil, dried mushrooms and their soaking liquid and the vermicelli and simmer for 5 minutes or until all of the vegetables are tender.

6 Remove the pan from the heat and stir in the pesto.

7 Serve with freshly grated Parmesan cheese, if using.

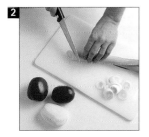

Chickpea (Garbanzo Bean) Soup

A thick vegetable soup which is a delicious meal in itself. Serve with Parmesan cheese and warm sun-dried tomato-flavoured ciabatta bread.

NUTRITIONAL INFORMATION

Calories	297	Sugars	.........0g
Protein	........11g	Fat	..........18g
Carbohydrate	...24g	Saturates	.......2g

5 MINS   15 MINS

SERVES 4

INGREDIENTS

2 tbsp olive oil

2 leeks, sliced

2 courgettes (zucchini), diced

2 garlic cloves, crushed

2 x 400 g/14 oz cans chopped tomatoes

1 tbsp tomato purée (paste)

1 fresh bay leaf

850 ml/1 ½ pints/3 ¾ cups chicken stock

400 g/14 oz can chickpeas (garbanzo beans), drained and rinsed

225 g/8 oz spinach

salt and pepper

TO SERVE

Parmesan cheese

sun-dried tomato bread

1 Heat the oil in a large saucepan, add the leeks and courgettes (zucchini) and cook briskly for 5 minutes, stirring constantly.

2 Add the garlic, tomatoes, tomato purée (paste), bay leaf, stock and chickpeas (garbanzo beans). Bring to the boil and simmer for 5 minutes.

3 Shred the spinach finely, add to the soup and cook for 2 minutes. Season.

4 Remove the bay leaf from the soup and discard.

5 Serve the soup with freshly grated Parmesan cheese and sun-dried tomato bread.

COOK'S TIP

Chickpeas (garbanzo beans) are used extensively in North African cuisine and are also found in Italian, Spanish, Middle Eastern and Indian cooking. They have a deliciously nutty flavour with a firm texture and are an excellent canned product.

Spinach & Mascarpone Soup

Spinach is the basis for this delicious soup, but use sorrel or watercress instead for a pleasant change.

NUTRITIONAL INFORMATION

Calories ....537 Sugars 2g
Protein ....6g Fat 53g
Carbohydrate ....9g Saturates 29g

  5 MINS   35 MINS

SERVES 4

I N G R E D I E N T S

60 g/2 oz/¼ cup butter

1 bunch spring onions (scallions), trimmed
    and chopped

2 celery sticks, chopped

350 g/12 oz/3 cups spinach or sorrel, or
    3 bunches watercress

850 ml /1 ½ pints/3 ½ cups vegetable stock

225 g/8 oz/1 cup Mascarpone cheese

1 tbsp olive oil

2 slices thick-cut bread, cut into cubes

½ tsp caraway seeds

salt and pepper

sesame bread sticks, to serve

1 Melt half the butter in a very large saucepan. Add the spring onions (scallions) and celery and cook gently for about 5 minutes, or until softened.

2 Pack the spinach, sorrel or watercress into the saucepan. Add the vegetable stock and bring to the boil; then reduce the heat and simmer, covered, for 15–20 minutes.

3 Transfer the soup to a blender or food processor and blend until smooth, or pass through a sieve. Return to the saucepan.

4 Add the Mascarpone cheese to the soup and heat gently, stirring, until smooth and blended. Taste and season with salt and pepper.

5 Heat the remaining butter with the oil in a frying pan (skillet). Add the bread cubes and fry in the hot oil until golden brown, adding the caraway seeds towards the end of cooking, so that they do not burn.

6 Ladle the soup into 4 warmed bowls. Sprinkle with the croûtons and serve at once, accompanied by the sesame bread sticks.

VARIATIONS

Any leafy vegetable can be used to make this soup to give variations to the flavour. For anyone who grows their own vegetables, it is the perfect recipe for experimenting with a glut of produce. Try young beetroot (beet) leaves or surplus lettuces for a change.

Calabrian Mushroom Soup

The Calabrian Mountains in southern Italy provide large amounts of wild mushrooms that are rich in flavour and colour.

NUTRITIONAL INFORMATION

Calories 452	Sugars 5g
Protein 15g	Fat 26g
Carbohydrate ...42g	Saturates 12g

 5 MINS   25–30 MINS

SERVES 4

I N G R E D I E N T S

2 tbsp olive oil

1 onion, chopped

450g/1 lb mixed mushrooms, such as ceps, oyster and button

300 ml/ ½ pint/1 ¼ cup milk

850 ml/1 ½ pints/3 ¾ cups hot vegetable stock

8 slices of rustic bread or French stick

2 garlic cloves, crushed

50 g/1 ¾ oz/3 tbsp butter, melted

75 g/2 ¾ oz Gruyère cheese, finely grated

salt and pepper

1 Heat the oil in a large frying pan (skillet) and cook the onion for 3–4 minutes or until soft and golden.

2 Wipe each mushroom with a damp cloth and cut any large mushrooms into smaller, bite-size pieces.

3 Add the mushrooms to the pan, stirring quickly to coat them in the oil.

4 Add the milk to the pan, bring to the boil, cover and leave to simmer for about 5 minutes. Gradually stir in the hot vegetable stock and season with salt and pepper to taste.

5 Under a preheated grill (broiler), toast the bread on both sides until golden.

6 Mix together the garlic and butter and spoon generously over the toast.

7 Place the toast in the bottom of a large tureen or divide it among 4 individual serving bowls and pour over the hot soup. Top with the grated Gruyère cheese and serve at once.

COOK'S TIP

Mushrooms absorb liquid, which can lessen the flavour and affect cooking properties. Therefore, carefully wipe them with a damp cloth rather than rinsing them in water.

Tomato & Pasta Soup

Plum tomatoes are ideal for making soups and sauces as they have denser, less watery flesh than rounder varieties.

NUTRITIONAL INFORMATION

Calories 503	Sugars 16g	
Protein 9g	Fat 28g	
Carbohydrate ...59g	Saturates 17g	

5 MINS   50–55 MINS

SERVES 4

INGREDIENTS

60 g/2 oz/4 tbsp unsalted butter

1 large onion, chopped

600 ml/1 pint/2 ½ cups vegetable stock

900 g/2 lb Italian plum tomatoes, skinned and roughly chopped

pinch of bicarbonate of soda (baking soda)

225 g/8 oz/2 cups dried fusilli

1 tbsp caster (superfine) sugar

150 ml/ ¼ pint/ ⅔ cup double (heavy) cream

salt and pepper

fresh basil leaves, to garnish

1 Melt the butter in a large pan, add the onion and fry for 3 minutes, stirring. Add 300 ml/ ½ pint/1 ¼ cups of vegetable stock to the pan, with the chopped tomatoes and bicarbonate of soda (baking

soda). Bring the soup to the boil and simmer for 20 minutes.

2 Remove the pan from the heat and set aside to cool. Purée the soup in a blender or food processor and pour through a fine strainer back into the saucepan.

3 Add the remaining vegetable stock and the fusilli to the pan, and season to taste with salt and pepper.

4 Add the sugar to the pan, bring to the boil, then lower the heat and simmer for about 15 minutes.

5 Pour the soup into a warm tureen, swirl the double (heavy) cream around the surface of the soup and garnish with fresh basil leaves. Serve immediately.

VARIATION

To make orange and tomato soup, simply use half the quantity of vegetable stock, topped up with the same amount of fresh orange juice and garnish the soup with orange rind.

Lettuce & Tofu Soup

This is a delicate, clear soup of shredded lettuce and small chunks of tofu (bean curd) with sliced carrot and spring onion (scallion).

NUTRITIONAL INFORMATION

Calories 113   Sugars 2g
Protein . . . . .5g   Fat 8g
Carbohydrate . . . .3g   Saturates 1g

 5 MINS   15 MINS

SERVES 4

INGREDIENTS

200 g/7 oz tofu (bean curd)

2 tbsp vegetable oil

1 carrot, sliced thinly

1 cm/½ inch piece ginger root,
    cut into thin shreds

3 spring onions (scallions), sliced
    diagonally

1.2 litres/2 pints/5 cups vegetable stock

2 tbsp soy sauce

2 tbsp dry sherry

1 tsp sugar

125 g/4½ oz/1½ cups cos (romaine) lettuce,
    shredded

salt and pepper

1 Using a sharp knife, cut the tofu (bean curd) into small cubes.

2 Heat the vegetable oil in a preheated wok or large saucepan, add the tofu (bean curd) and stir-fry until browned. Remove with a perforated spoon and drain on kitchen paper (paper towels).

3 Add the carrot, ginger root and spring onions (scallions) to the wok or saucepan and stir-fry for 2 minutes.

4 Add the vegetable stock, soy sauce, sherry and sugar. Stir well to mix all the ingredients. Bring to the boil and simmer for 1 minute.

5 Add the cos (romaine) lettuce to the wok or saucepan and stir until it has just wilted.

6 Return the tofu (bean curd) to the pan to reheat. Season with salt and pepper to taste and serve the soup immediately in warmed bowls.

COOK'S TIP

For a prettier effect, score grooves along the length of the carrot with a sharp knife before slicing. This will create a flower effect as the carrot is cut into rounds. You could also try slicing the carrot on the diagonal to make longer slices.

Clear Chicken & Egg Soup

This tasty chicken soup has the addition of poached eggs, making it both delicious and filling. Use fresh, home-made stock for a better flavour.

NUTRITIONAL INFORMATION

Calories	138	Sugars	.........1g
Protein	........16g	Fat	...........7g
Carbohydrate	....1g	Saturates	.......2g

 5 MINS   🕐 35 MINS

SERVES 4

I N G R E D I E N T S

1 tsp salt

1 tbsp rice wine vinegar

4 eggs

850 ml/1½ pints/3¾ cups
   chicken stock

1 leek, sliced

125 g/4½ oz broccoli florets

125 g/4½ oz/1 cup shredded
   cooked chicken

2 open-cap mushrooms, sliced

1 tbsp dry sherry

dash of chilli sauce

chilli powder, to garnish

VARIATION

You could use 4 dried Chinese mushrooms, rehydrated according to the packet instructions, instead of the open-cap mushrooms, if you prefer.

1 Bring a large saucepan of water to the boil and add the salt and rice wine vinegar.

2 Reduce the heat so that it is just simmering and carefully break the eggs into the water, one at a time. Poach the eggs for 1 minute.

3 Remove the poached eggs with a slotted spoon and set aside.

4 Bring the chicken stock to the boil in a separate pan and add the leek, broccoli, chicken, mushrooms and sherry and season with chilli sauce to taste. Cook for 10–15 minutes.

5 Add the poached eggs to the soup and cook for a further 2 minutes. Carefully transfer the soup and poached eggs to 4 soup bowls. Dust with a little chilli powder and serve immediately.

Lamb & Rice Soup

This is a very filling soup, as it contains rice and tender pieces of lamb. Serve before a light main course.

NUTRITIONAL INFORMATION

Calories 116   Sugars 0.2g
Protein . . . . .9g   Fat 4g
Carbohydrate . . .12g   Saturates 2g

  5 MINS   35 MINS

SERVES 4

I N G R E D I E N T S

150 g/5½ oz lean lamb

50 g/1¾ oz/¼ cup rice

850 ml/1½ pints/3¾ cups
  lamb stock

1 leek, sliced

1 garlic clove, thinly sliced

2 tsp light soy sauce

1 tsp rice wine vinegar

1 medium open-cap mushroom,
  thinly sliced

salt

1 Using a sharp knife, trim any fat from the lamb and cut the meat into thin strips. Set aside until required.

2 Bring a large pan of lightly salted water to the boil and add the rice. Bring back to the boil, stir once, reduce the heat and cook for 10–15 minutes, until tender.

3 Drain the rice, rinse under cold running water, drain again and set aside until required.

4 Meanwhile, put the lamb stock in a large saucepan and bring to the boil.

5 Add the lamb strips, leek, garlic, soy sauce and rice wine vinegar to the stock in the pan. Reduce the heat, cover and leave to simmer for 10 minutes, or until the lamb is tender and cooked through.

6 Add the mushroom slices and the rice to the pan and cook for a further 2–3 minutes, or until the mushroom is completely cooked through.

7 Ladle the soup into 4 individual warmed soup bowls and serve immediately.

VARIATION

Use a few dried Chinese mushrooms, rehydrated according to the packet instructions and chopped, as an alternative to the open-cap mushroom. Add the Chinese mushrooms with the lamb in step 4.

Chilli Fish Soup

Chinese mushrooms add an intense flavour to this soup which is unique.
If they are unavailable, use open-cap mushrooms, sliced.

NUTRITIONAL INFORMATION

Calories	166	Sugars	.........1g
Protein	........23g	Fat	...........7g
Carbohydrate	....4g	Saturates	.......1g

 15 MINS   15 MINS

SERVES 4

INGREDIENTS

15 g/½ oz Chinese dried mushrooms

2 tbsp sunflower oil

1 onion, sliced

100 g/3½ oz/1½ cups mangetout (snow peas)

100 g/3½ oz/1½ cups bamboo shoots

3 tbsp sweet chilli sauce

1.2 litres/2 pints/5 cups fish or vegetable stock

3 tbsp light soy sauce

2 tbsp fresh coriander (cilantro), plus extra to garnish

450 g/1 lb cod fillet, skinned and cubed

COOK'S TIP

Cod is used in this recipe as it is a meaty white fish. For real luxury, use monkfish tail instead.

There are many different varieties of dried mushrooms, but shiitake are best. They are not cheap, but a small amount will go a long way.

1 Place the mushrooms in a large bowl. Pour over enough boiling water to cover and leave to stand for 5 minutes. Drain the mushrooms thoroughly in a colander. Using a sharp knife, roughly chop the mushrooms.

2 Heat the sunflower oil in a preheated wok or large frying pan (skillet). Add the sliced onion to the wok and stir-fry for 5 minutes, or until softened.

3 Add the mangetout (snow peas), bamboo shoots, chilli sauce, stock and soy sauce to the wok and bring to the boil.

4 Add the coriander (cilantro) and cod and leave to simmer for 5 minutes or until the fish is cooked through.

5 Transfer the soup to warm bowls, garnish with extra coriander (cilantro), if wished, and serve hot.

Crab & Ginger Soup

Two classic ingredients in Chinese cooking are blended together in this recipe for a special soup.

NUTRITIONAL INFORMATION

Calories 32	Sugars 1g
Protein 6g	Fat 0.4g
Carbohydrate 1g	Saturates 0g

 10 MINS 25 MINS

SERVES 4

INGREDIENTS

1 carrot

1 leek

1 bay leaf

850 ml/1½ pints/3¾ cups fish stock

2 medium-sized cooked crabs

2.5-cm/1-inch piece fresh root ginger (ginger root), grated

1 tsp light soy sauce

½ tsp ground star anise

salt and pepper

1 Using a sharp knife, chop the carrot and leek into small pieces and place in a large saucepan with the bay leaf and fish stock.

2 Bring the mixture in the saucepan to the boil.

3 Reduce the heat, cover and leave to simmer for about 10 minutes, or until the vegetables are nearly tender.

4 Remove all of the meat from the cooked crabs. Break off and reserve the claws, break the joints and remove the meat, using a fork or skewer.

5 Add the crabmeat to the pan of fish stock, together with the ginger, soy sauce and star anise and bring to the boil. Leave to simmer for about 10 minutes, or until the vegetables are tender and the crab is heated through.

6 Season the soup then ladle into a warmed soup tureen or individual serving bowls and garnish with crab claws. Serve immediately.

VARIATION

If fresh crabmeat is unavailable, use drained canned crabmeat or thawed frozen crabmeat instead.

Mushroom Noodle Soup

A light, refreshing clear soup of mushrooms, cucumber and small pieces of rice noodles, flavoured with soy sauce and a touch of garlic.

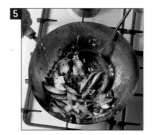

NUTRITIONAL INFORMATION

Calories 84	Sugars 1g
Protein 1g	Fat 8g
Carbohydrate 3g	Saturates 1g

 5 MINS   10 MINS

SERVES 4

I N G R E D I E N T S

125 g/4½ oz flat or open-cup mushrooms

½ cucumber

2 spring onions (scallions)

1 garlic clove

2 tbsp vegetable oil

25 g/1 oz/¼ cup Chinese rice noodles

¾ tsp salt

1 tbsp soy sauce

1 Wash the mushrooms and pat dry on kitchen paper (paper towels). Slice thinly. Do not remove the peel as this adds more flavour.

2 Halve the cucumber lengthways. Scoop out the seeds, using a teaspoon, and slice the cucumber thinly.

3 Chop the spring onions (scallions) finely and cut the garlic clove into thin strips.

4 Heat the vegetable oil in a large saucepan or wok.

5 Add the spring onions (scallions) and garlic to the pan or wok and stir-fry for 30 seconds. Add the mushrooms and stir-fry for 2–3 minutes.

6 Stir in 600 ml/1 pint/2½ cups water. Break the noodles into short lengths and add to the soup. Bring to the boil, stirring occasionally.

7 Add the cucumber slices, salt and soy sauce, and simmer for 2–3 minutes.

8 Serve the mushroom noodle soup in warmed bowls, distributing the noodles and vegetables evenly.

COOK'S TIP

Scooping the seeds out from the cucumber gives it a prettier effect when sliced, and also helps to reduce any bitterness, but if you prefer, you can leave them in.

Curried Chicken & Corn Soup

Tender cooked chicken strips and baby corn cobs are the main flavours in this delicious clear soup, with just a hint of ginger.

NUTRITIONAL INFORMATION

Calories 206	Sugars 5g
Protein 29g	Fat 5g
Carbohydrate . . .13g	Saturates 1g

 5 MINS   30 MINS

SERVES 4

I N G R E D I E N T S

175 g/6 oz can sweetcorn
  (corn), drained

850 ml/1½ pints/3¾ cups
  chicken stock

350 g/12 oz cooked, lean chicken,
  cut into strips

16 baby corn cobs

1 tsp Chinese curry powder

1-cm/½-inch piece fresh root ginger
  (ginger root), grated

3 tbsp light soy sauce

2 tbsp chopped chives

1 Place the canned sweetcorn (corn) in a food processor, together with 150 ml/¼ pint/⅔ cup of the chicken stock and process until the mixture forms a smooth purée.

2 Pass the sweetcorn purée through a fine sieve (strainer), pressing with the back of a spoon to remove any husks.

3 Pour the remaining chicken stock into a large saucepan and add the strips of cooked chicken. Stir in the sweetcorn (corn) purée.

4 Add the baby corn cobs and bring the soup to the boil. Boil the soup for 10 minutes.

5 Add the Chinese curry powder, grated fresh root ginger and light soy sauce and stir well to combine. Cook for a further 10–15 minutes.

6 Stir the chopped chives into the soup.

7 Transfer the curried chicken and corn soup to warm soup bowls and serve immediately.

COOK'S TIP

Prepare the soup up to 24 hours in advance without adding the chicken, cool, cover and store in the refrigerator. Add the chicken and heat the soup through thoroughly before serving.

Prawn (Shrimp) Soup

This soup is an interesting mix of colours and textures. The egg may be made into a flat omelette and added as thin strips if preferred.

NUTRITIONAL INFORMATION

Calories 123	Sugars 0.2g
Protein 13g	Fat 8g
Carbohydrate 1g	Saturates 1g

5 MINS 20 MINS

SERVES 4

I N G R E D I E N T S

2 tbsp sunflower oil

2 spring onions (scallions), thinly sliced
   diagonally

1 carrot, coarsely grated

125 g/4½ oz large closed cup mushrooms,
   thinly sliced

1 litre/1¾ pints/4 cups fish or
   vegetable stock

½ tsp Chinese five-spice powder

1 tbsp light soy sauce

125 g/4½ oz large peeled prawns (shrimp)
   or peeled tiger prawns (shrimp),
   defrosted if frozen

½ bunch watercress, trimmed and
   roughly chopped

1 egg, well beaten

salt and pepper

4 large prawns (shrimp) in shells, to garnish
   (optional)

1 Heat the oil in a wok, swirling it around until really hot. Add the spring onions (scallions) and stir-fry for a minute then add the carrots and mushrooms and continue to cook for about 2 minutes.

2 Add the stock and bring to the boil then season to taste with salt and pepper, five-spice powder and soy sauce and simmer for 5 minutes.

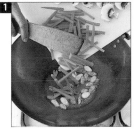 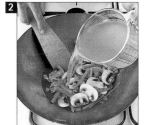 

3 If the prawns (shrimp) are really large, cut them in half before adding to the wok and simmer for 3-4 minutes.

4 Add the watercress to the wok and mix well, then slowly pour in the beaten egg in a circular movement so that it cooks in threads in the soup. Adjust the seasoning and serve each portion topped with a whole prawn (shrimp).

COOK'S TIP

The large open mushrooms with black gills give the best flavour but they tend to spoil the colour of the soup, making it very dark. Oyster mushrooms can also be used.

Chicken & Pasta Broth

This satisfying soup makes a good lunch or supper dish and you can use any vegetables that you have at hand.

NUTRITIONAL INFORMATION

Calories 295	Sugar 8g
Protein 25g	Fats 10g
Carbohydrates ...29g	Saturates 2g

5 MINS   20 MINS

SERVES 4

I N G R E D I E N T S

350 g/12 oz boneless chicken breasts

2 tbsp sunflower oil

1 medium onion, diced

225 g/8 oz/1½ cups carrots, diced

225 g/8 oz cauliflower florets

900 ml/1½ pints/3¾ cups chicken stock

2 tsp dried mixed herbs

125 g/4½ oz small pasta shapes

salt and pepper

Parmesan cheese (optional) and crusty bread, to serve

1 Finely dice the chicken, discarding any skin.

2 Heat the oil and quickly sauté the chicken and vegetables until they are lightly coloured.

3 Stir in the stock and herbs. Bring to the boil and add the pasta. Return to the boil, cover and simmer for 10 minutes.

4 Season to taste and sprinkle with Parmesan cheese (if using). Serve with crusty bread.

Lemon & Chicken Soup

This delicately flavoured summer soup is surprisingly easy to make, and tastes delicious.

NUTRITIONAL INFORMATION

Calories	506	Sugars	.........4g
Protein	........19g	Fat	..........31g
Carbohydrate	...41g	Saturates	......19g

5-10 MINS   1¼ HOURS

SERVES 4

INGREDIENTS

60 g/2 oz/4 tbsp butter

8 shallots, thinly sliced

2 carrots, thinly sliced

2 celery sticks (stalks), thinly sliced

225 g/8 oz boned chicken breasts,
   finely chopped

3 lemons

1.2 litres/2 pints/5 cups chicken stock

225 g/8 oz dried spaghetti, broken into
   small pieces

150 ml/¼ pint/⅝ cup double (heavy) cream

salt and white pepper

TO GARNISH

fresh parsley sprig

3 lemon slices, halved

COOK'S TIP

You can prepare this soup up to the end of step 3 in advance, so that all you need do before serving is heat it through before adding the pasta and the finishing touches.

1 Melt the butter in a large saucepan. Add the shallots, carrots, celery and chicken and cook over a low heat, stirring occasionally, for 8 minutes.

2 Thinly pare the lemons and blanch the lemon rind in boiling water for 3 minutes. Squeeze the juice from the lemons.

3 Add the lemon rind and juice to the pan, together with the chicken stock. Bring slowly to the boil over a low heat and simmer for 40 minutes, stirring occasionally.

4 Add the spaghetti to the pan and cook for 15 minutes. Season to taste with salt and white pepper and add the cream. Heat through, but do not allow the soup to boil or it will curdle.

5 Pour the soup into a tureen or individual bowls, garnish with the parsley and half slices of lemon and serve immediately.

Chicken & Leek Soup

This satisfying soup can be served as a main course. You can add rice and (bell) peppers to make it even more hearty, as well as colourful.

NUTRITIONAL INFORMATION

Calories 183	Sugar 4g	
Protein 21g	Fats 9g	
Carbohydrates 4g	Saturates 5g	

5 MINS   1¼ HOURS

SERVES 4–6

INGREDIENTS

25 g/1 oz/2 tbsp butter

350 g/12 oz boneless chicken

350 g/12 oz leeks, cut into 2.5-cm/
   1-inch pieces

1.2 litres/2 pints/5 cups chicken stock

1 bouquet garni sachet

8 pitted prunes, halved

salt and white pepper

cooked rice and diced (bell) peppers
   (optional)

1 Melt the butter in a large saucepan.

2 Add the chicken and leeks to the saucepan and fry for 8 minutes.

3 Add the chicken stock and bouquet garni sachet and stir well.

4 Season well with salt and pepper to taste.

5 Bring the soup to the boil and simmer for 45 minutes.

6 Add the prunes to the saucepan with some cooked rice and diced (bell) peppers (if using) and simmer for about 20 minutes.

7 Remove the bouquet garni sachet from the soup and discard. Serve the chicken and leek soup immediately.

VARIATION

Instead of the bouquet garni sachet, you can use a bunch of fresh mixed herbs, tied together with string. Choose herbs such as parsley, thyme and rosemary.

Red (Bell) Pepper Soup

This soup has a real Mediterranean flavour, using sweet red (bell) peppers, tomato, chilli and basil. It is great served with a warm olive bread.

NUTRITIONAL INFORMATION

Calories 55	Sugar 10g
Protein 2g	Fats 0.5g
Carbohydrates . . .11g	Saturates 0.1g

5 MINS   25 MINS

SERVES 4

INGREDIENTS

225 g/8 oz red (bell) peppers, seeded and sliced

1 onion, sliced

2 garlic cloves, crushed

1 green chilli, chopped

300 ml/½ pint/1½ cups passata (sieved tomatoes)

600 ml/1 pint/2½ cups vegetable stock

2 tbsp chopped basil

fresh basil sprigs, to garnish

1 Put the (bell) peppers in a large saucepan with the onion, garlic and chilli. Add the passata (sieved tomatoes) and vegetable stock and bring to the boil, stirring well.

2 Reduce the heat to a simmer and cook for 20 minutes or until the (bell) peppers have softened. Drain, reserving the liquid and vegetables separately.

3 Sieve the vegetables by pressing through a sieve (strainer) with the back of a spoon. Alternatively, blend in a food processor until smooth.

4 Return the vegetable purée to a clean saucepan with the reserved cooking liquid. Add the basil and heat through until hot. Garnish the soup with fresh basil sprigs and serve.

VARIATION

This soup is also delicious served cold with 150 ml/¼ pint/¼ cup of natural (unsweetened) yogurt swirled into it.

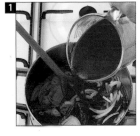  

Partan Bree

This traditional Scottish soup is thickened with a purée of rice and crab meat cooked in milk. Add soured cream, if liked, at the end of cooking.

NUTRITIONAL INFORMATION

Calories 112	Sugars 5g	
Protein 7g	Fat 2g	
Carbohydrate ...18g	Saturates 0.3g	

1 HOUR   35 MINS

SERVES 6

I N G R E D I E N T S

1 medium-sized boiled crab

90 g/3 oz/scant ½ cup long-grain rice

600 ml/1 pint/2½ cups skimmed milk

600 ml/1 pint/2½ cups Fish Stock

1 tbsp anchovy essence (paste)

2 tsp lime or lemon juice

1 tbsp chopped fresh parsley or I tsp
    chopped fresh thyme

3–4 tbsp soured cream (optional)

salt and pepper

snipped chives, to garnish

1 Remove and reserve all the brown and white meat from the crab, then crack the claws and remove and chop that meat; reserve the claw meat.

COOK'S TIP

If you are unable to buy a whole crab, use about 175 g/6 oz frozen crab meat and thaw thoroughly before use; or a 175 g/6 oz can of crab meat which just needs thorough draining.

2 Put the rice and milk into a saucepan and bring slowly to the boil. Cover and simmer gently for about 20 minutes.

3 Add the reserved white and brown crab meat and seasoning and simmer for a further 5 minutes.

4 Cool a little, then press through a sieve (strainer), or blend in a food processor or blender until smooth.

5 Pour the soup into a clean saucepan and add the fish stock and the reserved claw meat. Bring slowly to the boil, then add the anchovy essence (paste) and lime or lemon juice and adjust the seasoning.

6 Simmer for a further 2–3 minutes. Stir in the parsley or thyme and then swirl soured cream (if using) through each serving. Garnish with snipped chives.

Smoked Haddock Soup

Smoked haddock gives this soup a wonderfully rich flavour, while the mashed potatoes and cream thicken and enrich the stock.

NUTRITIONAL INFORMATION

Calories 169	Sugars 8g	
Protein 16g	Fat 5g	
Carbohydrate ...16g	Saturates 3g	

25 MINS 40 MINS

SERVES 4–6

INGREDIENTS

225 g/8 oz smoked haddock fillet

1 onion, chopped finely

1 garlic clove, crushed

600 ml/1 pint/2½ cups water

600 ml/I pint/2½ cups skimmed milk

225–350 g/8–12 oz/1–1½ cups hot mashed potatoes

30 g/1 oz/2 tbsp butter

about 1 tbsp lemon juice

6 tbsp low-fat natural fromage frais

4 tbsp fresh parsley, chopped

salt and pepper

1 Put the fish, onion, garlic and water into a saucepan. Bring to the boil, cover and simmer for 15–20 minutes.

2 Remove the fish from the pan, strip off the skin and remove all the bones. Flake the flesh finely.

3 Return the skin and bones to the cooking liquor and simmer for 10 minutes. Strain, discarding the skin and bone. Pour the liquor into a clean pan.

4 Add the milk, flaked fish and seasoning to the pan, bring to the boil and simmer for about 3 minutes.

5 Gradually whisk in sufficient mashed potato to give a fairly thick soup, then stir in the butter and sharpen to taste with lemon juice.

6 Add the fromage frais and 3 tablespoons of the chopped parsley. Reheat gently and adjust the seasoning. Sprinkle with the remaining parsley and serve immediately.

COOK'S TIP

Undyed smoked haddock may be used in place of the bright yellow fish; it will give a paler colour but just as much flavour. Alternatively, use smoked cod or smoked whiting.

Bacon, Bean & Garlic Soup

A mouth-wateringly healthy vegetable, bean and bacon soup with a garlic flavour. Serve with granary or wholemeal (whole wheat) bread.

NUTRITIONAL INFORMATION

Calories 261   Sugars 5g
Protein . . . . .23g   Fat 8g
Carbohydrate . . .25g   Saturates 2g

5 MINS   20 MINS

SERVES 4

INGREDIENTS

225 g/8 oz lean smoked back bacon slices

1 carrot, sliced thinly

1 celery stick, sliced thinly

1 onion, chopped

1 tbsp oil

3 garlic cloves, sliced

700 ml/1¼ pints/3 cups hot vegetable stock

200 g/7 oz can chopped tomatoes

1 tbsp chopped fresh thyme

about 400 g/14 oz can cannellini beans, drained

1 tbsp tomato purée (paste)

salt and pepper

grated Cheddar cheese, to garnish

COOK'S TIP

For a more substantial soup add 60 g/2 oz cup small pasta shapes or short lengths of spaghetti when you add the stock and tomatoes. You will also need to add an extra 150 ml/ ¼ pint/ ⅔ cup vegetable stock.

1 Chop 2 slices of the bacon and place in a bowl. Cook on HIGH power for 3–4 minutes until the fat runs out and the bacon is well cooked. Stir the bacon halfway through cooking to separate the pieces. Transfer to a plate lined with kitchen towels and leave to cool. When cool, the bacon pieces should be crisp and dry. Place the carrot, celery, onion and oil in a large bowl. Cover and cook on HIGH power for 4 minutes.

2 Chop the remaining bacon and add to the bowl with the garlic. Cover and cook on HIGH power for 2 minutes.

3 Add the stock, the contents of the can of tomatoes, the thyme, beans and tomato purée (paste). Cover and cook on HIGH power for 8 minutes, stirring halfway through. Season to taste. Ladle the soup into warmed bowls and sprinkle with the crisp bacon and grated cheese.

Spicy Dhal & Carrot Soup

This delicious, warming and nutritious soup includes a selection of spices to give it a 'kick'. It is simple to make and extremely good to eat.

NUTRITIONAL INFORMATION

Calories ....173 Sugars 11g
Protein ....9g Fat 5g
Carbohydrate ...24g Saturates 1g

10 MINS   50 MINS

SERVES 6

I N G R E D I E N T S

125 g/4½ oz split red lentils

1.2 litres/2 pints/5 cups vegetable
   stock

350 g/12 oz carrots, peeled and sliced

2 onions, peeled and chopped

1 x 250 g/9 oz can chopped tomatoes

2 garlic cloves, peeled and chopped

2 tbsp vegetable ghee or oil

1 tsp ground cumin

1 tsp ground coriander

1 fresh green chilli, seeded and chopped,
   or use 1 tsp minced chilli (from a jar)

½ tsp ground turmeric

15 ml/1 tbsp lemon juice

salt

300 ml/½ pint/1¼ cups skimmed milk

30 ml/2 tbsp chopped fresh coriander
   (cilantro)

yogurt, to serve

1 Place the lentils in a sieve and wash well under cold running water. Drain and place in a large saucepan with 850 ml/1½ pints/3½ cups of the vegetable stock, the carrots, onions, tomatoes and garlic. Bring the mixture to the boil, reduce the heat, cover and simmer for 30 minutes.

2 Meanwhile, heat the ghee or oil in a small pan, add the cumin, coriander, chilli and turmeric and fry gently for 1 minute.

3 Remove from the heat and stir in the lemon juice and salt to taste.

4 Purée the soup in batches in a blender or food processor. Return the soup to the saucepan, add the spice mixture and the remaining 300 ml/½ pint/ 1¼ cups stock or water and simmer for 10 minutes.

5 Add the milk to the soup and adjust the seasoning according to taste.

6 Stir in the chopped coriander (cilantro) and reheat gently. Serve hot, with a swirl of yogurt.

Spicy Lentil Soup

For a warming, satisfying meal on a cold day, this lentil dish is packed full of taste and goodness.

NUTRITIONAL INFORMATION

Calories 155	Sugars 4g	
Protein 11g	Fat 3g	
Carbohydrate ...22g	Saturates 0.4g	

1 HOUR   1¼ HOURS

SERVES 4

INGREDIENTS

125 g/4½ oz/½ cup red lentils

2 tsp vegetable oil

1 large onion, chopped finely

2 garlic cloves, crushed

1 tsp ground cumin

1 tsp ground coriander

1 tsp garam masala

2 tbsp tomato purée (paste)

1 litre/1¾ pints/4½ cups Fresh Vegetable Stock

about 350 g/12 oz can sweetcorn, drained

salt and pepper

TO SERVE

low-fat natural (unsweetened) yogurt

chopped fresh parsley

warmed pitta (pocket) bread

1 Rinse the red lentils in cold water. Drain the lentils well and put to one side.

2 Heat the oil in a large non-stick saucepan and fry the onion and garlic gently until softened but not browned.

3 Stir in the cumin, coriander, garam masala, tomato purée (paste) and 4 tablespoons of the stock. Mix well and simmer gently for 2 minutes.

4 Add the lentils and pour in the remaining stock. Bring to the boil, reduce the heat and simmer, covered, for 1 hour until the lentils are tender and the soup thickened. Stir in the sweetcorn and heat through for 5 minutes. Season well.

5 Ladle into warmed soup bowls and top each with a spoonful of yogurt and a sprinkling of parsley. Serve with warmed pitta (pocket) bread.

COOK'S TIP

Many of the ready-prepared ethnic breads available today either contain fat or are brushed with oil before baking. Always check the ingredients list for fat content.

Chunky Potato & Beef Soup

This is a real winter warmer – pieces of tender beef and chunky mixed vegetables are cooked in a liquor flavoured with sherry.

NUTRITIONAL INFORMATION

Calories 187	Sugars 3g	
Protein 14g	Fat 9g	
Carbohydrate ...12g	Saturates 2g	

5 MINS

35 MINS

SERVES 4

I N G R E D I E N T S

2 tbsp vegetable oil

225 g/8 oz lean braising or frying steak, cut into strips

225 g/8 oz new potatoes, halved

1 carrot, diced

2 celery sticks, sliced

2 leeks, sliced

850 ml/1½ pints/3¾ cups beef stock

8 baby sweetcorn cobs, sliced

1 bouquet garni

2 tbsp dry sherry

salt and pepper

chopped fresh parsley, to garnish

1 Heat the vegetable oil in a large saucepan.

2 Add the strips of meat to the saucepan and cook for 3 minutes, turning constantly.

3 Add the halved potatoes, diced carrot and sliced celery and leeks. Cook for a further 5 minutes, stirring.

4 Pour the beef stock into the saucepan and bring to the boil. Reduce the heat until the liquid is simmering, then add the sliced baby sweetcorn cobs and the bouquet garni.

5 Cook the soup for a further 20 minutes or until cooked through.

6 Remove the bouquet garni from the saucepan and discard. Stir the dry sherry into the soup and then season to taste with salt and pepper.

7 Pour the soup into warmed bowls and garnish with the chopped fresh parsley. Serve at once with crusty bread.

COOK'S TIP

Make double the quantity of soup and freeze the remainder in a rigid container for later use. When ready to use, leave in the refrigerator to defrost thoroughly, then heat until piping hot.

Mushroom & Ginger Soup

Thai soups are very quickly and easily put together, and are cooked so that each ingredient can still be tasted in the finished dish.

NUTRITIONAL INFORMATION

Calories 74	Sugars 1g	
Protein 3g	Fat 3g	
Carbohydrate 9g	Saturates 0.4g	

🄶   🄶

🍲 1½ HOURS   🕐 15 MINS

SERVES 4

I N G R E D I E N T S

15 g/½ oz/¼ cup dried Chinese
    mushrooms or 125 g/4½ oz/1⅓ cups field
    or chestnut (crimini) mushrooms

1 litre/1¾ pints/4 cups hot
    vegetable stock

125 g/4½ oz thread egg noodles

2 tsp sunflower oil

3 garlic cloves, crushed

2.5 cm/1 inch piece ginger,
    shredded finely

½ tsp mushroom ketchup

1 tsp light soy sauce

125 g/4½ oz/2 cups bean sprouts

coriander (cilantro) leaves, to garnish

1   Soak the dried Chinese mushrooms (if using) for at least 30 minutes in 300 ml/½ pint/1¼ cups of the hot vegetable stock. Remove the stalks and discard, then slice the mushrooms. Reserve the stock.

2   Cook the noodles for 2–3 minutes in boiling water. Drain and rinse. Set them aside.

3   Heat the oil over a high heat in a wok or large, heavy frying pan (skillet). Add the garlic and ginger, stir and add the mushrooms. Stir over a high heat for 2 minutes.

4   Add the remaining vegetable stock with the reserved stock and bring to the boil. Add the mushroom ketchup and soy sauce.

5   Stir in the bean sprouts and cook until tender. Put some noodles in each bowl and ladle the soup on top. Garnish with coriander (cilantro) leaves and serve immediately.

COOK'S TIP

Rice noodles contain no fat and are ideal for for anyone on a low-fat diet.

Yogurt & Spinach Soup

Whole young spinach leaves add vibrant colour to this unusual soup.
Serve with hot, crusty bread for a nutritious light meal.

NUTRITIONAL INFORMATION

Calories	227	Sugars	........13g
Protein	........14g	Fat	..........7g
Carbohydrate	...29g	Saturates	......2g

 15 MINS   30 MINS

SERVES 4

INGREDIENTS

600 ml/1 pint/2½ cups chicken stock

60 g/2 oz/4 tbsp long-grain rice, rinsed and drained

4 tbsp water

1 tbsp cornflour (cornstarch)

600 ml/1 pint/2½ cups low-fat natural yogurt

juice of 1 lemon

3 egg yolks, lightly beaten

350 g/12 oz young spinach leaves, washed and drained

salt and pepper

1 Pour the stock into a large pan, season and bring to the boil. Add the rice and simmer for 10 minutes, until barely cooked. Remove from the heat.

2 Combine the water and cornflour (cornstarch) to make a smooth paste.

3 Pour the yogurt into a second pan and stir in the cornflour (cornstarch) mixture. Set the pan over a low heat and bring the yogurt slowly to the boil, stirring with a wooden spoon in one direction only. This will stabilize the yogurt and prevent it from separating or curdling on contact with the hot stock. When the yogurt has reached boiling point, stand the pan on a heat diffuser and leave to simmer slowly for 10 minutes. Remove the pan from the heat and allow the mixture to cool slightly before stirring in the beaten egg yolks.

4 Pour the yogurt mixture into the stock, stir in the lemon juice and stir to blend thoroughly. Keep the soup warm, but do not allow it to boil.

5 Blanch the washed and drained spinach leaves in a large pan of boiling, salted water for 2–3 minutes until they begin to soften but have not wilted. Tip the spinach into a colander, drain well and stir it into the soup. Let the spinach warm through. Taste the soup and adjust the seasoning if necessary. Serve in wide shallow soup plates, with hot, fresh crusty bread.

Red Lentil Soup with Yogurt

Tasty red lentil soup flavoured with chopped coriander (cilantro). The yogurt adds a light piquancy to the soup.

NUTRITIONAL INFORMATION

Calories 280	Sugars 6g	
Protein 17g	Fat 7g	
Carbohydrate ...40g	Saturates 4g	

5 MINS   30 MINS

SERVES 4

INGREDIENTS

25 g/1 oz/2 tbsp butter

1 onion, chopped finely

1 celery stick, chopped finely

1 large carrot, grated

1 dried bay leaf

225 g/8 oz/1 cup red lentils

1.2 litres/2 pints/5 cups hot vegetable or chicken stock

2 tbsp chopped fresh coriander (cilantro)

4 tbsp low-fat natural (unsweetened) yogurt

salt and pepper

fresh coriander (cilantro) sprigs, to garnish

1 Place the butter, onion and celery in a large bowl. Cover and cook on HIGH power for 3 minutes.

2 Add the carrot, bay leaf and lentils. Pour over the stock. Cover and cook on HIGH power for 15 minutes, stirring halfway through.

3 Remove from the microwave oven and stand, covered, for 5 minutes.

4 Remove the bay leaf, then blend in batches in a food processor, until smooth. Alternatively, press the soup through a sieve (strainer).

5 Pour into a clean bowl. Season with salt and pepper to taste and stir in the coriander (cilantro). Cover and cook on HIGH power for 4–5 minutes until piping hot.

6 Serve in warmed bowls. Stir 1 tablespoon of yogurt into each serving and garnish with sprigs of fresh coriander (cilantro).

COOK'S TIP

For an extra creamy soup try adding low-fat crème fraîche or soured cream instead of yogurt.

Minted Pea & Yogurt Soup

A deliciously refreshing soup that is full of goodness. It is also extremely tasty served chilled.

NUTRITIONAL INFORMATION

Calories 208	Sugars 9g
Protein 10g	Fat 7g
Carbohydrate ...26g	Saturates 2g

10 MINS   25 MINS

SERVES 4

INGREDIENTS

2 tbsp vegetable ghee or oil

2 onions, peeled and coarsely chopped

225 g/8 oz potato, peeled and coarsely chopped

2 garlic cloves, peeled

2.5 cm/1 inch ginger root, peeled and chopped

1 tsp ground coriander

1 tsp ground cumin

1 tbsp plain (all-purpose) flour

850 ml/1½ pints/3½ cups vegetable stock

500 g/1 lb 2 oz frozen peas

2-3 tbsp chopped fresh mint, to taste

salt and freshly ground black pepper

150 ml/¼ pint/⅔ cup low-fat natural yogurt

½ tsp cornflour (cornstarch)

300 ml/½ pint/1¼ cups skimmed milk

a little extra yogurt, for serving (optional)

mint sprigs, to garnish

1 Heat the ghee or oil in a saucepan, add the onions and potato and cook gently for 3 minutes. Stir in the garlic, ginger, coriander, cumin and flour and cook for 1 minute, stirring. Add the stock, peas and half the mint and bring to the boil, stirring. Reduce the heat, cover and simmer gently for 15 minutes.

2 Purée the soup in a blender or food processor. Return the mixture to the pan and season with salt and pepper to taste. Blend the yogurt with the cornflour (cornstarch) and stir into the soup.

3 Add the milk and bring almost to the boil, stirring all the time. Cook very gently for 2 minutes. Serve hot, sprinkled with the remaining mint and a swirl of extra yogurt, if wished.

COOK'S TIP

The yogurt is mixed with a little cornflour (cornstarch) before being added to the hot soup – this helps to stabilize the yogurt and prevents it separating when heated.

Avocado & Mint Soup

A rich and creamy pale green soup made with avocados and enhanced by a touch of chopped mint. Serve chilled in summer or hot in winter.

NUTRITIONAL INFORMATION

Calories 199   Sugars 3g
Protein ....3g   Fat 18g
Carbohydrate ....7g   Saturates 6g

 15 MINS   35 MINS

SERVES 6

INGREDIENTS

40 g/1½ oz/3 tbsp butter or margarine

6 spring onions (scallions), sliced

1 garlic clove, crushed

25 g/1 oz/¼ cup plain (all-purpose) flour

600 ml/1 pint/2½ cups vegetable stock

2 ripe avocados

2–3 tsp lemon juice

pinch of grated lemon rind

150 ml/¼ pint/⅔ cup milk

150 ml/¼ pint/⅔ cup single (light) cream

1–1½ tbsp chopped mint

salt and pepper

mint sprigs, to garnish

MINTED GARLIC BREAD

125 g/4½ oz/½ cup butter

1–2 tbsp chopped mint

1–2 garlic cloves, crushed

1 wholemeal (whole wheat) or
   white French bread stick

1 Melt the butter or margarine in a large, heavy-based saucepan. Add the spring onions (scallions) and garlic clove and fry over a low heat, stirring occasionally, for about 3 minutes, until soft and translucent.

2 Stir in the flour and cook, stirring, for 1–2 minutes. Gradually stir in the stock, then bring to the boil. Simmer gently while preparing the avocados.

3 Peel the avocados, discard the stones (pits) and chop coarsely. Add to the soup with the lemon juice and rind and seasoning. Cover and simmer for about 10 minutes, until tender.

4 Cool the soup slightly, then press through a strainer with the back of a spoon or process in a food processor or blender until a smooth purée forms. Pour into a bowl.

5 Stir in the milk and cream, adjust the seasoning, then stir in the mint. Cover and chill thoroughly.

6 To make the minted garlic bread, soften the butter and beat in the mint and garlic. Cut the loaf into slanting slices but leave a hinge on the bottom crust. Spread each slice with the butter and reassemble the loaf. Wrap in foil and place in a preheated oven, 180°C/350°F/Gas Mark 4, for about 15 minutes.

7 Serve the soup garnished with a sprig of mint and accompanied by the minted garlic bread.

Thick Onion Soup

A delicious creamy soup with grated carrot and parsley for texture and colour. Serve with crusty cheese scones (biscuits) for a hearty lunch.

NUTRITIONAL INFORMATION

Calories ....277 Sugars 12g
Protein ....6g Fat 20g
Carbohydrate ...19g Saturates 8g

20 MINS   1HR 10 MINS

SERVES 6

INGREDIENTS

75 g/2¾ oz/5 tbsp butter

500 g/1 lb 2 oz onions, finely chopped

1 garlic clove, crushed

40 g/1½ oz/6 tbsp plain (all-purpose) flour

600 ml/1 pint/2½ cups vegetable stock

600 ml/1 pint/2½ cups milk

2–3 tsp lemon or lime juice

good pinch of ground allspice

1 bay leaf

1 carrot, coarsely grated

4–6 tbsp double (heavy) cream

2 tbsp chopped parsley

salt and pepper

CHEESE SCONES (BISCUITS)

225 g/8 oz/2 cups malted wheat or
   wholemeal (whole wheat) flour

2 tsp baking powder

60 g/2 oz/¼ cup butter

4 tbsp grated Parmesan cheese

1 egg, beaten

about 75 ml/3 fl oz/⅓ cup milk

1 Melt the butter in a saucepan and fry the onions and garlic over a low heat, stirring frequently, for 10–15 minutes, until soft, but not coloured. Stir in the flour and cook, stirring, for 1 minute, then gradually stir in the stock and bring to the boil, stirring frequently. Add the milk, then bring back to the boil.

2 Season to taste with salt and pepper and add 2 teaspoons of the lemon or lime juice, the allspice and bay leaf. Cover and simmer for about 25 minutes until the vegetables are tender. Discard the bay leaf.

3 Meanwhile, make the scones (biscuits). Combine the flour, baking powder and seasoning and rub in the butter until the mixture resembles fine breadcrumbs. Stir in 3 tablespoons of the cheese, the egg and enough milk to mix to a soft dough.

4 Shape into a bar about 2 cm/¾ inch thick. Place on a floured baking tray (cookie sheet) and mark into slices. Sprinkle with the remaining cheese and bake in a preheated oven, 220°C/425°F/ Gas Mark 7, for about 20 minutes, until risen and golden brown.

5 Stir the carrot into the soup and simmer for 2–3 minutes. Add more lemon or lime juice, if necessary. Stir in the cream and reheat. Garnish and serve with the warm scones (biscuits).

Gardener's Broth

This hearty soup uses a variety of green vegetables with a flavouring of ground coriander. A finishing touch of thinly sliced leeks adds texture.

NUTRITIONAL INFORMATION

Calories ....169 Sugars 5g
Protein ....4g Fat 13g
Carbohydrate ....8g Saturates 5g

 10 MINS   45 MINS

SERVES 6

INGREDIENTS

40 g/1½ oz/3 tbsp butter

1 onion, chopped

1–2 garlic cloves, crushed

1 large leek

225 g/8 oz Brussels sprouts

125 g/4½ oz French (green) or runner
   (string) beans

1.2 litres/2 pints/5 cups vegetable stock

125 g/4½ oz/1 cup frozen peas

1 tbsp lemon juice

½ tsp ground coriander

4 tbsp double (heavy) cream

salt and pepper

MELBA TOAST

4–6 slices white bread

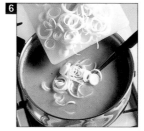

1 Melt the butter in a saucepan. Add the onion and garlic and fry over a low heat, stirring occasionally, until they begin to soften, but not colour.

2 Slice the white part of the leek very thinly and reserve; slice the remaining leek. Slice the Brussels sprouts and thinly slice the beans.

3 Add the green part of the leeks, the Brussels sprouts and beans to the saucepan. Add the stock and bring to the boil. Simmer for 10 minutes.

4 Add the frozen peas, seasoning, lemon juice and coriander and continue to simmer for 10–15 minutes, until the vegetables are tender.

5 Cool the soup a little, then press through a strainer or process in a food processor or blender until smooth. Pour into a clean pan.

6 Add the reserved slices of leek to the soup, bring back to the boil and simmer for about 5 minutes, until the leek is tender. Adjust the seasoning, stir in the cream and reheat gently.

7 To make the melba toast, toast the bread on both sides under a preheated grill (broiler). Cut horizontally through the slices, then toast the uncooked sides until they curl up. Serve immediately with the soup.

Speedy Beetroot (Beet) Soup

Quick and easy to prepare in a microwave oven, this deep red soup of puréed beetroot (beets) and potatoes makes a stunning first course.

NUTRITIONAL INFORMATION

Calories . . . . . . .120 Sugars 11g
Protein . . . . .4g Fat 2g
Carbohydrate . . .22g Saturates 1g

 20 MINS   30 MINS

SERVES 6

INGREDIENTS

1 onion, chopped

350 g/12 oz potatoes, diced

1 small cooking apple, peeled,
   cored and grated

3 tbsp water

1 tsp cumin seeds

500 g/1 lb 2 oz cooked beetroot (beets),
   peeled and diced

1 bay leaf

pinch of dried thyme

1 tsp lemon juice

600 ml/1 pint/2½ cups hot vegetable stock

4 tbsp soured cream

salt and pepper

few dill sprigs, to garnish

1 Place the onion, potatoes, apple and water in a large bowl. Cover and cook on HIGH power for 10 minutes.

2 Stir in the cumin seeds and cook on HIGH power for 1 minute.

3 Stir in the beetroot (beets), bay leaf, thyme, lemon juice and hot vegetable stock. Cover and cook on HIGH power for 12 minutes, stirring halfway through the cooking time.

4 Leave to stand, uncovered, for 5 minutes. Remove and discard the bay leaf. Strain the vegetables and reserve the liquid. Process the vegetables with a little of the reserved liquid in a food processor or blender until they are smooth and creamy. Alternatively, either mash the vegetables with a potato masher or press them through a strainer with the back of a wooden spoon.

5 Pour the vegetable purée into a clean bowl with the reserved liquid and mix well. Season to taste. Cover and cook on HIGH power for 4–5 minutes, until the soup is piping hot.

6 Serve the soup in warmed bowls. Swirl 1 tablespoon of soured cream into each serving and garnish with a few sprigs of fresh dill.

Starters & Snacks

All of these recipes are easy to prepare and appetizing. They are colourful and flavoursome, providing an excellent beginning to any dinner party or just for an everyday snack. Depending on the main course, whet your guests'

appetite with a tasty Dipping Platter, Chinese Omelette or a Pâté or delicious vegetable nibbles. Other quick and tasty snacks provide interesting colours and textures and can all be rustled up at speed. In addition, all these quick recipes will satisfy your hunger pangs and taste buds. All of these dishes are sure to get your meal off to the right start.

Heavenly Garlic Dip

Anyone who loves garlic will adore this dip – it is very potent! Serve it at a barbecue and dip raw vegetables or chunks of French bread into it.

NUTRITIONAL INFORMATION

Calories	344	Sugars	.........2g
Protein	.........6g	Fat	..........34g
Carbohydrate	....3g	Saturates	.......5g

 15 MINS   20 MINS

SERVES 4

INGREDIENTS

2 bulbs garlic

6 tbsp olive oil

1 small onion, finely chopped

2 tbsp lemon juice

3 tbsp tahini (sesame seed paste)

2 tbsp chopped parsley

salt and pepper

TO SERVE

fresh vegetable crudités

French bread or warmed pitta
(pocket) breads

1 Separate the bulbs of garlic into individual cloves. Place them on a baking tray (cookie sheet) and roast in a preheated oven, 200°C/400°F/Gas Mark 6, for 8–10 minutes. Set aside to cool for a few minutes.

2 When they are cool enough to handle, peel the garlic cloves and then chop them finely.

3 Heat the olive oil in a saucepan or frying pan (skillet) and add the garlic and onion. Fry over a low heat, stirring occasionally, for 8–10 minutes, until softened. Remove the pan from the heat.

4 Mix in the lemon juice, tahini (sesame seed paste) and parsley. Season to taste with salt and pepper. Transfer to a small heatproof bowl and keep warm at one side of the barbecue.

5 Serve with fresh vegetable crudités, chunks of French bread or warm pitta (pocket) breads.

VARIATION

If you come across smoked garlic, use it in this recipe – it tastes wonderful. There is no need to roast the smoked garlic, so omit the first step. This dip can also be used to baste kebabs (kabobs) and vegetarian burgers.

Mint & Cannellini Bean Dip

This dip is ideal for pre-dinner drinks or for handing around at a party. The cannellini beans require soaking overnight, so prepare in advance.

NUTRITIONAL INFORMATION

Calories 208	Sugars 1g
Protein 10g	Fat 12g
Carbohydrate ...16g	Saturates 2g

 40 MINS   30 MINS

SERVES 6

INGREDIENTS

175 g/6 oz/1 cup dried cannellini beans

1 small garlic clove, crushed

1 bunch spring onions (scallions),
   roughly chopped

handful of mint leaves

2 tbsp tahini (sesame seed paste)

2 tbsp olive oil

1 tsp ground cumin

1 tsp ground coriander

lemon juice

salt and pepper

sprigs of mint, to garnish

TO SERVE

fresh vegetable crudités, such as
   cauliflower florets, carrots, cucumber,
   radishes and (bell) peppers

1 Soak the cannellini beans overnight in plenty of cold water.

2 Rinse and drain the beans, put them into a large saucepan and cover them with cold water. Bring to the boil and boil rapidly for 10 minutes. Reduce the heat, cover and simmer until tender.

3 Drain the beans and transfer them to a bowl or food processor. Add the garlic, spring onions (scallions), mint, tahini (sesame seed paste) and olive oil.

4 Process the mixture for about 15 seconds or mash well by hand, until smooth.

5 Transfer the mixture to a bowl, stir in the cumin, coriander and lemon juice and season to taste with salt and pepper. Mix thoroughly, cover and leave in a cool place for 30 minutes to allow the flavours to develop fully.

6 Spoon the dip into serving bowls, garnish with sprigs of fresh mint and surround with vegetable crudités. Serve at room temperature.

Buttered Nut & Lentil Dip

This tasty dip is very easy to make. It is perfect to have at barbecues, as it gives your guests something to nibble while they are waiting.

NUTRITIONAL INFORMATION

Calories 395	Sugars 4g
Protein 12g	Fat 31g
Carbohydrate ...18g	Saturates 10g

 5–10 MINS 40 MINS

SERVES 4

INGREDIENTS

60 g/2 oz/¼ cup butter

1 small onion, chopped

90 g/3 oz/⅓ cup red lentils

300 ml/½ pint/1¼ cups vegetable stock

60 g/2 oz/½ cup blanched almonds

60 g/2 oz/½ cup pine nuts

½ tsp ground coriander

½ tsp ground cumin

½ tsp grated root ginger

1 tsp chopped fresh coriander (cilantro)

salt and pepper

sprigs of fresh coriander
    (cilantro) to garnish

TO SERVE

fresh vegetable crudités

bread sticks

VARIATION

Green or brown lentils can be used, but they will take longer to cook than red lentils. If you wish, substitute peanuts for the almonds. Ground ginger can be used instead of fresh – substitute ½ teaspoon and add it with the other spices.

1 Melt half the butter in a saucepan and fry the onion over a medium heat, stirring frequently, until golden brown.

2 Add the lentils and vegetable stock. Bring to the boil, then reduce the heat and simmer gently, uncovered, for about 25–30 minutes, until the lentils are tender. Drain well.

3 Melt the remaining butter in a small frying pan (skillet). Add the almonds and pine nuts and fry them over a low heat, stirring frequently, until golden brown. Remove from the heat.

4 Put the lentils, almonds and pine nuts, with any remaining butter, into a food processor blender. Add the ground coriander, cumin, ginger and fresh coriander (cilantro). Process for about 15–20 seconds, until the mixture is smooth. Alternatively, press the lentils through a strainer to purée them and then mix with the finely chopped nuts, spices and herbs.

5 Season the dip with salt and pepper and garnish with sprigs of fresh coriander (cilantro). Serve with fresh vegetable crudités and bread sticks.

Cheese, Garlic & Herb Pâté

This wonderful soft cheese pâté is fragrant with the aroma of fresh herbs and garlic. Serve with triangles of Melba toast for a perfect starter.

NUTRITIONAL INFORMATION

Calories ....392　Sugars 1g
Protein ....17g　Fat 28g
Carbohydrate ...18g　Saturates 18g

 20 MINS　　🕙 10 MINS

SERVES 4

I N G R E D I E N T S

15 g/½ oz/1 tbsp butter

1 garlic clove, crushed

3 spring onions (scallions), finely chopped

125 g/4½ oz/½ cup full-fat soft cheese

2 tbsp chopped mixed herbs,
　such as parsley, chives, marjoram,
　oregano and basil

175 g/6 oz/1½ cups finely grated mature
　(sharp) Cheddar cheese

pepper

4–6 slices of white bread from a
　medium-cut sliced loaf

mixed salad leaves (greens) and cherry
tomatoes, to serve

T O　G A R N I S H

ground paprika

herb sprigs

1 Melt the butter in a small frying pan (skillet) and gently fry the garlic and spring onions (scallions) together for 3–4 minutes, until softened. Allow to cool.

2 Beat the soft cheese in a large mixing bowl until smooth, then add the garlic and spring onions (scallions). Stir in the herbs, mixing well.

3 Add the Cheddar and work the mixture together to form a stiff paste. Cover and chill until ready to serve.

4 To make the Melba toast, toast the slices of bread on both sides, and then cut off the crusts. Using a sharp bread knife, cut through the slices horizontally to make very thin slices. Cut into triangles and then lightly grill (broil) the untoasted sides until golden.

5 Arrange the mixed salad leaves (greens) on 4 serving plates with the cherry tomatoes. Pile the cheese pâté on top and sprinkle with a little paprika. Garnish with sprigs of fresh herbs and serve with the Melba toast.

Walnut, Egg & Cheese Pâté

This unusual pâté, flavoured with parsley and dill, can be served with crackers, crusty bread or toast. The pâté requires chilling until set.

NUTRITIONAL INFORMATION

Calories 438	Sugars 2g	
Protein 21g	Fat 38g	
Carbohydrate 2g	Saturates 18g	

  20 MINS 2 MINS

SERVES 2

INGREDIENTS

1 celery stick

1–2 spring onions (scallions), trimmed

25 g/1 oz/¼ cup shelled walnuts

1 tbsp chopped fresh parsley

1 tsp chopped fresh dill or ½ tsp dried dill

1 garlic clove, crushed

dash of vegetarian Worcestershire sauce

125 g/4½ oz/½ cup cottage cheese

60 g/2 oz/½ cup blue cheese, such as
   Stilton or Danish Blue

1 hard-boiled (hard-cooked) egg

25 g/1 oz/2 tbsp butter

salt and pepper

herbs, to garnish

crackers, toast or crusty bread and
   crudités, to serve

COOK'S TIP

You can also use this as a stuffing for vegetables. Cut the tops off extra-large tomatoes, scoop out the seeds and fill with the pâté, piling it well up, or spoon into the hollows of celery sticks cut into 5 cm/2 inch pieces.

1 Finely chop the celery, slice the spring onions (scallions) very finely and chop the walnuts evenly. Place in a bowl.

2 Add the chopped herbs and garlic and Worcestershire sauce to taste and mix well, then stir the cottage cheese evenly through the mixture.

3 Grate the blue cheese and hard-boiled (hard-cooked) egg finely into the pâté mixture, and season with salt and pepper.

4 Melt the butter and stir through the pâté, then spoon into one serving dish or two individual dishes, but do not press down firmly. Chill until set.

5 Garnish with fresh herbs and serve with crackers, toast or fresh, crusty bread and a few crudités, if liked.

Smoked Fish & Potato Pâté

This smoked fish pâté is given a tart fruity flavour by the gooseberries, which complement the fish perfectly.

NUTRITIONAL INFORMATION

Calories	418	Sugars 4g
Protein	........18g	Fat 25g
Carbohydrate	...32g	Saturates 6g

20 MINS   10 MINS

SERVES 4

I N G R E D I E N T S

650 g/1 lb 7 oz floury (mealy) potatoes, diced

300 g/10½ oz smoked mackerel, skinned and flaked

75 g/2¾ oz cooked gooseberries

2 tsp lemon juice

2 tbsp low-fat crème fraîche

1 tbsp capers

1 gherkin, chopped

1 tbsp chopped dill pickle

1 tbsp chopped fresh dill

salt and pepper

lemon wedges, to garnish

toast or warm crusty bread, to serve

1 Cook the diced potatoes in a saucepan of boiling water for 10 minutes until tender, then drain well.

2 Place the cooked potatoes in a food processor or blender.

3 Add the skinned and flaked smoked mackerel and process for 30 seconds until fairly smooth. Alternatively, place the ingredients in a bowl and mash with a fork.

4 Add the cooked gooseberries, lemon juice and crème fraîche to the fish and potato mixture. Blend for a further 10 seconds or mash well.

5 Stir in the capers, chopped gherkin and dill pickle, and chopped fresh dill. Season well with salt and pepper.

6 Turn the fish pâté into a serving dish, garnish with lemon wedges and serve with slices of toast or warm crusty bread cut into chunks or slices.

COOK'S TIP

Use stewed, canned or bottled cooked gooseberries for convenience and to save time, or when fresh gooseberries are out of season.

Lentil Pâté

Red lentils are used in this spicy recipe for speed as they do not require pre-soaking. You can substitute other types of lentils, if preferred.

NUTRITIONAL INFORMATION

Calories	267	Sugars	........12g
Protein	........14g	Fat	...........8g
Carbohydrate	...37g	Saturates	.......1g

 30 MINS 1¼ HOURS

SERVES 4

INGREDIENTS

1 tbsp vegetable oil, plus extra for greasing

1 onion, chopped

2 garlic cloves, crushed

1 tsp garam masala

½ tsp ground coriander

850 ml/1½ pints/3¾ cups vegetable stock

175 g/6 oz/¾ cup red lentils

1 small egg

2 tbsp milk

2 tbsp mango chutney

2 tbsp chopped parsley

fresh parsley sprigs, to garnish

salad leaves (greens) and toast, to serve

1 Heat the oil in a large saucepan and sauté the onion and garlic, stirring constantly, for 2–3 minutes. Add the spices and cook for a further 30 seconds.

2 Stir in the stock and lentils and bring the mixture to the boil. Reduce the heat and simmer for 20 minutes, until the lentils are cooked and softened. Remove the pan from the heat and drain off any excess moisture.

3 Put the mixture in a food processor and add the egg, milk, mango chutney and parsley. Process until smooth.

4 Grease and line the base of a 450 g/ 1 lb loaf tin (pan) and spoon in the mixture, levelling the surface. Cover and cook in a preheated oven, 200°C/400°F/ Gas Mark 6, for 40–45 minutes, or until firm to the touch.

5 Cool in the tin (pan) for 20 minutes, then transfer to the refrigerator.

6 Turn out the pâté on to a serving plate, slice and garnish with fresh parsley. Serve with salad leaves (greens) and toast.

COOK'S TIP

It is always better to make your own stock, if you have time, rather than use stock cubes, as the flavour of homemade stock is far superior.

Mixed Bean Pâté

This is a really quick starter to prepare if canned beans are used. Choose a wide variety of beans for colour and flavour.

NUTRITIONAL INFORMATION

Calories ....126 Sugars 3g
Protein ....5g Fat 6g
Carbohydrate ...13g Saturates 1g

 45 MINS   0 MINS

SERVES 4

INGREDIENTS

400 g/14 oz can mixed beans, drained

2 tbsp olive oil

juice of 1 lemon

2 garlic cloves, crushed

1 tbsp chopped coriander (cilantro)

2 spring onions (scallions), chopped

salt and pepper

shredded spring onions (scallions),
   to garnish

1 Rinse the beans thoroughly under cold running water and drain well.

2 Transfer the beans to a food processor or blender and process until smooth. Alternatively, place the beans in a bowl and mash thoroughly with a fork or potato masher.

3 Add the olive oil, lemon juice, garlic, coriander (cilantro) and spring onions (scallions) and blend until fairly smooth. Season with salt and pepper to taste.

4 Transfer the pâté to a serving bowl and chill in the refrigerator for at least 30 minutes.

5 Garnish with shredded spring onions (scallions) and serve.

Toasted Nibbles

These tiny cheese balls are rolled in fresh herbs, toasted nuts or paprika to make tasty nibbles for parties, buffets, or pre-dinner drinks.

NUTRITIONAL INFORMATION

Calories 310	Sugars 1g
Protein 15g	Fat 27g
Carbohydrate 1g	Saturates 12g

🍲 40 MINS   🕐 5 MINS

SERVES 4

I N G R E D I E N T S

125 g/4½ oz/½ cup ricotta cheese

125 g/4½ oz/1 cup finely grated Double
 Gloucester (brick) cheese

2 tsp chopped parsley

60 g/2 oz/½ cup chopped mixed nuts

3 tbsp chopped herbs, such as parsley,
 chives, marjoram, lovage and chervil

2 tbsp mild paprika

pepper

herb sprigs, to garnish

1 Mix together the ricotta and Double Gloucester (brick) cheeses. Add the parsley and pepper and work together until thoroughly combined.

2 Form the mixture into small balls and place on a plate. Cover and chill in the refrigerator for about 20 minutes, until they are firm.

3 Scatter the chopped nuts on to a baking tray (cookie sheet) and place them under a preheated grill (broiler) until lightly browned. Take care as they can easily burn. Leave them to cool.

4 Sprinkle the nuts, herbs and paprika into 3 separate small bowls. Remove the cheese balls from the refrigerator and

divide into 3 equal piles. Roll 1 quantity of the cheese balls in the nuts, 1 quantity in the herbs and 1 quantity in the paprika until they are all well coated.

5 Arrange the coated cheese balls alternately on a large serving platter. Chill in the refrigerator until ready to serve and then garnish with sprigs of fresh herbs.

Tzatziki & Black Olive Dip

Tzatziki is a Greek dish, made with yogurt, mint and cucumber.
It tastes superb with warm pitta (pocket) bread.

NUTRITIONAL INFORMATION

Calories 381	Sugars 8g	
Protein 11g	Fat 15g	
Carbohydrate . . .52g	Saturates 2g	

🍴 1 HOUR   🕐 3 MINS

SERVES 4

INGREDIENTS

½ cucumber

225 g/8 oz/1 cup thick natural
   (unsweetened) yogurt

1 tbsp chopped mint

salt and pepper

4 pitta (pocket) breads

DIP

2 garlic cloves, crushed

125 g/4½ oz/1 cup pitted black olives

4 tbsp olive oil

2 tbsp lemon juice

1 tbsp chopped parsley

TO GARNISH

mint sprigs

parsley sprigs

COOK'S TIP

Sprinkling the cucumber
with salt draws out some of its
moisture, making it crisper. If
you are in a hurry, you can omit
this procedure. Use green olives
instead of black ones if you prefer.

1 To make the tzatziki, peel the cucumber and chop roughly. Sprinkle it with salt and leave to stand for 15–20 minutes. Rinse with cold water and drain well.

2 Mix the cucumber, yogurt and mint together. Season to taste with salt and pepper and transfer to a serving bowl. Cover and chill for 20–30 minutes.

3 To make the black olive dip, put the crushed garlic and olives into a blender or food processor and process for 15–20 seconds. Alternatively, chop them very finely.

4 Add the olive oil, lemon juice and parsley to the blender or food processor and process for a few more seconds. Alternatively, mix with the chopped garlic and olives and mash together. Season with salt and pepper.

5 Wrap the pitta (pocket) breads in foil and place over a barbecue for 2–3 minutes, turning once to warm through. Alternatively, heat in the oven or under the grill (broiler). Cut into pieces and serve with the tzatziki and black olive dip, garnished with sprigs of fresh mint and parsley.

Hummus & Garlic Toasts

Hummus is a real favourite spread on these flavoursome garlic toasts for a delicious starter or snack.

NUTRITIONAL INFORMATION

Calories 731	Sugars 2g	
Protein 22g	Fat 55g	
Carbohydrate . . .39g	Saturates 8g	

20 MINS   3 MINS

SERVES 4

I N G R E D I E N T S

H U M M U S

400 g/14 oz can chickpeas
(garbanzo beans)

juice of 1 large lemon

6 tbsp tahini (sesame seed paste)

2 tbsp olive oil

2 garlic cloves, crushed

salt and pepper

chopped coriander (cilantro) and
black olives, to garnish

T O A S T S

1 ciabatta loaf (Italian bread), sliced

2 garlic cloves, crushed

1 tbsp chopped coriander (cilantro)

4 tbsp olive oil

COOK'S TIP

Make the hummus 1 day in advance, and chill, covered, in the refrigerator until required. Garnish and serve.

1 To make the hummus, firstly drain the chickpeas (garbanzo beans), reserving a little of the liquid. Put the chickpeas (garbanzo beans) and liquid in a food processor and process, gradually adding the reserved liquid and lemon juice. Blend well after each addition until smooth.

2 Stir in the tahini (sesame seed paste) and all but 1 teaspoon of the olive oil. Add the garlic, season to taste and blend again until smooth.

3 Spoon the hummus into a serving dish and smooth the top. Drizzle the remaining olive oil over the top, garnish with chopped coriander (cilantro) and olives. Set aside in the refrigerator to chill while you are preparing the toasts.

4 Place the slices of ciabatta (Italian bread) on a grill (broiler) rack in a single layer.

5 Mix the garlic, coriander (cilantro) and olive oil together and drizzle over the bread slices. Cook under a hot grill (broiler), turning once, for about 2–3 minutes, until golden brown. Serve the toasts immediately with the hummus.

Onions à la Grecque

This is a well-known method of cooking vegetables
and is perfect with shallots or onions, served with a crisp salad.

NUTRITIONAL INFORMATION

Calories	200	Sugars	........26g
Protein	.........2g	Fat	...........9g
Carbohydrate	...28g	Saturates	.......1g

 10 MINS   15 MINS

SERVES 4

I N G R E D I E N T S

450 g/1 lb shallots

3 tbsp olive oil

3 tbsp clear honey

2 tbsp garlic wine vinegar

3 tbsp dry white wine

1 tbsp tomato purée (paste)

2 celery stalks, sliced

2 tomatoes, seeded and chopped

salt and pepper

chopped celery leaves, to garnish

1 Peel the shallots. Heat the oil in a large saucepan, add the shallots and cook, stirring, for 3–5 minutes, or until they begin to brown.

2 Add the honey and cook over a high heat for a further 30 seconds, then add the garlic wine vinegar and dry white wine, stirring well.

3 Stir in the tomato purée (paste), celery and tomatoes and bring the mixture to the boil. Cook over a high heat for 5–6 minutes. Season to taste and leave to cool slightly.

4 Garnish with chopped celery leaves and serve warm. Alternatively chill in the refrigerator before serving.

(Bell) Pepper Salad

Colourful marinated Mediterranean vegetables make a tasty starter.
Serve with fresh bread or Tomato Toasts.

NUTRITIONAL INFORMATION

Calories	234	Sugars	.........4g
Protein	.........6g	Fat	..........17g
Carbohydrate	...15g	Saturates	.......2g

🥪 5–10 MINS   🕐 35 MINS

SERVES 4

INGREDIENTS

1 onion

2 red (bell) peppers

2 yellow (bell) peppers

3 tbsp olive oil

2 large courgettes (zucchini), sliced

2 garlic cloves, sliced

1 tbsp balsamic vinegar

50 g/1¾ oz anchovy fillets, chopped

25 g/1 oz/¼ cup black olives,
   halved and pitted

1 tbsp chopped fresh basil

salt and pepper

TOMATO TOASTS

small stick of French bread

1 garlic clove, crushed

1 tomato, peeled and chopped

2 tbsp olive oil

1 Cut the onion into wedges. Core and deseed the (bell) peppers and cut into thick slices.

2 Heat the oil in a large heavy-based frying pan (skillet). Add the onion, (bell) peppers, courgettes (zucchini) and garlic and fry gently for 20 minutes, stirring occasionally.

3 Add the vinegar, anchovies, olives and seasoning to taste, mix thoroughly and leave to cool.

4 Spoon on to individual plates and sprinkle with the basil.

5 To make the tomato toasts, cut the French bread diagonally into 1 cm/ ½ inch slices.

6 Mix the garlic, tomato, oil and seasoning together, and spread thinly over each slice of bread.

7 Place the bread on a baking tray (cookie sheet), drizzle with the olive oil and bake in a preheated oven, 220°C/425°F/Gas Mark 7, for 5–10 minutes until crisp. Serve the Tomato Toasts with the (Bell) Pepper Salad.

Bruschetta with Tomatoes

Using ripe tomatoes and the best olive oil will make this Tuscan dish absolutely delicious.

NUTRITIONAL INFORMATION

Calories . . . . . . .330　Sugars 4g
Protein . . . . .8g　Fat 14g
Carbohydrate . . .45g　Saturates 2g

 15 MINS　 5 MINS

SERVES 4

I N G R E D I E N T S

300 g/10½ oz cherry tomatoes

4 sun-dried tomatoes

4 tbsp extra virgin olive oil

16 fresh basil leaves, shredded

2 garlic cloves, peeled

8 slices ciabatta

salt and pepper

1 Using a sharp knife, cut the cherry tomatoes in half.

2 Using a sharp knife, slice the sun-dried tomatoes into strips.

3 Place the cherry tomatoes and sun-dried tomatoes in a bowl. Add the olive oil and the shredded basil leaves and toss to mix well. Season to taste with a little salt and pepper.

4 Using a sharp knife, cut the garlic cloves in half. Lightly toast the ciabatta bread.

5 Rub the garlic, cut-side down, over both sides of the lightly toasted ciabatta bread.

6 Top the ciabatta bread with the tomato mixture and serve.

Cured Meats, Olives & Tomatoes

This is a typical *antipasto* dish with the cold cured meats, stuffed olives and fresh tomatoes, basil and balsamic vinegar.

NUTRITIONAL INFORMATION

Calories	312	Sugars	.........1g
Protein	.........12g	Fat	..........28g
Carbohydrate	....2g	Saturates	.......1g

 10 MINS   5 MINS

SERVES 4

INGREDIENTS

4 plum tomatoes

1 tbsp balsamic vinegar

6 canned anchovy fillets, drained and rinsed

2 tbsp capers, drained and rinsed

125 g/4 ½ oz green olives, pitted

175 g/6 oz mixed, cured meats, sliced

8 fresh basil leaves

1 tbsp extra virgin olive oil

salt and pepper

crusty bread, to serve

1 Using a sharp knife, cut the tomatoes into evenly-sized slices. Sprinkle the tomato slices with the balsamic vinegar and a little salt and pepper to taste, and set aside.

2 Chop the anchovy fillets into pieces measuring about the same length as the olives.

3 Push a piece of anchovy and a caper into each olive.

4 Arrange the sliced meat on 4 individual serving plates together with the tomatoes, filled olives and basil leaves.

5 Lightly drizzle the olive oil over the sliced meat, tomatoes and olives.

6 Serve the cured meats, olives and tomatoes with plenty of fresh crusty bread.

COOK'S TIP

The cured meats for this recipe are up to your individual taste. They can include a selection of Parma ham (prosciutto), pancetta, bresaola (dried salt beef) and salame di Milano (pork and beef sausage).

Baked Fennel

Fennel is used extensively in northern Italy. It is a very versatile vegetable, which is good cooked or used raw in salads.

NUTRITIONAL INFORMATION

Calories 111   Sugars 6g
Protein ....7g   Fat 7g
Carbohydrate ....7g   Saturates 3g

 10 MINS   35 MINS

SERVES 4

INGREDIENTS

2 fennel bulbs

2 celery sticks, cut into 7.5 cm/3 inch sticks

6 sun-dried tomatoes, halved

200 g/7 oz passata (tomato paste)

2 tsp dried oregano

50 g/1¾ oz Parmesan cheese, grated

1 Using a sharp knife, trim the fennel, discarding any tough outer leaves, and cut the bulb into quarters.

2 Bring a large pan of water to the boil, add the fennel and celery and cook for 8–10 minutes or until just tender. Remove with a perforated spoon and drain.

3 Place the fennel pieces, celery and sun-dried tomatoes in a large ovenproof dish.

4 Mix the passata (tomato paste) and oregano and pour the mixture over the fennel.

5 Sprinkle with the Parmesan cheese and bake in a preheated oven at 190°C/375°F/Gas Mark 5 for 20 minutes or until hot. Serve as a starter with bread or as a vegetable side dish.

Figs & Parma Ham (Prosciutto)

This colourful fresh salad is delicious at any time of the year. Prosciutto di Parma is said to be the best ham in the world.

NUTRITIONAL INFORMATION

Calories	...121	Sugars	...6g
Protein	...1g	Fat	...11g
Carbohydrate	...6g	Saturates	...2g

 15 MINS 5 MINS

SERVES 4

INGREDIENTS

40 g/1½ oz rocket (arugula)

4 fresh figs

4 slices Parma ham (prosciutto)

4 tbsp olive oil

1 tbsp fresh orange juice

1 tbsp clear honey

1 small red chilli

1 Tear the rocket (arugula) into more manageable pieces and arrange on 4 serving plates.

2 Using a sharp knife, cut each of the figs into quarters and place them on top of the rocket (arugula) leaves.

3 Using a sharp knife, cut the Parma ham (prosciutto) into strips and scatter over the rocket (arugula) and figs.

4 Place the oil, orange juice and honey in a screw-top jar. Shake the jar until the mixture emulsifies and forms a thick dressing. Transfer to a bowl.

5 Using a sharp knife, dice the chilli, remembering not to touch your face before you have washed your hands (see Cook's Tip, below). Add the chopped chilli to the dressing and mix well.

6 Drizzle the dressing over the Parma ham (prosciutto), rocket (arugula) and figs, tossing to mix well. Serve at once.

COOK'S TIP

Chillies can burn the skin for several hours after chopping, so it is advisable to wear gloves when you are handling the very hot varieties.

Deep-Fried Seafood

Deep-fried seafood is popular all around the Mediterranean, where fish of all kinds is fresh and abundant.

NUTRITIONAL INFORMATION

Calories	393	Sugars	.......0.2g
Protein	........27g	Fat	..........26g
Carbohydrate	...12g	Saturates	.......3g

5 MINS   15 MINS

SERVES 4

I N G R E D I E N T S

200 g/7 oz prepared squid

200 g/7 oz blue (raw) tiger prawns
  (shrimp), peeled

150 g/5 ½ oz whitebait

oil, for deep-frying

50 g/1 ½ oz plain (all-purpose) flour

1 tsp dried basil

salt and pepper

TO SERVE

garlic mayonnaise

lemon wedges

1 Carefully rinse the squid, prawns (shrimp) and whitebait under cold running water, completely removing any dirt or grit.

2 Using a sharp knife, slice the squid into rings, leaving the tentacles whole.

3 Heat the oil in a large saucepan to 180°–190°C/350°–375°F or until a cube of bread browns in 30 seconds.

4 Place the flour in a bowl, add the basil and season with salt and pepper to taste. Mix together well.

5 Roll the squid, prawns (shrimp) and whitebait in the seasoned flour until coated all over. Carefully shake off any excess flour.

6 Cook the seafood in the heated oil, in batches, for 2–3 minutes or until crispy and golden all over. Remove all of the seafood with a perforated spoon and leave to drain thoroughly on kitchen paper.

7 Transfer the deep-fried seafood to serving plates and serve with garlic mayonnaise (see page 30) and a few lemon wedges.

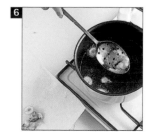

Mussels in White Wine

This soup of mussels, cooked in white wine with onions and cream, can be served as an appetizer or a main dish with plenty of crusty bread.

NUTRITIONAL INFORMATION

Calories 396	Sugars 2g	
Protein 23g	Fat 24g	
Carbohydrate 8g	Saturates 15g	

5–10 MINS | 25 MINS

SERVES 4

INGREDIENTS

about 3 litres/5¼ pints/12 cups fresh
  mussels

60 g/2 oz/¼ cup butter

1 large onion, chopped very finely

2–3 garlic cloves, crushed

350 ml/12 fl oz/1½ cups dry white wine

150 ml/¼ pint/⅔ cup water

2 tbsp lemon juice

good pinch of finely grated lemon rind

1 bouquet garni sachet

1 tbsp plain (all-purpose) flour

4 tbsp single (light) or double (thick) cream

2–3 tbsp chopped fresh parsley

salt and pepper

warm crusty bread, to serve

  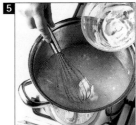

1 Scrub the mussels in several changes of cold water to remove all mud, sand, barnacles, etc. Pull off all the 'beards'. All of the mussels must be tightly closed; if they don't close when given a sharp tap, they must be discarded.

2 Melt half the butter in a large saucepan. Add the onion and garlic, and fry gently until soft but not coloured.

3 Add the wine, water, lemon juice and rind, bouquet garni and plenty of seasoning. Bring to the boil then cover and simmer for 4–5 minutes.

4 Add the mussels to the pan, cover tightly and simmer for 5 minutes, shaking the pan frequently, until all the mussels have opened. Discard any mussels which have not opened. Remove the bouquet garni.

5 Remove the empty half shell from each mussel. Blend the remaining butter with the flour and whisk into the soup, a little at a time. Simmer gently for 2–3 minutes until slightly thickened.

6 Add the cream and half the parsley to the soup and reheat gently. Adjust the seasoning. Ladle the mussels and soup into warmed large soup bowls, sprinkle with the remaining parsley and serve with plenty of warm crusty bread.

Tagliarini with Gorgonzola

This simple, creamy pasta sauce is a classic Italian recipe. You could use Danish blue cheese instead of the Gorgonzola, if you prefer.

NUTRITIONAL INFORMATION

Calories 904	Sugars 4g	
Protein 27g	Fat 53g	
Carbohydrate . . .83g	Saturates 36g	

🧈 5 MINS   🕐 20 MINS

SERVES 4

INGREDIENTS

25 g/1 oz/2 tbsp butter

225 g/8 oz Gorgonzola cheese, roughly crumbled

150 ml/¼ pint/⅝ cup double (heavy) cream

30 ml/2 tbsp dry white wine

1 tsp cornflour (cornstarch)

4 fresh sage sprigs, finely chopped

400 g/14 oz dried tagliarini

2 tbsp olive oil

salt and white pepper

1 Melt the butter in a heavy-based pan. Stir in 175 g/6 oz of the cheese and melt, over a low heat, for about 2 minutes.

2 Add the cream, wine and cornflour (cornstarch) and beat with a whisk until fully incorporated.

COOK'S TIP

Gorgonzola is one of the world's oldest veined cheeses and, arguably, its finest. When buying, always check that it is creamy yellow with delicate green veining. Avoid hard or discoloured cheese. It should have a rich, piquant aroma, not a bitter smell.

3 Stir in the sage and season to taste with salt and white pepper. Bring to the boil over a low heat, whisking constantly, until the sauce thickens. Remove from the heat and set aside while you cook the pasta.

4 Bring a large saucepan of lightly salted water to the boil. Add the tagliarini and 1 tbsp of the olive oil. Cook the pasta for 8–10 minutes or until just tender, drain thoroughly and toss in the remaining olive oil. Transfer the pasta to a serving dish and keep warm.

5 Reheat the sauce over a low heat, whisking constantly. Spoon the Gorgonzola sauce over the tagliarini, generously sprinkle over the remaining cheese and serve immediately.

Ciabatta Rolls

Sandwiches are always a welcome snack, but can be mundane. These crisp rolls filled with roast (bell) peppers and cheese are irresistible.

NUTRITIONAL INFORMATION

Calories 328   Sugars 6g
Protein ....8g   Fat 19g
Carbohydrate ...34g   Saturates 9g

15 MINS   10 MINS

SERVES 4

INGREDIENTS

4 ciabatta rolls

2 tbsp olive oil

1 garlic clove, crushed

FILLING

1 red (bell) pepper

1 green (bell) pepper

1 yellow (bell) pepper

4 radishes, sliced

1 bunch watercress

100 g/3½ oz/8 tbsp cream cheese

1 Slice the ciabatta rolls in half. Heat the olive oil and crushed garlic in a saucepan. Pour the garlic and oil mixture over the cut surfaces of the rolls and leave to stand.

2 Halve the (bell) peppers and place, skin side uppermost, on a grill (broiler) rack. Cook under a hot grill (broiler) for 8–10 minutes, until just beginning to char. Remove the (bell) peppers from the grill (broiler), peel and slice thinly.

3 Arrange the radish slices on one half of each roll with a few watercress leaves. Spoon the cream cheese on top. Pile the (bell) peppers on top of the cream cheese and top with the other half of the roll. Serve immediately.

Aubergine Dipping Platter

Dipping platters are a very sociable dish, bringing together all the diners at the table.

NUTRITIONAL INFORMATION

Calories 81	Sugars 4g	
Protein 4g	Fat 5g	
Carbohydrate 5g	Saturates 1g	

 15 MINS   10 MINS

SERVES 4

INGREDIENTS

1 aubergine (eggplant), peeled and cut into 2.5 cm/1 inch cubes

3 tbsp sesame seeds, roasted in a dry pan over a low heat

1 tsp sesame oil

grated rind and juice of ½ lime

1 small shallot, diced

1 tsp sugar

1 red chilli, deseeded and sliced

125 g/4½ oz/1¼ cups broccoli florets

2 carrots, cut into matchsticks

125 g/4½ oz/8 baby corn, cut in half lengthways

2 celery stalks, cut into matchsticks

1 baby red cabbage, cut into 8 wedges, the leaves of each wedge held together by the core

salt and pepper

 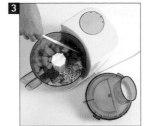 

1 Cook the diced aubergine (eggplant) in a saucepan of boiling water for 7–8 minutes.

2 Meanwhile, grind the sesame seeds with the oil in a food processor or pestle and mortar.

3 Add the aubergine (eggplant), lime rind and juice, shallot, ½ tsp salt, pepper, sugar and chilli in that order to the sesame seeds. Process, or chop and mash by hand, until smooth.

4 Adjust the seasoning to taste then spoon the dip into a bowl.

5 Serve the aubergine (eggplant) dipping platter surrounded by the broccoli, carrots, baby corn, celery and red cabbage.

VARIATION

You can vary the selection of vegetables depending on your preference or whatever you have at hand. Other vegetables you could use are cauliflower florets and cucumber sticks.

Son-in-Law Eggs

This recipe is supposedly so called because it is an easy dish for a son-in-law to cook to impress his new mother-in-law!

NUTRITIONAL INFORMATION

Calories . . . . . . .229 Sugars 8g
Protein . . . . .9g Fat 18g
Carbohydrate . . . .8g Saturates 3g

🥘 15 MINS   🕐 15 MINS

SERVES 4

I N G R E D I E N T S

6 eggs, hard-boiled (hard-cooked)
  and shelled

4 tbsp sunflower oil

1 onion, sliced thinly

2 fresh red chillies, sliced

2 tbsp sugar

1 tbsp water

2 tsp tamarind pulp

1 tbsp liquid seasoning, such
  as Maggi

rice, to serve

1 Prick the hard-boiled (hard-cooked) eggs 2 or 3 times with a cocktail stick (toothpick).

2 Heat the sunflower oil in a wok and fry the eggs until crispy and golden. Drain on absorbent kitchen paper (paper towels).

3 Halve the eggs lengthways and put on a serving dish.

4 Reserve one tablespoon of the oil, pour off the rest, then heat the tablespoonful in the wok. Cook the onion and chillies over a high heat until golden and slightly crisp. Drain on kitchen paper (paper towels).

5 Heat the sugar, water, tamarind pulp and liquid seasoning in the wok and simmer for 5 minutes until thickened.

6 Pour the sauce over the eggs and spoon over the onion and chillies. Serve immediately with rice.

COOK'S TIP

Tamarind pulp is sold in oriental stores, and is quite sour. If it is not available, use twice the amount of lemon juice in its place.

  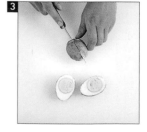

Crispy Seaweed

This tasty Chinese starter is not all that it seems – the 'seaweed' is in fact pak choi which is then fried, salted and tossed with pine kernels.

NUTRITIONAL INFORMATION

Calories	214	Sugars	14g
Protein	6g	Fat	15g
Carbohydrate	15g	Saturates	2g

 10 MINS   5 MINS

SERVES 4

I N G R E D I E N T S

1 kg/2 lb 4 oz pak choi

groundnut oil, for deep-frying (about 850 ml/1½ pints/3¾ cups)

1 tsp salt

1 tbsp caster (superfine) sugar

50 g/1¾ oz/2½ tbsp toasted pine kernels (nuts)

1 Rinse the pak choi leaves under cold running water and then pat dry thoroughly with absorbent kitchen paper (paper towels).

2 Discarding any tough outer leaves, roll each pak choi leaf up, then slice

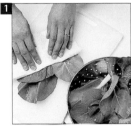  

through thinly so that the leaves are finely shredded. Alternatively, use a food processor to shred the pak choi.

3 Heat the groundnut oil in a large wok or heavy-based frying pan (skillet).

4 Carefully add the shredded pak choi leaves to the wok or frying pan (skillet) and fry for about 30 seconds or until they shrivel up and become crispy

(you will probably need to do this in several batches, depending on the size of the wok).

5 Remove the crispy seaweed from the wok with a slotted spoon and drain on absorbent kitchen paper (paper towels).

6 Transfer the crispy seaweed to a large bowl and toss with the salt, sugar and pine kernels (nuts). Serve immediately.

COOK'S TIP

The tough, outer leaves of pak choi are discarded as these will spoil the overall taste and texture of the dish.

Use savoy cabbage instead of the pak choi if it is unavailable, drying the leaves thoroughly before frying.

Spicy Sweetcorn Fritters

Cornmeal can be found in most supermarkets or health food shops.
Yellow in colour, it acts as a binding agent in this recipe.

NUTRITIONAL INFORMATION

Calories	.... .213	Sugars	.........6g
Protein	.........5g	Fat	...........8g
Carbohydrate	...30g	Saturates	.......1g

 5 MINS   15 MINS

SERVES 4

I N G R E D I E N T S

225 g/8 oz/¾ cup canned or frozen
sweetcorn

2 red chillies, deseeded and very finely
chopped

2 cloves garlic, crushed

10 lime leaves, very finely chopped

2 tbsp fresh coriander (cilantro),
chopped

1 large egg

75 g/2¾ oz/½ cup cornmeal

100 g/3½ oz fine green beans, very finely
sliced

groundnut oil, for frying

1 Place the sweetcorn, chillies, garlic, lime leaves, coriander (cilantro), egg and cornmeal in a large mixing bowl, and stir to combine.

2 Add the green beans to the ingredients in the bowl and mix well, using a wooden spoon.

3 Divide the mixture into small, evenly sized balls. Flatten the balls of mixture between the palms of your hands to form rounds.

4 Heat a little groundnut oil in a preheated wok or large frying pan (skillet) until really hot. Cook the fritters, in batches, until brown and crispy on the outside, turning occasionally.

5 Leave the fritters to drain on absorbent kitchen paper (paper towels) while frying the remaining fritters.

6 Transfer the fritters to warm serving plates and serve immediately.

COOK'S TIP

Kaffir lime leaves are dark green, glossy leaves that have a lemony-lime flavour. They can be bought from specialist Asian stores either fresh or dried. Fresh leaves impart the most delicious flavour.

Chinese Omelette

This is a fairly filling omelette, as it contains chicken and prawns (shrimp). It is cooked as a whole omelette and then sliced for serving.

NUTRITIONAL INFORMATION

Calories	309	Sugars	0g
Protein	34g	Fat	19g
Carbohydrate	0.2g	Saturates	5g

  5 MINS 5 MINS

SERVES 4

I N G R E D I E N T S

8 eggs

225 g/8 oz/2 cups cooked chicken, shredded

12 tiger prawns (jumbo shrimp), peeled and deveined

2 tbsp chopped chives

2 tsp light soy sauce

dash of chilli sauce

2 tbsp vegetable oil

1 Lightly beat the eggs in a large mixing bowl.

2 Add the shredded chicken and tiger prawns (jumbo shrimp) to the eggs, mixing well.

3 Stir in the chopped chives, light soy sauce and chilli sauce, mixing well to combine all the ingredients.

4 Heat the vegetable oil in a large preheated frying pan (skillet) over a medium heat.

5 Add the egg mixture to the frying pan (skillet), tilting the pan to coat the base completely.

6 Cook over a medium heat, gently stirring the omelette with a fork, until the surface is just set and the underside is a golden brown colour.

7 When the omelette is set, slide it out of the pan, with the aid of a palette knife (spatula).

8 Cut the Chinese omelette into squares or slices and serve immediately. Alternatively, serve the omelette as a main course for two people.

VARIATION

You could add extra flavour to the omelette by stirring in 3 tablespoons of finely chopped fresh coriander (cilantro) or 1 teaspoon of sesame seeds with the chives in step 3.

Pork Sesame Toasts

This classic Chinese appetizer is also a great nibble for serving at parties – but be sure to make plenty!

NUTRITIONAL INFORMATION

Calories . . . . . . .674 Sugars 2g
Protein . . . . .33g Fat 46g
Carbohydrate . . .33g Saturates 7g

5 MINS   35 MINS

SERVES 4

I N G R E D I E N T S

250 g/9 oz lean pork

250 g/9 oz/⅔ cup uncooked peeled prawns (shrimp), deveined

4 spring onions (scallions), trimmed

1 garlic clove, crushed

1 tbsp chopped fresh coriander (cilantro) leaves and stems

1 tbsp fish sauce

1 egg

8–10 slices of thick-cut white bread

3 tbsp sesame seeds

150 ml/¼ pint/⅔ cup vegetable oil

salt and pepper

T O   G A R N I S H

sprigs of fresh coriander (cilantro)

red (bell) pepper, sliced finely

1 Put the pork, prawns (shrimp), spring onions (scallions), garlic, coriander (cilantro), fish sauce, egg and seasoning into a food processor or blender. Process for a few seconds until the ingredients are finely chopped. Transfer the mixture to a bowl. Alternatively, chop the pork, prawns (shrimp) and spring onions (scallions) very finely, and mix with the garlic, coriander (cilantro), fish sauce, beaten egg and seasoning until all the ingredients are well combined.

2 Spread the pork and prawn (shrimp) mixture thickly over the bread so that it reaches right up to the edges. Cut off the crusts and slice each piece of bread into 4 squares or triangles.

3 Sprinkle the topping liberally with sesame seeds.

4 Heat the oil in a wok or frying pan (skillet). Fry a few pieces of the bread, topping side down first so that it sets the egg, for about 2 minutes or until golden brown. Turn the pieces over to cook on the other side, about 1 minute.

5 Drain the pork and prawn (shrimp) toasts and place them on kitchen paper (paper towels). Fry the remaining pieces. Serve garnished with sprigs of fresh coriander (cilantro) and strips of red (bell) pepper.

Sesame Ginger Chicken

Chunks of chicken breast are marinated in a mixture of lime juice, garlic, sesame oil and fresh ginger to give them a great flavour.

NUTRITIONAL INFORMATION

Calories	204	Sugars	.........0g
Protein	........28g	Fat	..........10g
Carbohydrate	....1g	Saturates	.......2g

  2¼ HOURS   10 MINS

SERVES 4

I N G R E D I E N T S

4 wooden satay sticks, soaked in
   warm water

500 g/1 lb 2 oz boneless chicken
   breasts

sprigs of fresh mint, to garnish

MARINADE

1 garlic clove, crushed

1 shallot, chopped very finely

2 tbsp sesame oil

1 tbsp fish sauce or light soy sauce

finely grated rind of 1 lime or
   ½ lemon

2 tbsp lime juice or lemon juice

1 tsp sesame seeds

2 tsp finely grated fresh ginger root

2 tsp chopped fresh mint

salt and pepper

COOK'S TIP

The kebabs taste delicious if dipped into an accompanying bowl of hot chilli sauce.

1 To make the marinade, put the crushed garlic, chopped shallot, sesame oil, fish sauce or soy sauce, lime or lemon rind and juice, sesame seeds, grated ginger root and chopped mint into a large non-metallic bowl. Season with a little salt and pepper and mix together until all the ingredients are thoroughly combined.

2 Remove the skin from the chicken breasts and cut the flesh into chunks.

3 Add the chicken to the marinade, stirring to coat the chicken completely in the mixture. Cover with cling film (plastic wrap) and chill in the refrigerator for at least 2 hours so that the flavours are absorbed.

4 Thread the chicken on to wooden satay sticks. Place them on the rack of a grill (broiler) pan and baste with the marinade.

5 Place the kebabs under a preheated grill (broiler) for about 8–10 minutes. Turn them frequently, basting them with the remaining marinade.

6 Serve the chicken skewers at once, garnished with sprigs of fresh mint.

Spicy Salt & Pepper Prawns

For best results, use raw tiger prawns (shrimp) in their shells. They are 7-10 cm/3-4 inches long, and you should get 18-20 per 500 g/1 lb 2 oz.

NUTRITIONAL INFORMATION

Calories 160	Sugars 0.2g	
Protein 17g	Fat 10g	
Carbohydrate ...0.5g	Saturates 1g	

 35 MINS   20 MINS

SERVES 4

INGREDIENTS

250-300 g/9-10½ oz raw prawns (shrimp) in their shells, defrosted if frozen

1 tbsp light soy sauce

1 tsp Chinese rice wine or dry sherry

2 tsp cornflour (cornstarch)

vegetable oil, for deep-frying

2-3 spring onions (scallions), to garnish

SPICY SALT AND PEPPER

1 tbsp salt

1 tsp ground Szechuan peppercorns

1 tsp five-spice powder

1 Pull the soft legs off the prawns (shrimp), but keep the body shell on. Dry well on absorbent kitchen paper (paper towels).

2 Place the prawns (shrimp) in a bowl with the soy sauce, rice wine or sherry and cornflour (cornstarch). Turn the prawns (shrimp) to coat thoroughly in the mixture and leave to marinate for about 25-30 minutes.

3 To make the Spicy Salt and Pepper, mix the salt, ground Szechuan peppercorns and five-spice powder together. Place in a dry frying pan (skillet) and stir-fry for about 3-4 minutes over a low heat, stirring constantly to prevent the spices burning on the bottom of the pan. Remove from the heat and allow to cool.

4 Heat the vegetable oil in a preheated wok or large frying pan (skillet) until smoking, then deep-fry the prawns (shrimp) in batches until golden brown. Remove the prawns (shrimp) from the wok with a slotted spoon and drain on kitchen paper (paper towels).

5 Place the spring onions (scallions) in a bowl, pour on 1 tablespoon of the hot oil and leave for 30 seconds. Serve the prawns (shrimp) garnished with the spring onions (scallions), and with the Spicy Salt and Pepper as a dip.

COOK'S TIP

The roasted spice mixture made with Szechuan peppercorns is used throughout China as a dip for deep-fried food. The peppercorns are sometimes roasted first and then ground. Dry-frying is a way of releasing the flavours of the spices.

Crostini alla Fiorentina

Serve as a starter, or simply spread on small pieces of crusty fried bread (crostini) as an appetizer with drinks.

NUTRITIONAL INFORMATION

Calories 393	Sugars 2g	
Protein 17g	Fat 25g	
Carbohydrate ...19g	Saturates 9g	

   10 MINS   40–45 MINS

SERVES 4

INGREDIENTS

3 tbsp olive oil

1 onion, chopped

1 celery stalk, chopped

1 carrot, chopped

1–2 garlic cloves, crushed

125 g/4½ oz chicken livers

125 g/4½ oz calf's, lamb's or pig's liver

150 ml/¼ pint/⅔ cup red wine

1 tbsp tomato purée (paste)

2 tbsp chopped fresh parsley

3–4 canned anchovy fillets, chopped finely

2 tbsp stock or water

25–40 g/1–1½ oz/2–3 tbsp butter

1 tbsp capers

salt and pepper

small pieces of fried crusty bread, to serve

chopped parsley, to garnish

1 Heat the oil in a pan, add the onion, celery, carrot and garlic, and cook gently for 4–5 minutes or until the onion is soft, but not coloured.

2 Meanwhile, rinse and dry the chicken livers. Dry the calf's or other liver, and slice into strips. Add the liver to the pan and fry gently for a few minutes until the strips are well sealed on all sides.

3 Add half of the wine and cook until it has mostly evaporated. Then add the rest of the wine, tomato purée (paste), half of the parsley, the anchovy fillets, stock or water, a little salt and plenty of black pepper.

4 Cover the pan and leave to simmer, stirring occasionally, for 15–20 minutes or until tender and most of the liquid has been absorbed.

5 Leave the mixture to cool a little, then either coarsely mince or put into a food processor and process to a chunky purée.

6 Return to the pan and add the butter, capers and remaining parsley. Heat through gently until the butter melts. Adjust the seasoning and turn out into a bowl. Serve warm or cold spread on the slices of crusty bread and sprinkled with chopped parsley.

Chicken or Beef Satay

In this dish, strips of chicken or beef are threaded on to skewers, grilled (broiled) and served with a spicy peanut sauce.

NUTRITIONAL INFORMATION

Calories 314   Sugars 8g
Protein . . . . .32g   Fat 16g
Carbohydrate . . .10g   Saturates 4g

2¼ HOURS   15 MINS

SERVES 6

INGREDIENTS

4 boneless, skinned chicken breasts or
   750 g/1 lb 10 oz rump steak, trimmed

MARINADE

1 small onion, finely chopped

1 garlic clove, crushed

2.5 cm/1 inch piece ginger root, peeled
   and grated

2 tbsp dark soy sauce

2 tsp chilli powder

1 tsp ground coriander

2 tsp dark brown sugar

1 tbsp lemon or lime juice

1 tbsp vegetable oil

SAUCE

300 ml/½ pint/1¼ cups coconut milk

4 tbsp/⅓ cup crunchy peanut butter

1 tbsp fish sauce

1 tsp lemon or lime juice

salt and pepper

1 Using a sharp knife, trim any fat from the chicken or beef then cut into thin strips, about 7 cm/3 inches long.

2 To make the marinade, place all the ingredients in a shallow dish and mix well. Add the chicken or beef strips and turn in the marinade until well coated.

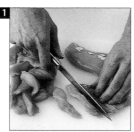

Cover with cling film (plastic wrap) and leave to marinate for 2 hours or overnight in the refrigerator.

3 Remove the meat from the marinade and thread the pieces, concertina style, on pre-soaked bamboo or thin wooden skewers.

4 Grill (broil) the chicken and beef satays for 8-10 minutes, turning and

brushing occasionally with the marinade, until cooked through.

5 Meanwhile, to make the sauce, mix the coconut milk with the peanut butter, fish sauce and lemon or lime juice in a saucepan. Bring to the boil and cook for 3 minutes. Season to taste.

6 Transfer the sauce to a serving bowl and serve with the cooked satays.

Pasta & Anchovy Sauce

This is an ideal dish for cooks in a hurry, as it is prepared in minutes from store-cupboard ingredients.

NUTRITIONAL INFORMATION

Calories 712   Sugars 4g
Protein . . . . .25g   Fat 34g
Carbohydrate . . .81g   Saturates 8g

  10 MINS   25 MINS

SERVES 4

INGREDIENTS

90 ml/3 fl oz olive oil

2 garlic cloves, crushed

60 g/2 oz can anchovy fillets, drained

450 g/1 lb dried spaghetti

60 g/2 oz pesto sauce (see page 223)

2 tbsp finely chopped fresh oregano

90 g/3 oz/1 cup grated Parmesan cheese,
    plus extra for serving (optional)

salt and pepper

2 fresh oregano sprigs, to garnish

1 Reserve 1 tbsp of the oil and heat the remainder in a small saucepan. Add the garlic and fry for 3 minutes.

2 Lower the heat, stir in the anchovies and cook, stirring occasionally, until the anchovies have disintegrated.

3 Bring a large saucepan of lightly salted water to the boil. Add the spaghetti and the remaining olive oil and cook for 8–10 minutes or until just tender, but still firm to the bite.

4 Add the Pesto Sauce and chopped fresh oregano to the anchovy mixture and then season with pepper to taste.

5 Drain the spaghetti, using a slotted spoon, and transfer to a warm serving dish. Pour the Pesto Sauce over the spaghetti and then sprinkle over the grated Parmesan cheese.

6 Garnish with oregano sprigs and serve with extra cheese, if using.

COOK'S TIP

If you find canned anchovies rather too salty, soak them in a saucer of cold milk for 5 minutes, drain and pat dry with kitchen paper (kitchen towels) before using. The milk absorbs the salt.

Fish & Seafood

The wealth of species and flavours of fish and seafood that the world's oceans and rivers provide is immense. Each country combines its local catch with the region's favourite herbs and spices to create a variety of dishes. All of the recipes featured

here are easy to prepare and delicious to eat. Moreover, not only are fish and seafood are quick to cook, but they are packed full with nutritional goodness. Naturally low in fat, yet rich in minerals and proteins, fish and seafood are important to help balance any diet. The variety of fish and fish prices helps us to choose dishes to suit both mood and pocket.

Seafood Salad

Seafood is plentiful in Italy and each region has its own seafood salad. The dressing needs to be chilled for several hours so prepare in advance.

NUTRITIONAL INFORMATION

Calories 471   Sugars 2g
Protein . . . . .34g   Fat 33g
Carbohydrate . . . .4g   Saturates 5g

45-55 MINS   40 MINS

SERVES 4

INGREDIENTS

175 g/6 oz squid rings, defrosted if frozen

600 ml/1 pint/2½ cups water

150 ml/¼ pint/⅔ cup dry white wine

225 g/8 oz hake or monkfish, cut into cubes

16–20 mussels, scrubbed and debearded

20 clams in shells, scrubbed, if available
   (otherwise use extra mussels)

125–175 g/4½–6 oz peeled prawns
   (shrimp)

3–4 spring onions (scallions), trimmed and
   sliced (optional)

radicchio and curly endive leaves, to serve

lemon wedges, to garnish

DRESSING

6 tbsp olive oil

1 tbsp wine vinegar

2 tbsp chopped fresh parsley

1–2 garlic cloves, crushed

salt and pepper

GARLIC MAYONNAISE

5 tbsp thick mayonnaise

2–3 tbsp fromage frais or natural yogurt

2 garlic cloves, crushed

1 tbsp capers

2 tbsp chopped fresh parsley or mixed herbs

1 Poach the squid in the water and wine for 20 minutes or until nearly tender. Add the fish and continue to cook gently for 7–8 minutes or until tender. Strain, reserving the fish. Pour the stock into a clean pan.

2 Bring the fish stock to the boil and add the mussels and clams. Cover the pan and simmer gently for about 5 minutes or until the shells open. Discard any that remain closed.

3 Drain the shellfish and remove from their shells. Put into a bowl with the cooked fish and add the prawns (shrimp) and spring onions (scallions), if using.

4 For the dressing, whisk together the oil, vinegar, parsley, garlic, salt and pepper to taste. Pour over the fish, mixing well. Cover and chill for several hours.

5 Arrange small leaves of radicchio and curly endive on 4 plates and spoon the fish salad into the centre. Garnish with lemon wedges. Combine all the ingredients for the garlic mayonnaise and serve with the salad.

Mussel Salad

A colourful combination of cooked mussels tossed together with char-grilled red (bell) peppers and salad leaves in a lemon dressing.

NUTRITIONAL INFORMATION

Calories ....124 Sugars 5g
Protein ....16g Fat 5g
Carbohydrate ....5g Saturates 1g

 40 MINS   10 MINS

SERVES 4

INGREDIENTS

2 large red (bell) peppers

350 g/12 oz cooked shelled mussels, thawed if frozen

1 head of radicchio

25 g/1 oz rocket (arugula) leaves

8 cooked New Zealand mussels in their shells

TO SERVE

lemon wedges

crusty bread

DRESSING

1 tbsp olive oil

1 tbsp lemon juice

1 tsp finely grated lemon rind

2 tsp clear honey

1 tsp French mustard

1 tbsp snipped fresh chives

salt and pepper

1 Preheat the grill (broiler) to hot. Halve and deseed the (bell) peppers and place them skin-side up on the rack.

2 Cook for 8–10 minutes until the skin is charred and blistered and the flesh is soft. Leave to cool for 10 minutes, then peel off the skin.

3 Slice the (bell) pepper flesh into thin strips and place in a bowl. Gently mix in the shelled mussels and set aside until required.

4 To make the dressing, mix all of the ingredients until well blended.

5 Mix into the (bell) pepper and mussel mixture until coated.

6 Remove the central core of the radicchio and shred the leaves. Place in a serving bowl with the rocket (arugula) leaves and toss together.

7 Pile the mussel mixture into the centre of the leaves and arrange the large mussels in their shells around the edge of the dish. Serve with lemon wedges and crusty bread.

Sweet & Sour Tuna Salad

Flageolet (small navy) beans, courgettes (zucchini) and tomatoes are briefly cooked in a sweet and sour sauce, before being mixed with tuna.

NUTRITIONAL INFORMATION

Calories . . . . . . .245 Sugars 5g
Protein . . . . .22g Fat 8g
Carbohydrate . . .24g Saturates 1g

15 MINS   10 MINS

SERVES 4

INGREDIENTS

2 tbsp olive oil

1 onion, chopped

2 garlic cloves, chopped

2 courgettes (zucchini), sliced

4 tomatoes, skinned

400 g/14 oz can flageolet (small navy) beans, drained and rinsed

10 black olives, halved and pitted

1 tbsp capers

1 tsp caster (superfine) sugar

1 tbsp wholegrain mustard

1 tbsp white wine vinegar

200 g/7 oz can tuna fish, drained

2 tbsp chopped fresh parsley

chopped fresh parsley, to garnish

crusty bread, to serve

1 Heat the oil in a frying pan (skillet) and fry the onion, garlic for 5 minutes until soft.

2 Add the courgettes (zucchini) and cook for 3 minutes, stirring occasionally.

3 Cut the tomatoes in half then into thin wedges.

4 Add the tomatoes to the pan with the beans, olives, capers, sugar, mustard and vinegar.

5 Simmer for 2 minutes, stirring gently, then allow to cool slightly.

6 Flake the tuna fish and stir into the bean mixture with the parsley.

7 Garnish with parsley and serve lukewarm with crusty bread.

COOK'S TIP

Capers are the flower buds of the caper bush, which is native to the Mediterranean region. Capers are preserved in vinegar and salt and give a distinctive flavour to this salad. They are much used in Italian and Provençale cooking.

Smoked Trout & Apple Salad

Smoked trout and horseradish are natural partners, but with apple and watercress this makes a wonderful first course.

NUTRITIONAL INFORMATION

Calories	133	Sugars	........11g
Protein	........12g	Fat	...........5g
Carbohydrate	....11g	Saturates	......1g

  10 MINS   0 MINS

SERVES 4

I N G R E D I E N T S

2 orange-red dessert (eating) apples, such as Cox's Orange

2 tbsp French dressing

½ bunch watercress

1 smoked trout, about 175 g/6 oz

HORSERADISH DRESSING

125 ml/4 fl oz/½ cup low-fat natural yogurt

½–1 tsp lemon juice

1 tbsp horseradish sauce

milk (optional)

salt and pepper

TO GARNISH

1 tbsp chopped chives

chive flowers (optional)

1 Leaving the skin on, cut the apples into quarters and remove the core. Slice the apples into a bowl and toss in the French dressing to prevent them from browning.

2 Break the watercress into sprigs and arrange on 4 serving plates.

3 Skin the trout and take out the bone. Carefully remove any fine bones that remain. Flake the trout into fairly large pieces and arrange between the watercress with the apple.

4 To make the horseradish dressing, whisk all the ingredients together, adding a little milk if too thick, then drizzle over the trout. Sprinkle the chopped chives and flowers (if using) over the trout, then serve.

COOK'S TIP

To make Melba toast, toast thinly sliced bread then cut off the crusts and carefully slice in half horizontally using a sharp knife. Cut in half diagonally and place toasted side down in a warm oven for 15–20 minutes until the edges start to curl and the toast is crisp.

Tuna, Bean & Anchovy Salad

Serve as part of a selection of *antipasti*, or for a summer lunch with hot garlic bread.

NUTRITIONAL INFORMATION

Calories 397	Sugars 8g
Protein 23g	Fat 30g
Carbohydrate ...10g	Saturates 4g

🥟 35 MINS   🕐 0 MINS

SERVES 4

INGREDIENTS

500 g/1 lb 2 oz tomatoes

200 g/7 oz can tuna fish, drained

2 tbsp chopped fresh parsley

½ cucumber

1 small red onion, sliced

225 g/8 oz cooked green beans

1 small red (bell) pepper, cored and
   deseeded

1 small crisp lettuce

6 tbsp Italian-style dressing

3 hard-boiled (hard-cooked) eggs

60 g/2 oz can anchovies, drained

12 black olives, pitted

1 Cut the tomatoes into wedges, flake the tuna and put both into the bowl with the parsley.

2 Cut the cucumber in half lengthways, then cut into slices. Slice the onion. Add the cucumber and onion to the bowl.

3 Cut the beans in half, chop the (bell) pepper and add both to the bowl with the lettuce leaves. Pour over the dressing and toss to mix, then spoon into a salad bowl. Cut the eggs into quarters, arrange over the top with the anchovies and scatter with the olives.

Neapolitan Seafood Salad

This delicious mix of seafood, salad leaves (greens) and ripe tomatoes conjures up all the warmth and sunshine of Naples.

NUTRITIONAL INFORMATION

Calories	1152	Sugars	.........3g
Protein	........67g	Fat	..........81g
Carbohydrate	...35g	Saturates	......12g

   6½ HOURS   🕐 25 MINS

SERVES 4

INGREDIENTS

450 g/1 lb prepared squid,
    cut into strips

750 g/1 lb 10 oz cooked mussels

450 g/1 lb cooked cockles in brine

150 ml/¼ pint/⅔ cup white wine

300 ml/½ pint/1¼ cups olive oil

225 g/8 oz/2 cups dried campanelle or
    other small pasta shapes

juice of 1 lemon

1 bunch chives, snipped

1 bunch fresh parsley,
finely chopped

4 large tomatoes

mixed salad leaves (greens)

salt and pepper

sprig of fresh basil, to garnish

VARIATION

You can substitute cooked scallops for the mussels and clams in brine for the cockles, if you prefer. The seafood needs to be marinated for 6 hours, so prepare well in advance.

1 Put all of the seafood into a large bowl, pour over the wine and half of the olive oil, and set aside for 6 hours.

2 Put the seafood mixture into a saucepan and simmer over a low heat for 10 minutes. Set aside to cool.

3 Bring a large saucepan of lightly salted water to the boil. Add the pasta and 1 tbsp of the remaining olive oil and cook for 8–10 minutes or until tender, but still firm to the bite. Drain thoroughly and refresh in cold water.

4 Strain off about half of the cooking liquid from the seafood and discard the rest. Mix in the lemon juice, chives, parsley and the remaining olive oil. Season to taste with salt and pepper. Drain the pasta and add to the seafood.

5 Cut the tomatoes into quarters. Shred the salad leaves (greens) and arrange them at the base of a salad bowl. Spoon in the seafood salad and garnish with the tomatoes and a sprig of basil. Serve.

Seafood Stir-Fry

This combination of assorted seafood and tender vegetables flavoured with ginger makes an ideal light meal served with thread noodles.

NUTRITIONAL INFORMATION

Calories 226	Sugars 5g
Protein 35g	Fat 7g
Carbohydrate 6g	Saturates 1g

5 MINS   15 MINS

SERVES 4

INGREDIENTS

100 g/3½ oz small, thin asparagus spears, trimmed

1 tbsp sunflower oil

2.5 cm/1 inch piece root (fresh) ginger, cut into thin strips

1 medium leek, shredded

2 medium carrots, julienned

100 g/3½ oz baby sweetcorn cobs, quartered lengthwise

2 tbsp light soy sauce

1 tbsp oyster sauce

1 tsp clear honey

450 g/1 lb cooked, assorted shellfish, thawed if frozen

freshly cooked egg noodles, to serve

TO GARNISH

4 large cooked prawns

small bunch fresh chives, freshly snipped

1 Bring a small saucepan of water to the boil and blanch the asparagus for 1–2 minutes.

2 Drain the asparagus, set aside and keep warm.

3 Heat the oil in a wok or large frying pan (skillet) and stir-fry the ginger, leek, carrot and sweetcorn for about 3 minutes. Do not allow the vegetables to brown.

4 Add the soy sauce, oyster sauce and honey to the wok or frying pan (skillet).

5 Stir in the cooked shellfish and continue to stir-fry for 2–3 minutes until the vegetables are just tender and the shellfish are thoroughly heated through. Add the blanched asparagus and stir-fry for about 2 minutes.

6 To serve, pile the cooked noodles on to 4 warm serving plates and spoon the seafood and vegetable stir fry over them.

7 Garnish with the cooked prawns and freshly snipped chives and serve immediately. Serve garnished with a large prawn and freshly snipped chives.

Fillets of Red Mullet & Pasta

This simple recipe perfectly complements the sweet flavour and delicate texture of the fish.

NUTRITIONAL INFORMATION

Calories 457   Sugars 3g
Protein ....39g   Fat 12g
Carbohydrate ...44g   Saturates 5g

 15 MINS   1 HOUR

SERVES 4

INGREDIENTS

1 kg/2 lb 4 oz red mullet fillets

300 ml/½ pint/1¼ cups dry white wine

4 shallots, finely chopped

1 garlic clove, crushed

3 tbsp finely chopped mixed fresh herbs

finely grated rind and juice of 1 lemon

pinch of freshly grated nutmeg

3 anchovy fillets, roughly chopped

2 tbsp double (heavy) cream

1 tsp cornflour (cornstarch)

450 g/1 lb dried vermicelli

1 tbsp olive oil

salt and pepper

TO GARNISH

1 fresh mint sprig

lemon slices

lemon rind

1 Put the red mullet fillets in a large casserole. Pour over the wine and add the shallots, garlic, herbs, lemon rind and juice, nutmeg and anchovies. Season. Cover and bake in a preheated oven at 180°C/350°F/Gas Mark 4 for 35 minutes.

2 Transfer the mullet to a warm dish. Set aside and keep warm.

3 Pour the cooking liquid into a pan and bring to the boil. Simmer for 25 minutes, until reduced by half. Mix the cream and cornflour (cornstarch) and stir into the sauce to thicken.

4 Meanwhile, bring a pan of lightly salted water to the boil. Add the vermicelli and oil and cook for 8–10 minutes, until tender but still firm to the bite. Drain the pasta and transfer to a warm serving dish.

5 Arrange the red mullet fillets on top of the vermicelli and pour over the sauce. Garnish with a fresh mint sprig, slices of lemon and strips of lemon rind and serve immediately.

Trout with Smoked Bacon

Most trout available nowadays is farmed rainbow trout, however, if you can, buy wild brown trout for this recipe.

NUTRITIONAL INFORMATION

Calories ....802 Sugars 8g
Protein ....68g Fat 36g
Carbohydrate ...54g Saturates 10g

 35 MINS   25 MINS

SERVES 4

INGREDIENTS

butter, for greasing

4 x 275 g/9½ oz trout, gutted and cleaned

12 anchovies in oil, drained and chopped

2 apples, peeled, cored and sliced

4 fresh mint sprigs

juice of 1 lemon

12 slices rindless smoked fatty bacon

450 g/1 lb dried tagliatelle

1 tbsp olive oil

salt and pepper

TO GARNISH

2 apples, cored and sliced

4 fresh mint sprigs

1 Grease a deep baking tray (cookie sheet) with butter.

2 Open up the cavities of each trout and rinse with warm salt water.

3 Season each cavity with salt and pepper. Divide the anchovies, sliced apples and mint sprigs between each of the cavities. Sprinkle the lemon juice into each cavity.

4 Carefully cover the whole of each trout, except the head and tail, with three slices of smoked bacon in a spiral.

5 Arrange the trout on the baking tray (cookie sheet) with the loose ends of bacon tucked underneath. Season with pepper and bake in a preheated oven at 200°C/400°F/Gas Mark 6 for 20 minutes, turning the trout over after 10 minutes.

6 Meanwhile, bring a large pan of lightly salted water to the boil. Add the tagliatelle and olive oil and cook for about 12 minutes, until tender but still firm to the bite. Drain the pasta and transfer to a large, warm serving dish.

7 Remove the trout from the oven and arrange on the tagliatelle. Garnish with sliced apples and fresh mint sprigs and serve immediately.

Poached Salmon with Penne

Fresh salmon and pasta in a mouth-watering lemon and watercress sauce – a wonderful summer evening treat.

NUTRITIONAL INFORMATION

Calories	968	Sugars	.........3g
Protein	........59g	Fat	..........58g
Carbohydrate	...49g	Saturates	......19g

 10 MINS   30 MINS

SERVES 4

INGREDIENTS

4 x 275 g/9½ oz fresh salmon steaks

60 g/2 oz/4 tbsp butter

175 ml/6 fl oz/¾ cup dry white wine

sea salt

8 peppercorns

fresh dill sprig

fresh tarragon sprig

1 lemon, sliced

450 g/1 lb dried penne

2 tbsp olive oil

lemon slices and fresh watercress,
   to garnish

LEMON & WATERCRESS SAUCE

25 g/1 oz/2 tbsp butter

25 g/1 oz/¼ cup plain (all-purpose) flour

150 ml/¼ pint/⅝ cup warm milk

juice and finely grated rind of 2 lemons

60 g/2 oz watercress, chopped

salt and pepper

1 Put the salmon in a large, non-stick pan. Add the butter, wine, a pinch of sea salt, the peppercorns, dill, tarragon and lemon. Cover, bring to the boil, and simmer for 10 minutes.

2 Using a fish slice, carefully remove the salmon. Strain and reserve the cooking liquid. Remove and discard the salmon skin and centre bones. Place on a warm dish, cover and keep warm.

3 Meanwhile, bring a saucepan of salted water to the boil. Add the penne and 1 tbsp of the oil and cook for 8–10 minutes, until tender but still firm to the bite. Drain and sprinkle over the remaining olive oil. Place on a warm serving dish, top with the salmon steaks and keep warm.

4 To make the sauce, melt the butter and stir in the flour for 2 minutes. Stir in the milk and about 7 tbsp of the reserved cooking liquid. Add the lemon juice and rind and cook, stirring, for a further 10 minutes.

5 Add the watercress to the sauce, stir gently and season to taste with salt and pepper.

6 Pour the sauce over the salmon and penne, garnish with slices of lemon and fresh watercress and serve.

Prawn (Shrimp) Pasta Bake

This dish is ideal for a substantial supper. You can use whatever pasta you like, but the tricolour varieties will give the most colourful results.

NUTRITIONAL INFORMATION

Calories 723	Sugars 9g	
Protein 56g	Fat 8g	
Carbohydrate ...114g	Saturates 2g	

  10 MINS 50 MINS

SERVES 4

INGREDIENTS

225 g/8 oz tricolour pasta shapes

1 tbsp vegetable oil

175 g/6 oz button mushrooms, sliced

1 bunch spring onions (scallions), trimmed and chopped

400 g/14 oz can tuna in brine, drained and flaked

175 g/6 oz peeled prawns (shrimp), thawed if frozen

2 tbsp cornflour (cornstarch)

425 ml/15 fl oz/1¾ cups skimmed milk

4 medium tomatoes, sliced thinly

25 g/1 oz fresh breadcrumbs

25 g/1 oz reduced-fat Cheddar cheese, grated

salt and pepper

TO SERVE

wholemeal bread

fresh salad

1 Preheat the oven to 190°C/375°F/Gas Mark 5. Bring a large saucepan of water to the boil and cook the pasta according to the instructions on the packet. Drain well.

2 Meanwhile, heat the vegetable oil in a frying pan (skillet) and fry the mushrooms and all but a handful of the spring onions (scallions) for 4–5 minutes until softened.

3 Place the cooked pasta in a bowl and mix in the spring onions (scallions), mushrooms, tuna and prawns (shrimp).

4 Blend the cornflour (cornstarch) with a little milk to make a paste. Pour the remaining milk into a saucepan and stir in the paste. Heat, stirring, until the sauce begins to thicken. Season well. Add the sauce to the pasta mixture and mix well. Transfer to an ovenproof gratin dish and place on a baking tray (cookie sheet).

5 Arrange the tomato slices over the pasta and sprinkle with the breadcrumbs and cheese. Bake for 25–30 minutes until golden. Serve sprinkled with the reserved spring onions (scallions) and accompanied with bread and salad.

Spaghetti al Tonno

The classic Italian combination of pasta and tuna is enhanced in this recipe with a delicious parsley sauce.

NUTRITIONAL INFORMATION

Calories 1065	Sugars 3g
Protein 27g	Fat 85g
Carbohydrate . . .52g	Saturates 18g

 10 MINS   15 MINS

SERVES 4

INGREDIENTS

200 g/7 oz can tuna, drained

60 g/2 oz can anchovies, drained

250 ml/9 fl oz/1⅛ cups olive oil

60 g/2 oz/1 cup roughly chopped
   flat leaf parsley

150 ml/¼ pint/⅔ cup crème fraîche

450 g/1 lb dried spaghetti

25 g/1 oz/2 tbsp butter

salt and pepper

black olives, to garnish

crusty bread, to serve

1 Remove any bones from the tuna. Put the tuna into a food processor or blender, together with the anchovies, 225 ml/ 8 fl oz/1 cup of the olive oil and the flat leaf parsley. Process until the sauce is very smooth.

VARIATION

If liked, you could add 1–2 garlic cloves to the sauce, substitute 25 g/1 oz/½ cup chopped fresh basil for half the parsley and garnish with capers instead of black olives.

2 Spoon the crème fraîche into the food processor or blender and process again for a few seconds to blend thoroughly. Season with salt and pepper to taste.

3 Bring a large pan of lightly salted water to the boil. Add the spaghetti and the remaining olive oil and cook for 8–10 minutes until tender, but still firm to the bite.

4 Drain the spaghetti, return to the pan and place over a medium heat. Add the butter and toss well to coat. Spoon in the sauce and quickly toss into the spaghetti, using 2 forks.

5 Remove the pan from the heat and divide the spaghetti between 4 warm individual serving plates. Garnish with the olives and serve immediately with warm, crusty bread.

Pasta Shells with Mussels

Serve this aromatic seafood dish to family and friends who admit to a love of garlic.

NUTRITIONAL INFORMATION

Calories	686	Sugars	.........2g
Protein	........30g	Fat	..........45g
Carbohydrate	...36g	Saturates	......27g

🍳 15 MINS   🕐 25 MINS

SERVES 6

INGREDIENTS

1.25 kg/2 lb 12 oz mussels

225 ml/8 fl oz/1 cup dry white wine

2 large onions, chopped

115 g/4 oz/½ cup unsalted butter

6 large garlic cloves, finely chopped

5 tbsp chopped fresh parsley

300 ml/½ pint/1¼ cups double
   (heavy) cream

400 g/14 oz dried pasta shells

1 tbsp olive oil

salt and pepper

crusty bread, to serve

1 Scrub and debeard the mussels under cold running water. Discard any mussels that do not close immediately when sharply tapped. Put the mussels into a large saucepan, together with the wine and half of the onions. Cover and cook over a medium heat, shaking the pan frequently, for 2–3 minutes, or until the shells open.

2 Remove the pan from the heat. Drain the mussels and reserve the cooking liquid. Discard any mussels that have not opened. Strain the cooking liquid through a clean cloth into a glass jug (pitcher) or bowl and reserve.

3 Melt the butter in a pan over a medium heat. Add the remaining onion and fry until translucent. Stir in the garlic and cook for 1 minute. Gradually stir in the reserved cooking liquid. Stir in the parsley and cream and season to taste with salt and pepper. Bring to simmering point over a low heat.

4 Meanwhile, bring a large pan of lightly salted water to the boil. Add the pasta and oil and cook for 8–10 minutes until just tender, but still firm to the bite. Drain the pasta, return to the pan, cover and keep warm.

5 Reserve a few mussels for the garnish and remove the remainder from their shells. Stir the shelled mussels into the cream sauce and warm briefly.

6 Transfer the pasta to a serving dish. Pour over the sauce and toss to coat. Garnish with the reserved mussels.

Mussel & Scallop Spaghetti

Juicy mussels and scallops poached gently in white wine are the perfect accompaniment to pasta to make a sophisticated meal.

NUTRITIONAL INFORMATION

Calories 301	Sugars 1g
Protein 42g	Fat 5g
Carbohydrate . . .17g	Saturates 1g

🥄 55 MINS   🕐 30 MINS

SERVES 4

I N G R E D I E N T S

225 g/8 oz dried wholemeal (wholewheat) spaghetti

60 g/2 oz/2 slices rindless lean back bacon, chopped

2 shallots, chopped finely

2 celery stick, chopped finely

150 ml/¼ pint/⅔ cup dry white wine

150 ml/¼ pint/⅔ cup fish stock

500 g/1 lb 2 oz fresh mussels, prepared

225 g/8 oz shelled queen or China bay scallops

1 tbsp chopped fresh parsley

salt and pepper

1 Cook the spaghetti in a saucepan of boiling water according to the packet instructions, or until the pasta is cooked but still 'al dente' (firm to the bite) – this will take about 10 minutes.

2 Meanwhile, gently dry-fry the bacon in a large non-stick frying pan (skillet) for 2–3 minutes. Stir in the shallots, celery and wine. Simmer gently, uncovered, for 5 minutes until softened.

3 Add the stock, mussels and scallops, cover and cook for a further 6–7 minutes. Discard any mussels that remain unopened after cooking.

4 Drain the spaghetti and add to the frying pan (skillet). Add the parsley, season to taste and toss together. Continue to cook for 1–2 minutes to heat through. Pile on to warmed serving plates, spooning over the cooking juices.

COOK'S TIP

Wholemeal (wholewheat) pasta doesn't have any egg added to the dough, so it is low in fat, and higher in fibre than other pastas.

Seafood Medley

You can use almost any kind of sea fish in this recipe. Red sea bream is an especially good choice.

NUTRITIONAL INFORMATION

Calories	699	Sugars	.........4g
Protein	........56g	Fat	..........35g
Carbohydrate	...35g	Saturates	......20g

  20 MINS 30 MINS

SERVES 4

INGREDIENTS

12 raw tiger prawns (shrimp)

12 raw (small) shrimp

450 g/1 lb fillet of sea bream

60 g/2 oz/4 tbsp butter

12 scallops, shelled

125 g/4½ oz freshwater prawns (shrimp)

juice and finely grated rind of 1 lemon

pinch of saffron powder or threads

1 litre/1¾ pints/4 cups vegetable stock

150 ml/¼ pint/⅔ cup rose petal vinegar

450 g/1 lb dried farfalle

1 tbsp olive oil

150 ml/¼ pint/⅔ cup white wine

1 tbsp pink peppercorns

115 g/4 oz baby carrots

150 ml/¼ pint/⅔ cup double (heavy) cream or fromage frais

salt and pepper

1 Peel and devein the prawns (shrimp) and (small) shrimp. Thinly slice the sea bream. Melt the butter in a frying pan (skillet), add the sea bream, scallops, prawns (shrimp) and (small) shrimp and cook for 1–2 minutes.

2 Season with pepper to taste. Add the lemon juice and grated rind. Very carefully add a pinch of saffron powder or a few strands of saffron to the cooking juices (not to the seafood).

3 Remove the seafood from the pan, set aside and keep warm.

4 Return the pan to the heat and add the stock. Bring to the boil and reduce by one third. Add the rose petal vinegar and cook for 4 minutes, until reduced.

5 Bring a pan of salted water to the boil. Add the farfalle and oil and cook for 8–10 minutes until tender, but still firm to the bite. Drain the pasta, transfer to a serving plate and top with the seafood.

6 Add the wine, peppercorns, and carrots to the pan and reduce the sauce for 6 minutes. Add the cream or fromage frais and simmer for 2 minutes.

7 Pour the sauce over the seafood and pasta and serve immediately.

Spaghetti & Seafood Sauce

Peeled prawns (shrimp) from the freezer can become the star ingredient in this colourful and tasty dish.

NUTRITIONAL INFORMATION

Calories	498	Sugars	.........5g
Protein	........32g	Fat	..........23g
Carbohydrate	...43g	Saturates	......11g

30 MINS   35 MINS

SERVES 4

INGREDIENTS

225 g/8 oz dried spaghetti, broken into
   15 cm/6 inch lengths

2 tbsp olive oil

300 ml/½ pint/1¼ cups chicken stock

1 tsp lemon juice

1 small cauliflower, cut into florets

2 carrots, thinly sliced

115 g/4 oz mangetout (snow peas)

60 g/2 oz/4 tbsp butter

1 onion, sliced

225 g/8 oz courgettes (zucchini), sliced

1 garlic clove, chopped

350 g/12 oz frozen, cooked, peeled prawns
   (shrimp), defrosted

2 tbsp chopped fresh parsley

25 g/1 oz/⅓ cup freshly grated
   Parmesan cheese

½ tsp paprika

salt and pepper

4 unpeeled, cooked prawns (shrimp),
   to garnish

1 Bring a pan of lightly salted water to the boil. Add the spaghetti and 1 tbsp of the olive oil and cook for 8–10 minutes until tender, but still firm to the bite. Drain the spaghetti and return to the pan. Toss with the remaining olive oil, cover and keep warm.

2 Bring the chicken stock and lemon juice to the boil. Add the cauliflower and carrots and cook for 3–4 minutes. Remove from the pan and set aside. Add the mangetout (snow peas) to the pan and cook for 1–2 minutes. Set aside with the other vegetables.

3 Melt half of the butter in a frying pan (skillet) over a medium heat. Add the onion and courgettes (zucchini) and fry for about 3 minutes. Add the garlic and prawns (shrimp) and cook for a further 2–3 minutes, until thoroughly heated through.

4 Stir in the reserved vegetables and heat through. Season to taste and stir in the remaining butter.

5 Transfer the spaghetti to a warm serving dish. Pour over the sauce and add the chopped parsley. Toss well with 2 forks until coated. Sprinkle over the Parmesan cheese and paprika, garnish with the unpeeled prawns (shrimp) and serve immediately.

Seafood Chow Mein

Use whatever seafood is available for this delicious noodle dish – mussels or crab would also be suitable.

NUTRITIONAL INFORMATION

Calories 281	Sugars 1g	
Protein 15g	Fat 18g	
Carbohydrate . . .16g	Saturates 2g	

 15 MINS 15 MINS

SERVES 4

I N G R E D I E N T S

90 g/3 oz squid, cleaned

3-4 fresh scallops

90 g/3 oz raw prawns (shrimp), shelled

½ egg white, lightly beaten

1 tbsp cornflour (cornstarch) paste

275 g/9½ oz egg noodles

5-6 tbsp vegetable oil

2 tbsp light soy sauce

60 g/2 oz mangetout (snow peas)

½ tsp salt

½ tsp sugar

1 tsp Chinese rice wine

2 spring onions (scallions), finely shredded

a few drops of sesame oil

COOK'S TIP

Chinese rice wine, made from glutinous rice, is also known as 'yellow wine' because of its golden amber colour. If it is unavailable, a good dry or medium sherry is an acceptable substitute.

1 Open up the squid and score the inside in a criss-cross pattern, then cut into pieces about the size of a postage stamp. Soak the squid in a bowl of boiling water until all the pieces curl up. Rinse in cold water and drain.

2 Cut each scallop into 3-4 slices. Cut the prawns (shrimp) in half lengthways if large. Mix the scallops and prawns (shrimp) with the egg white and cornflour (cornstarch) paste.

3 Cook the noodles in boiling water according to the packet instructions, then drain and rinse under cold water. Drain well, then toss with about 1 tablespoon of oil.

4 Heat 3 tablespoons of oil in a preheated wok. Add the noodles and 1 tablespoon of the soy sauce and stir-fry for 2-3 minutes. Remove to a large serving dish.

5 Heat the remaining oil in the wok and add the mangetout (snow peas) and seafood. Stir-fry for about 2 minutes, then add the salt, sugar, wine, remaining soy sauce and about half the spring onions (scallions). Blend well and add a little stock or water if necessary. Pour the seafood mixture on top of the noodles and sprinkle with sesame oil. Garnish with the remaining spring onions (scallions) and serve.

Cellophane Noodles & Prawns

Tiger prawns (jumbo shrimp) are cooked with orange juice, (bell) peppers, soy sauce and vinegar and served on a bed of cellophane noodles.

NUTRITIONAL INFORMATION

Calories 118	Sugar 4g
Protein 7g	Fat 4g
Carbohydrate ...15g	Saturates 1g

 10 MINS   25 MINS

SERVES 4

INGREDIENTS

175 g/6 oz cellophane noodles

1 tbsp vegetable oil

1 garlic clove, crushed

2 tsp grated fresh root ginger

24 raw tiger prawns (jumbo shrimp), peeled and deveined

1 red (bell) pepper, seeded and thinly sliced

1 green (bell) pepper, seeded and thinly sliced

1 onion, chopped

2 tbsp light soy sauce

juice of 1 orange

2 tsp wine vinegar

pinch of brown sugar

150 ml/¼ pint/⅔ cup fish stock

1 tbsp cornflour (cornstarch)

2 tsp water

orange slices, to garnish

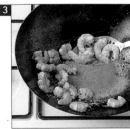  

1 Cook the noodles in a pan of boiling water for 1 minute. Drain well, rinse under cold water and then drain again.

2 Heat the oil in a wok and stir-fry the garlic and ginger for 30 seconds.

3 Add the prawns (shrimp) and stir-fry for 2 minutes. Remove with a slotted spoon and keep warm.

4 Add the (bell) peppers and onion to the wok and stir-fry for 2 minutes. Stir in the soy sauce, orange juice, vinegar, sugar and stock. Return the prawns (shrimp) to the wok and cook for 8-10 minutes, until cooked through.

5 Blend the cornflour (cornstarch) with the water and stir into the wok. Bring to the boil, add the noodles and cook for 1-2 minutes. Garnish and serve.

VARIATION

Lime or lemon juice and slices may be used instead of the orange. Use 3-5½ tsp of these juices.

Sweet & Sour Noodles

This delicious dish combines sweet and sour flavours with the addition of egg, rice noodles, king prawns (shrimp) and vegetables for a real treat.

NUTRITIONAL INFORMATION

Calories	352	Sugars	........14g
Protein	........23g	Fat	..........17g
Carbohydrate	...29g	Saturates	.......3g

 10 MINS   10 MINS

SERVES 4

I N G R E D I E N T S

3 tbsp fish sauce

2 tbsp distilled white vinegar

2 tbsp caster (superfine) or palm sugar

2 tbsp tomato purée (paste)

2 tbsp sunflower oil

3 cloves garlic, crushed

350 g/12 oz rice noodles, soaked in boiling water for 5 minutes

8 spring onions (scallions), sliced

175 g/6 oz carrot, grated

150 g/5½ oz/1¼ cups bean sprouts

2 eggs, beaten

225 g/8 oz peeled king prawns (shrimp)

50 g/1¾ oz/½ cup chopped peanuts

1 tsp chilli flakes, to garnish

1 Mix together the fish sauce, vinegar, sugar and tomato purée (paste).

2 Heat the sunflower oil in a large preheated wok.

3 Add the garlic to the wok and stir-fry for 30 seconds.

4 Drain the noodles thoroughly and add them to the wok together with the fish sauce and tomato purée (paste) mixture. Mix well to combine.

5 Add the spring onions (scallions), carrot and bean sprouts to the wok and stir-fry for 2–3 minutes.

6 Move the contents of the wok to one side, add the beaten eggs to the empty part of the wok and cook until the egg sets. Add the noodles, prawns (shrimp) and peanuts to the wok and mix well. Transfer to warm serving dishes and garnish with chilli flakes. Serve hot.

COOK'S TIP

Chilli flakes may be found in the spice section of large supermarkets.

Noodles with Prawns (Shrimp)

This is a simple dish using egg noodles and large prawns (shrimp), which give the dish a wonderful flavour, texture and colour.

NUTRITIONAL INFORMATION

Calories	142	Sugars	.......0.4g
Protein	........11g	Fat	...........7g
Carbohydrate	....11g	Saturates	.......1g

 5 MINS   🕐 10 MINS

SERVES 4

I N G R E D I E N T S

225 g/8 oz thin egg noodles

2 tbsp peanut oil

1 garlic clove, crushed

½ tsp ground star anise

1 bunch spring onions (scallions), cut into 5-cm/2-inch pieces

24 raw tiger prawns (jumbo shrimp), peeled with tails intact

2 tbsp light soy sauce

2 tsp lime juice

lime wedges, to garnish

1 Blanch the noodles in a saucepan of boiling water for about 2 minutes.

2 Drain the noodles well, rinse under cold water and drain thoroughly again. Keep warm and set aside until required.

3 Heat the peanut oil in a preheated wok or large frying pan (skillet) until almost smoking.

4 Add the crushed garlic and ground star anise to the wok and stir-fry for 30 seconds.

5 Add the spring onions (scallions) and tiger prawns (jumbo shrimp) to the wok and stir-fry for 2-3 minutes.

6 Stir in the light soy sauce, lime juice and noodles and mix well.

7 Cook the mixture in the wok for about 1 minute until thoroughly heated through and all the ingredients are thoroughly incorporated.

8 Spoon the noodle and prawn mixture into a warm serving dish. Transfer to serving bowls, garnish with lime wedges and serve immediately.

COOK'S TIP

If fresh egg noodles are available, these require very little cooking: simply place in boiling water for about 3 minutes, then drain and toss in oil. Noodles can be boiled and eaten plain, or stir-fried with meat and vegetables for a light meal or snack.

Noodles with Chilli & Prawn

This is a simple dish to prepare and is packed with flavour, making it an ideal choice for special occasions.

NUTRITIONAL INFORMATION

Calories 259	Sugars 9g
Protein 28g	Fat 8g
Carbohydrate ...20g	Saturates 1g

  10 MINS   5 MINS

SERVES 4

INGREDIENTS

250 g/9 oz thin glass noodles

2 tbsp sunflower oil

1 onion, sliced

2 red chillies, deseeded and very finely chopped

4 lime leaves, thinly shredded

1 tbsp fresh coriander (cilantro)

2 tbsp palm or caster (superfine) sugar

2 tbsp fish sauce

450 g/1 lb raw tiger prawns (jumbo shrimp), peeled

1 Place the noodles in a large bowl. Pour over enough boiling water to cover the noodles and leave to stand for 5 minutes. Drain thoroughly and set aside until required.

COOK'S TIP

If you cannot buy raw tiger prawns (jumbo shrimp), use cooked prawns (shrimp) instead and cook them with the noodles for 1 minute only, just to heat through.

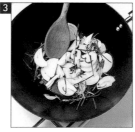  

2 Heat the sunflower oil in a large preheated wok or frying pan (skillet) until it is really hot.

3 Add the onion, red chillies and lime leaves to the wok and stir-fry for 1 minute.

4 Add the coriander (cilantro), palm or caster (superfine) sugar, fish sauce and prawns (shrimp) to the wok or frying pan (skillet) and stir-fry for a further 2 minutes or until the prawns (shrimp) turn pink.

5 Add the drained noodles to the wok, toss to mix well, and stir-fry for 1–2 minutes or until heated through.

6 Transfer the noodles and prawns (shrimp) to warm serving bowls and serve immediately.

Chilli (Small) Shrimp Noodles

Cellophane or 'glass' noodles are made from mung beans. They are sold dried, so they need soaking before use.

NUTRITIONAL INFORMATION

Calories	152	Sugars	.........2g
Protein	........11g	Fat	...........8g
Carbohydrate	...10g	Saturates	.......1g

25 MINS   🕐 10 MINS

SERVES 4

I N G R E D I E N T S

2 tbsp light soy sauce

1 tbsp lime or lemon juice

1 tbsp fish sauce

125 g/4½ oz firm tofu (bean curd), cut into chunks

125 g/4½ oz cellophane noodles

2 tbsp sesame oil

4 shallots, sliced finely

2 garlic cloves, crushed

1 small red chilli, deseeded and chopped finely

2 celery sticks, sliced finely

2 carrots, sliced finely

125 g/4½ oz/⅔ cup cooked, peeled (small) shrimps

60 g/2 oz/1 cup bean sprouts

T O   G A R N I S H

celery leaves

fresh chillies

1 Mix together the light soy sauce, lime or lemon juice and fish sauce in a small bowl. Add the tofu (bean curd) cubes and toss them until coated in the mixture. Cover and set aside for 15 minutes.

2 Put the noodles into a large bowl and cover with warm water. Leave them to soak for about 5 minutes, and then drain them well.

3 Heat the sesame oil in a wok or large frying pan (skillet). Add the shallots, garlic and red chilli, and stir-fry for 1 minute.

4 Add the sliced celery and carrots to the wok or pan and stir-fry for a further 2–3 minutes.

5 Tip the drained noodles into the wok or frying pan (skillet) and cook, stirring, for 2 minutes, then add the (small) shrimps, bean sprouts and tofu (bean curd), with the soy sauce mixture. Cook over a medium high heat for 2–3 minutes until heated through.

6 Transfer the mixture in the wok to a serving dish and garnish with celery leaves and chillies.

Noodles with Cod & Mango

Fish and fruit are tossed with a trio of (bell) peppers in this spicy dish served with noodles for a quick, healthy meal.

NUTRITIONAL INFORMATION

Calories 274	Sugars 11g
Protein 25g	Fat 8g
Carbohydrate ...26g	Saturates 1g

 10 MINS   25 MINS

SERVES 4

I N G R E D I E N T S

250 g/9 oz packet egg noodles

450 g/1 lb skinless cod fillet

1 tbsp paprika

2 tbsp sunflower oil

1 red onion, sliced

1 orange (bell) pepper, deseeded and sliced

1 green (bell) pepper, deseeded and sliced

100 g/3½ oz baby corn cobs, halved

1 mango, sliced

100 g/3½ oz/1 cup bean sprouts

2 tbsp tomato ketchup

2 tbsp soy sauce

2 tbsp medium sherry

1 tsp cornflour (cornstarch)

1 Place the egg noodles in a large bowl and cover with boiling water. Leave to stand for about 10 minutes.

2 Rinse the cod fillet and pat dry with absorbent kitchen paper (paper towels). Cut the cod flesh into thin strips.

3 Place the cod strips in a large bowl. Add the paprika and toss well to coat the fish.

4 Heat the sunflower oil in a large preheated wok.

5 Add the onion, (bell) peppers and baby corn cobs to the wok and stir-fry for about 5 minutes.

6 Add the cod to the wok together with the sliced mango and stir-fry for a further 2–3 minutes or until the fish is tender.

7 Add the bean sprouts to the wok and toss well to combine.

8 Mix together the tomato ketchup, soy sauce, sherry and cornflour (cornstarch). Add the mixture to the wok and cook, stirring occasionally, until the juices thicken.

9 Drain the noodles thoroughly and transfer to warm serving bowls. Transfer the cod and mango stir-fry to separate serving bowls and serve the dish immediately.

Oyster Sauce Noodles

Chicken and noodles are cooked and then tossed in an oyster sauce and egg mixture in this delicious recipe.

NUTRITIONAL INFORMATION

Calories 278	Sugars 2g	
Protein 30g	Fat 12g	
Carbohydrate ...13g	Saturates 3g	

🍲 5 MINS   🕐 25 MINS

SERVES 4

I N G R E D I E N T S

250 g/9 oz egg noodles

450 g/1 lb chicken thighs

2 tbsp groundnut oil

100 g/3½ oz carrots, sliced

3 tbsp oyster sauce

2 eggs

3 tbsp cold water

1 Place the egg noodles in a large bowl or dish. Pour enough boiling water over the noodles to cover and leave to stand for 10 minutes.

2 Meanwhile, remove the skin from the chicken thighs. Cut the chicken flesh into small pieces, using a sharp knife.

VARIATION

Flavour the eggs with soy sauce or hoisin sauce as an alternative to the oyster sauce, if you prefer.

3 Heat the groundnut oil in a large preheated wok or frying pan (skillet), swirling the oil around the base of the wok until it is really hot.

4 Add the pieces of chicken and the carrot slices to the wok and stir-fry for about 5 minutes.

5 Drain the noodles thoroughly. Add the noodles to the wok and stir-fry for a

further 2–3 minutes or until the noodles are heated through.

6 Beat together the oyster sauce, eggs and 3 tablespoons of cold water. Drizzle the mixture over the noodles and stir-fry for a further 2–3 minutes or until the eggs set.

7 Transfer the mixture in the wok to warm serving bowls and serve hot.

Fried Rice with Prawns

Use either large peeled prawns (shrimp) or tiger prawns (jumbo shrimp) for this rice dish.

NUTRITIONAL INFORMATION

Calories 599   Sugars 0g
Protein . . . . .26g   Fat 16g
Carbohydrate . . .94g   Saturates 3g

5 MINS   35 MINS

SERVES 4

INGREDIENTS

300 g/10½ oz/1½ cups long-grain rice

2 eggs

4 tsp cold water

salt and pepper

3 tbsp sunflower oil

4 spring onions (scallions), thinly sliced
  diagonally

1 garlic clove, crushed

125 g/4½ oz closed-cup or button
  mushrooms, thinly sliced

2 tbsp oyster or anchovy sauce

1 x 200 g/7 oz can water chestnuts, drained
  and sliced

250 g/9 oz peeled prawns (shrimp),
  defrosted if frozen

½ bunch watercress, roughly chopped

watercress sprigs, to garnish (optional)

1 Cook the rice in boiling salted water, stir well, cover the wok tightly and simmer for 12-13 minutes.

2 Beat each egg separately with 2 teaspoons of cold water and salt and pepper.

3 Heat 2 teaspoons of sunflower oil in a wok or large frying pan (skillet), swirling it around until really hot. Pour in the first egg, swirl it around and leave to cook undisturbed until set. Remove to a plate or board and repeat with the second egg. Cut the omelettes into 2.5 cm/1 inch squares.

4 Heat the remaining oil in the wok and when really hot add the spring onions (scallions) and garlic and stir-fry for 1 minute. Add the mushrooms and continue to cook for a further 2 minutes.

5 Stir in the oyster or anchovy sauce and seasoning and add the water chestnuts and prawns (shrimp); stir-fry for 2 minutes.

6 Stir in the cooked rice and stir-fry for 1 minute, then add the watercress and omelette squares and stir-fry for a further 1-2 minutes until piping hot. Serve at once garnished with sprigs of watercress, if liked.

Crab Fried Rice

Canned crabmeat is used in this recipe for convenience, but fresh white crabmeat could be used – quite deliciously – in its place.

NUTRITIONAL INFORMATION

Calories .... 225 Sugars 1g
Protein .... 12g Fat 11g
Carbohydrate ... 20g Saturates 2g

5 MINS   25 MINS

SERVES 4

I N G R E D I E N T S

150 g/5½ oz/⅔ cup long-grain rice

2 tbsp peanut oil

125 g/4½ oz canned white crabmeat, drained

1 leek, sliced

150 g/5½ oz/⅔ cup bean sprouts

2 eggs, beaten

1 tbsp light soy sauce

2 tsp lime juice

1 tsp sesame oil

salt

sliced lime, to garnish

1 Cook the rice in a saucepan of boiling salted water for 15 minutes. Drain well, rinse under cold running water and drain again thoroughly.

2 Heat the peanut oil in a preheated wok until it is really hot.

3 Add the crabmeat, leek and bean sprouts to the wok and stir-fry for 2–3 minutes. Remove the mixture from the wok with a slotted spoon and set aside until required.

4 Add the eggs to the wok and cook, stirring occasionally, for 2–3 minutes, until they begin to set.

5 Stir the rice and the crabmeat, leek and bean sprout mixture into the eggs in the wok.

6 Add the soy sauce and lime juice to the mixture in the wok. Cook for 1 minute, stirring to combine, and sprinkle with the sesame oil.

7 Transfer the crab fried rice to a serving dish, garnish with the sliced lime and serve immediately.

COOK'S TIP

To prepare fresh crab, twist off the claws and legs, crack with a heavy knife and pick out the meat with a skewer. Discard the gills and pull out the under shell; discard the stomach sac. Pull the soft meat from the shell. Cut open the body section and prise out the meat with a skewer.

Rice with Crab & Mussels

Shellfish makes an ideal partner for rice. Mussels and crab add flavour and texture to this spicy dish.

NUTRITIONAL INFORMATION

Calories	336	Sugars	.........4g
Protein	........32g	Fat	..........10g
Carbohydrate	...33g	Saturates	.......1g

 20 MINS 10 MINS

SERVES 4

INGREDIENTS

300 g/10½ oz/1½ cups long-grain rice

175 g/6 oz white crab meat, fresh, canned or frozen (defrosted if frozen), or 8 crab sticks, defrosted if frozen

2 tbsp sesame or sunflower oil

2.5 cm/1 inch piece ginger root, grated

4 spring onions (scallions), thinly sliced diagonally

125 g/4½ oz mangetout (snow peas), cut into 2-3 pieces

½ tsp turmeric

1 tsp ground cumin

2 x 200 g/7 oz jars mussels, well drained, or 350 g/12 oz frozen mussels, defrosted

1 x 425 g/15 oz can bean sprouts, well drained

salt and pepper

1 Cook the rice in boiling salted water, stir well, cover the wok tightly and simmer for 12-13 minutes.

2 Extract the crab meat, if using fresh crab (see right). Flake the crab meat or cut the crab sticks into 3 or 4 pieces.

3 Heat the oil in a preheated wok and stir-fry the ginger and spring onions (scallions) for a minute or so. Add the mangetout (snow peas) and continue to cook for a further minute. Sprinkle the turmeric, cumin and seasoning over the vegetables and mix well.

4 Add the crab meat and mussels and stir-fry for 1 minute. Stir in the cooked rice and bean sprouts and stir-fry for 2 minutes or until hot and well mixed.

5 Adjust the seasoning to taste and serve immediately.

Aromatic Seafood Rice

This is one of those easy, delicious meals where the rice and fish are cooked together in one pan. Remove the whole spices before serving.

NUTRITIONAL INFORMATION

Calories 380   Sugar 2g
Protein ....40g   Fats 13g
Carbohydrates ...26g   Saturates 5g

20 MINS   25 MINS

SERVES 4

INGREDIENTS

225 g/8 oz/1¼ cups basmati rice

2 tbsp ghee or vegetable oil

1 onion, peeled and chopped

1 garlic clove, peeled and crushed

1 tsp cumin seeds

½–1 tsp chilli powder

4 cloves

1 cinnamon stick or a piece of cassia bark

2 tsp curry paste

225 g/8 oz peeled prawns (shrimp)

500g/1 lb 2 oz white fish fillets (such as monkfish, cod or haddock), skinned and boned and cut into bite-sized pieces

salt and freshly ground black pepper

600 ml/1 pint/2½ cups boiling water

60 g/2 oz/⅓ cup frozen peas

60 g/2 oz/⅓ cup frozen sweetcorn kernels

1–2 tbsp lime juice

2 tbsp toasted desiccated (shredded) coconut

coriander (cilantro) sprigs and lime slices, to garnish

1 Place the rice in a sieve and wash well under cold running water until the water runs clear, then drain well.

2 Heat the ghee or oil in a saucepan, add the onion, garlic, spices and curry paste and fry very gently for 1 minute.

3 Stir in the rice and mix well until coated in the spiced oil. Add the prawns (shrimp) and white fish and season well with salt and pepper. Stir lightly, then pour in the boiling water.

4 Cover and cook gently for 10 minutes, without uncovering the pan. Add the peas and corn, cover and continue cooking for a further 8 minutes. Remove from the heat and allow to stand for 10 minutes.

5 Uncover the pan, fluff up the rice with a fork and transfer to a warm serving platter.

6 Sprinkle the dish with the lime juice and toasted coconut, and serve garnished with coriander (cilantro) sprigs and lime slices.

Indian Cod with Tomatoes

Quick and easy – cod steaks are cooked in a rich tomato and coconut sauce to produce tender, succulent results.

NUTRITIONAL INFORMATION

Calories 194	Sugars 6g
Protein 21g	Fat 9g
Carbohydrate 7g	Saturates 1g

 5 MINS   25 MINS

SERVES 4

I N G R E D I E N T S

3 tbsp vegetable oil

4 cod steaks, about 2.5 cm/1 inch thick

salt and freshly ground black pepper

1 onion, peeled and finely chopped

2 garlic cloves, peeled and crushed

1 red (bell) pepper, seeded and chopped

1 tsp ground coriander

1 tsp ground cumin

1 tsp ground turmeric

½ tsp garam masala

1 x 400 g/14 oz can chopped tomatoes

150 ml/¼ pint/⅔ cup coconut milk

1-2 tbsp chopped fresh coriander (cilantro) or parsley

VARIATION

The mixture may be flavoured with a tablespoonful of curry powder or curry paste (mild, medium or hot, according to personal preference) instead of the mixture of spices at step 2, if wished.

  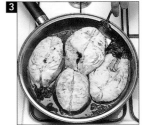

1 Heat the oil in a frying pan, add the fish steaks, season with salt and pepper and fry until browned on both sides (but not cooked through). Remove from the pan and reserve.

2 Add the onion, garlic, red (bell) pepper and spices and cook very gently for 2 minutes, stirring frequently. Add the tomatoes, bring to the boil and simmer for 5 minutes.

3 Add the fish steaks to the pan and simmer gently for 8 minutes or until the fish is cooked through.

4 Remove from the pan and keep warm on a serving dish. Add the coconut milk and coriander (cilantro) or parsley to the pan and reheat gently.

5 Spoon the sauce over the cod steaks and serve immediately.

Plaice Fillets with Grapes

Fish is ideal for a quick meal, especially when cut into strips as in this recipe – it takes only minutes to cook.

NUTRITIONAL INFORMATION

Calories ....226 Sugars 6g
Protein ....23g Fat 9g
Carbohydrate ....9g Saturates 4g

 5 MINS   ◷ 10 MINS

SERVES 4

INGREDIENTS

500 g/1 lb 2 oz plaice fillets, skinned

4 spring onions (scallions), white and green parts, sliced diagonally

125 ml/4 fl oz/½ cup dry white wine

1 tbsp cornflour (cornstarch)

2 tbsp skimmed milk

2 tbsp chopped fresh dill

50 ml/2 fl oz/¼ cup double (heavy) cream

125 g/4½ oz seedless white (green) grapes

1 tsp lemon juice

salt and pepper

fresh dill sprigs, to garnish

TO SERVE

basmati rice

courgette ribbons

1 Cut the fish into strips about 4 cm/1¾ inches long and put into a frying pan (skillet) with the spring onions (scallions), wine and seasoning.

2 Bring to the boil, cover and simmer for 4 minutes. Carefully transfer the fish to a warm serving dish. Cover and keep warm.

3 Mix the cornflour (cornstarch) and milk then add to the pan with the dill and cream. Bring to the boil, and boil, stirring, for 2 minutes until thickened.

4 Add the grapes and lemon juice and heat through gently for 1–2 minutes, then pour over the fish. Garnish with dill and serve with rice and courgette ribbons.

COOK'S TIP

Dill has a fairly strong aniseed flavour that goes very well with fish. The feathery leaves are particularly attractive when used as a garnish.

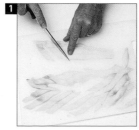

Plaice with Mushrooms

The moist texture of grilled (broiled) fish is complemented by the texture of the mushrooms.

NUTRITIONAL INFORMATION

Calories 243	Sugars 2g	
Protein 30g	Fat 13g	
Carbohydrate 2g	Saturates 3g	

 10 MINS   20 MINS

SERVES 4

INGREDIENTS

4 × 150 g/5½ oz white-skinned plaice fillets

2 tbsp lime juice

celery salt and pepper

90 g/3 oz/⅓ cup low-fat spread

300 g/10½ oz/2½ cups mixed small mushrooms such as button, oyster, shiitake, chanterelle or morel, sliced or quartered

4 tomatoes, skinned, seeded and chopped

basil leaves, to garnish

mixed salad, to serve

1 Line a grill (broiler) rack with baking parchment and place the fish on top.

2 Sprinkle over the lime juice and season with celery salt and pepper.

3 Place under a preheated moderate grill (broiler) and cook for 7–8 minutes without turning, until just cooked. Keep warm.

4 Meanwhile, gently melt the low fat spread in a non-stick frying pan (skillet), add the mushrooms and fry for 4–5 minutes over a low heat until cooked through.

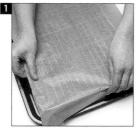  

5 Gently heat the tomatoes in a small saucepan.

6 Spoon the mushrooms, with any pan juices, and the tomatoes over the plaice.

7 Garnish the grilled (broiled) plaice with the basil leaves and serve with a mixed salad.

COOK'S TIP

Mushrooms are ideal in a low-fat diet, as they are packed full of flavour and contain no fat. More 'meaty' types of mushroom, such as chestnut (crimini), will take slightly longer to cook.

Delicately Spiced Trout

The firm, sweet flesh of the trout is enhanced by the sweet-spicy flavour of the marinade and cooking juices.

NUTRITIONAL INFORMATION

Calories 374   Sugars 13g
Protein ....38g   Fat 19g
Carbohydrate ...14g   Saturates 3g

45 MINS   20 MINS

SERVES 4

INGREDIENTS

4 trout, each weighing 175–250 g/
  6–9 oz, cleaned

3 tbsp oil

1 tsp fennel seeds

1 tsp onion seeds

1 garlic clove, crushed

150 ml/¼ pint/⅔ cup coconut milk or fish
  stock

3 tbsp tomato purée (paste)

60 g/2 oz/⅓ cup sultanas (golden raisins)

½ tsp garam masala

TO GARNISH

25 g/1 oz/¼ cup chopped cashew nuts

lemon wedges

sprigs of fresh coriander (cilantro)

MARINADE

4 tbsp lemon juice

2 tbsp chopped fresh coriander (cilantro)

1 tsp ground cumin

½ tsp salt

½ tsp ground black pepper

1 Slash the trout skin in several places on both sides with a sharp knife.

2 To make the marinade, mix all the ingredients together in a bowl.

3 Put the trout in a shallow dish and pour over the marinade. Leave to marinate for 30–40 minutes; turn the fish over during the marinating time.

4 Heat the oil in a Balti pan or wok and fry the fennel seeds and onion seeds until they start popping.

5 Add the crushed garlic, coconut milk or fish stock, and tomato purée (paste) and bring the mixture in the wok to the boil.

6 Add the sultanas (golden raisins), garam masala and trout with the juices from the marinade. Cover and simmer for 5 minutes. Turn the trout over and simmer for a further 10 minutes.

7 Serve garnished with the nuts, lemon and coriander (cilantro) sprigs.

Lemony Monkfish Skewers

A simple basting sauce is brushed over these tasty kebabs. When served with crusty bread, they make a perfect light meal.

NUTRITIONAL INFORMATION

Calories 191   Sugars 2g
Protein . . . . .21g   Fat 11g
Carbohydrate . . . .1g   Saturates 1g

🕙 10 MINS   🕐 15 MINS

SERVES 4

I N G R E D I E N T S

450 g/1 lb monkfish tail

2 courgettes (zucchini)

1 lemon

12 cherry tomatoes

8 bay leaves

S A U C E

3 tbsp olive oil

2 tbsp lemon juice

1 tsp chopped, fresh thyme

½ tsp lemon pepper

salt

T O   S E R V E

green salad leaves

fresh, crusty bread

1 Cut the monkfish into 5 cm/2 inch chunks.

2 Cut the courgettes (zucchini) into thick slices and the lemon into wedges.

3 Thread the monkfish, courgettes (zucchini), lemon, tomatoes and bay leaves on to 4 skewers.

4 To make the basting sauce, combine the oil, lemon juice, thyme, lemon pepper and salt to taste in a small bowl.

5 Brush the basting sauce liberally all over the fish, lemon, tomatoes and bay leaves on the skewers.

6 Cook the skewers on the barbecue (grill) for about 15 minutes over medium-hot coals, basting them frequently with the sauce, until the fish is cooked through. Transfer the skewers to plates and serve with green salad leaves and wedges of crusty bread.

VARIATION

Use plaice (flounder) fillets instead of the monkfish, if you prefer. Allow two fillets per person, and skin and cut each fillet lengthways into two. Roll up each piece and thread them on to the skewers.

Smoky Fish Skewers

The combination of fresh and smoked fish gives these kebabs a special flavour. Choose thick fish fillets to get good-sized pieces.

NUTRITIONAL INFORMATION

Calories 221	Sugars 0g	
Protein 33g	Fat 10g	
Carbohydrate 0g	Saturates 1g	

4 HOURS   10 MINS

SERVES 4

INGREDIENTS

350 g/12 oz smoked cod fillet

350 g/12 oz cod fillet

8 large raw prawns (shrimp)

8 bay leaves

fresh dill, to garnish (optional)

MARINADE

4 tbsp sunflower oil, plus a little for
    brushing

2 tbsp lemon or lime juice

rind of ½ lemon or lime, grated

¼ tsp dried dill

salt and pepper

1 Skin both types of cod and cut the flesh into bite-size pieces. Peel the prawns (shrimp), leaving just the tail.

2 To make the marinade, combine the oil, lemon or lime juice and rind, dill and salt and pepper to taste in a shallow, non-metallic dish.

3 Place the prepared fish in the marinade and stir together until the fish is well coated on all sides. Leave the fish to marinate for 1–4 hours.

4 Thread the fish on to 4 skewers, alternating the 2 types of cod with the prawns (shrimp) and bay leaves.

5 Cover the rack with lightly oiled kitchen foil and place the fish skewers on top of the foil.

6 Barbecue (grill) the fish skewers over hot coals for 5-10 minutes, basting with any remaining marinade, turning once.

7 Garnish the skewers with fresh dill (if using) and serve immediately.

COOK'S TIP

Cod fillet can be rather flaky, so choose the thicker end which is easier to cut into chunky pieces. Cook the fish on kitchen foil rather directly on the rack, so that if the fish breaks away from the skewer, it is not wasted.

Oriental Shellfish Kebabs

These shellfish and vegetable kebabs are ideal for serving at parties. They are quick and easy to prepare and take next to no time to cook.

NUTRITIONAL INFORMATION

Calories 93	Sugars 1g
Protein 15g	Fat 2g
Carbohydrate 2g	Saturates 0.3g

🐚 🐚 🐚

2½ HOURS   🕐 5 MINS

MAKES 12

INGREDIENTS

350 g/12 oz raw tiger prawns (jumbo shrimp), peeled leaving tails intact

350 g/12 oz scallops, cleaned, trimmed and halved (quartered if large)

1 bunch spring onions (scallions), sliced into 2.5 cm/1 inch pieces

1 medium red (bell) pepper, deseeded and cubed

100 g/3½ oz baby corn cobs, trimmed and sliced into 1 cm/½ inch pieces

3 tbsp dark soy sauce

½ tsp hot chilli powder

½ tsp ground ginger

1 tbsp sunflower oil

1 red chilli, deseeded and sliced, to garnish

DIP

4 tbsp dark soy sauce

4 tbsp dry sherry

2 tsp clear honey

2.5 cm/1 inch piece root (fresh) ginger, peeled and grated

1 spring onion (scallion), trimmed and sliced very finely

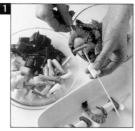

1 Divide the prawns (shrimp), scallops, spring onions (scallions), (bell) pepper and baby corn into 12 portions and thread on to the skewers (soaked for 10 minutes in water to prevent them from burning). Cover the ends with foil so that they do not burn and place in a shallow dish.

2 Mix the soy sauce, chilli powder and ground ginger and coat the kebabs. Cover and chill for about 2 hours.

3 Preheat the grill (broiler) to hot. Arrange the kebabs on the rack, brush with oil and cook for 2–3 minutes on each side until the prawns (shrimp) turn pink, the scallops become opaque and the vegetables soften.

4 Mix together the dip ingredients.

5 Remove the foil and transfer the kebabs to a warm serving platter. Garnish with sliced chilli and serve with the dip.

Scallop Skewers

As the scallops are marinated, it is not essential that they are fresh; frozen shellfish are fine for a barbecue (grill).

NUTRITIONAL INFORMATION

Calories 182	Sugars 0g	
Protein 29g	Fat 7g	
Carbohydrate 0g	Saturates 1g	

 30 MINS   10 MINS

SERVES 4

I N G R E D I E N T S

grated zest and juice of 2 limes

2 tbsp finely chopped lemon grass or 1 tbsp
  lemon juice

2 garlic cloves, crushed

1 green chilli, deseeded and chopped

16 scallops, with corals

2 limes, each cut into 8 segments

2 tbsp sunflower oil

1 tbsp lemon juice

salt and pepper

T O   S E R V E

60 g/2 oz/1 cup rocket (arugula) salad

200 g/7 oz/3 cups mixed salad leaves
  (greens)

1 Soak 8 skewers in warm water for at
least 10 minutes before you use them
to prevent the food from sticking.

2 Combine the lime juice and zest,
lemon grass, garlic and chilli together
in a pestle and mortar or spice grinder to
make a paste.

3 Thread 2 scallops on to each of the
soaked skewers. Cover the ends with
foil to prevent them from burning.

4 Alternate the scallops with the lime
segments.

5 Whisk together the oil, lemon juice,
salt and pepper to make the dressing.

6 Coat the scallops with the spice paste
and place over a medium barbecue,
basting occasionally.

7 Cook for 10 minutes, turning once.

8 Toss the rocket (arugula), mixed salad
leaves (greens) and dressing together
well. Put into a serving bowl.

9 Serve the scallops piping hot, 2
skewers on each plate, with the salad.

Meat Dishes

A whole variety of ways in which meat can be cooked is included in this chapter to create a sumptuous selection of dishes. Barbeques, stir-fries, roasts and casseroles are

combined to offer a wealth of textures and flavours. Classic and traditional recipes feature alongside more exotic dishes taken from all around the world, incorporating exciting new ingredients

alongside family favourites such as pork chops and lamb cutlets. The dishes in this chapter range from easy, economic mid-week suppers to sophisticated and elegant main courses for special occasions.

Creamed Strips of Sirloin

This quick and easy dish tastes superb and would make a delicious treat for a special occasion.

NUTRITIONAL INFORMATION

Calories 796   Sugars 2g
Protein . . . . .29g   Fat 63g
Carbohydrate . . .26g   Saturates 39g

15 MINS   30 MINS

SERVES 4

INGREDIENTS

75 g/2¾ oz/6 tbsp butter

450 g/1 lb sirloin steak, trimmed
   and cut into thin strips

175 g/6 oz button mushrooms, sliced

1 tsp mustard

pinch of freshly grated root ginger

2 tbsp dry sherry

150 ml/¼ pint/⅔ cup double (heavy) cream

salt and pepper

4 slices hot toast, cut into triangles,
   to serve

PASTA

450 g/1 lb dried rigatoni

2 tbsp olive oil

2 fresh basil sprigs

115 g/4 oz/8 tbsp butter

1 Melt the butter in a large frying pan (skillet) and gently fry the steak over a low heat, stirring frequently, for 6 minutes. Using a slotted spoon, transfer the steak to an ovenproof dish and keep warm.

2 Add the sliced mushrooms to the frying pan (skillet) and cook for 2–3 minutes in the juices remaining in the pan. Add the mustard, ginger, salt and pepper. Cook for 2 minutes, then add the sherry and cream. Cook for a further 3 minutes, then pour the cream sauce over the steak.

3 Bake the steak and cream mixture in a preheated oven, at 190°C/375°F/Gas Mark 5, for 10 minutes.

4 Meanwhile, cook the pasta. Bring a large saucepan of lightly salted water to the boil. Add the rigatoni, olive oil and 1 of the basil sprigs and boil rapidly for 10 minutes, until tender but still firm to the bite. Drain the pasta and transfer to a warm serving plate. Toss the pasta with the butter and garnish with a sprig of basil.

5 Serve the creamed steak strips with the pasta and triangles of warm toast.

COOK'S TIP

Dried pasta will keep for up to 6 months. Keep it in the packet and reseal it once you have opened it, or transfer the pasta to an airtight jar.

Beef & Spaghetti Surprise

This delicious Sicilian recipe originated as a handy way of using up leftover cooked pasta.

NUTRITIONAL INFORMATION

Calories	797	Sugars	.........7g
Protein	........31g	Fat	..........60g
Carbohydrate	...35g	Saturates	......16g

30 MINS   1½ HOURS

SERVES 4

I N G R E D I E N T S

150 ml/¼ pint/⅔ cup olive oil, plus extra
   for brushing

2 aubergines (eggplants)

350 g/12 oz/3 cups minced (ground) beef

1 onion, chopped

2 garlic cloves, crushed

2 tbsp tomato purée (paste)

400 g/14 oz can chopped tomatoes

1 tsp Worcestershire sauce

1 tsp chopped fresh marjoram or oregano
   or ½ tsp dried marjoram or oregano

60 g/2 oz/½ cup stoned (pitted) black
   olives, sliced

1 green, red or yellow (bell) pepper, cored,
   seeded and chopped

175 g/6 oz dried spaghetti

115 g/4 oz/1 cup freshly grated
   Parmesan cheese

salt and pepper

fresh oregano or parsley sprigs,
   to garnish

1 Brush a 20 cm/8 inch loose-based round cake tin (pan) with oil, line the base with baking parchment and brush with oil.

2 Slice the aubergines (eggplants). Heat a little oil in a pan and fry the aubergines (eggplant), in batches, for 3–4 minutes or until browned on both sides. Add more oil, as necessary. Drain on kitchen paper (paper towels).

3 Put the minced (ground) beef, onion and garlic in a saucepan and cook over a medium heat, stirring occasionally, until browned. Add the tomato purée (paste), tomatoes, Worcestershire sauce, marjoram or oregano and salt and pepper to taste. Leave to simmer, stirring occasionally, for 10 minutes. Add the olives and (bell) pepper and cook for a further 10 minutes.

4 Bring a pan of salted water to the boil. Add the spaghetti and 1 tbsp oil and cook for 8–10 minutes until tender, but still firm to the bite. Drain and turn the spaghetti into a bowl. Add the meat mixture and cheese and toss with 2 forks.

5 Arrange aubergine (eggplant) slices over the base and up the sides of the tin (pan). Add the spaghetti, pressing down firmly, and then cover with the rest of the aubergine (eggplant) slices. Bake in a preheated oven at 200°C/400°F/Gas Mark 6 for 40 minutes. Leave to stand for 5 minutes, then invert on to a serving dish. Discard the baking parchment. Garnish with the fresh herbs and serve.

Beef & Pasta Bake

The combination of Italian and Indian ingredients makes a surprisingly delicious recipe. Marinate the steak in advance to save time.

NUTRITIONAL INFORMATION

Calories	1050	Sugars	4g
Protein	47g	Fat	81g
Carbohydrate	37g	Saturates	34g

6¼ HOURS 1¼ HOURS

SERVES 4

INGREDIENTS

900g/2 lb steak, cut into cubes

150 ml/¼ pint/⅔ cup beef stock

450g/1 lb dried macaroni

300 ml/½ pint/1¼ cups double
   (heavy) cream

½ tsp garam masala

salt

fresh coriander (cilantro) and flaked
   (slivered) almonds, to garnish

KORMA PASTE

60 g/2 oz/½ cup blanched almonds

6 garlic cloves

2.5 cm/1 inch piece fresh root ginger,
   coarsely chopped

6 tbsp beef stock

1 tsp ground cardamom

4 cloves, crushed

1 tsp cinnamon

2 large onions, chopped

1 tsp coriander seeds

2 tsp ground cumin seeds

pinch of cayenne pepper

6 tbsp of sunflower oil

1 To make the korma paste, grind the almonds finely using a pestle and mortar. Put the ground almonds and the rest of the korma paste ingredients into a food processor or blender and process to make a very smooth paste.

2 Put the steak in a shallow dish and spoon over the korma paste, turning to coat the steak well. Leave in the refrigerator to marinate for 6 hours.

3 Transfer the steak and korma paste to a large saucepan, and simmer over a low heat, adding a little beef stock if required, for 35 minutes.

4 Meanwhile, bring a large saucepan of lightly salted water to the boil. Add the macaroni and cook for 10 minutes until tender, but still firm to the bite. Drain the pasta thoroughly and transfer to a deep casserole. Add the steak, double (heavy) cream and garam masala.

5 Bake in a preheated oven at 200°C/ 400°F/Gas Mark 6 for 30 minutes. Remove the casserole from the oven and allow to stand for about 10 minutes. Garnish the bake with fresh coriander (cilantro) and serve.

Fresh Spaghetti & Meatballs

This well-loved Italian dish is famous across the world. Make the most of it by using high-quality steak for the meatballs.

NUTRITIONAL INFORMATION

Calories 665	Sugars 9g
Protein 39g	Fat 24g
Carbohydrate . . .77g	Saturates 8g

 45 MINS   1¼ HOURS

SERVES 4

I N G R E D I E N T S

150 g/5½ oz/2½ cups brown breadcrumbs

150 ml/¼ pint/⅔ cup milk

25 g/1 oz/2 tbsp butter

25 g/1 oz/¼ cup wholemeal
   (whole-wheat) flour

200 ml/7 fl oz/⅞ cup beef stock

400 g/14 oz can chopped tomatoes

2 tbsp tomato purée (paste)

1 tsp sugar

1 tbsp finely chopped fresh tarragon

1 large onion, chopped

450 g/1 lb/4 cups minced steak

1 tsp paprika

4 tbsp olive oil

450 g/1 lb fresh spaghetti

salt and pepper

fresh tarragon sprigs, to garnish

1 Place the breadcrumbs in a bowl, add the milk and set aside to soak for about 30 minutes.

2 Melt half of the butter in a pan. Add the flour and cook, stirring constantly, for 2 minutes. Gradually stir in the beef stock and cook, stirring constantly, for a further 5 minutes. Add the tomatoes, tomato purée (paste), sugar and tarragon. Season well and simmer for 25 minutes.

3 Mix the onion, steak and paprika into the breadcrumbs and season to taste. Shape the mixture into 14 meatballs.

4 Heat the oil and remaining butter in a frying pan (skillet) and fry the meatballs, turning, until brown all over. Place in a deep casserole, pour over the tomato sauce, cover and bake in a preheated oven, at 180°C/350°F/Gas Mark 4, for 25 minutes.

5 Bring a large saucepan of lightly salted water to the boil. Add the fresh spaghetti, bring back to the boil and cook for about 2–3 minutes or until tender, but still firm to the bite.

6 Meanwhile, remove the meatballs from the oven and allow them to cool for 3 minutes. Serve the meatballs and their sauce with the spaghetti, garnished with tarragon sprigs.

Meatballs in Red Wine Sauce

A different twist is given to this traditional pasta dish with a rich, but subtle, sauce.

NUTRITIONAL INFORMATION

Calories 811	Sugars 7g	
Protein 30g	Fat 43g	
Carbohydrate ...76g	Saturates 12g	

 45 MINS   1½ HOURS

SERVES 4

I N G R E D I E N T S

150 ml/¼ pint/⅔ cup milk

150 g/5½ oz/2 cups white breadcrumbs

25 g/1 oz/2 tbsp butter

9 tbsp olive oil

225 g/8 oz/3 cups sliced
   oyster mushrooms

25 g/1 oz/¼ cup wholemeal
(whole-wheat) flour

200 ml/7 fl oz/⅞ cup beef stock

150 ml/¼ pint/⅔ cup red wine

4 tomatoes, skinned and chopped

1 tbsp tomato purée (paste)

1 tsp brown sugar

1 tbsp finely chopped fresh basil

12 shallots, chopped

450 g/1 lb/4 cups minced (ground) steak

1 tsp paprika

450 g/1 lb dried egg tagliarini

salt and pepper

fresh basil sprigs, to garnish

1 Pour the milk into a bowl and soak the breadcrumbs in the milk for 30 minutes.

2 Heat half of the butter and 4 tbsp of the oil in a pan. Fry the mushrooms for 4 minutes, then stir in the flour and cook for 2 minutes. Add the stock and wine and simmer for 15 minutes. Add the tomatoes, tomato purée (paste), sugar and basil. Season and simmer for 30 minutes.

3 Mix the shallots, steak and paprika with the breadcrumbs and season to taste. Shape the mixture into 14 meatballs.

4 Heat 4 tbsp of the remaining oil and the remaining butter in a large frying pan (skillet). Fry the meatballs, turning frequently, until brown all over. Transfer to a deep casserole, pour over the red wine and the mushroom sauce, cover and bake in a preheated oven, at 180°C/350°F/Gas Mark 4, for 30 minutes.

5 Bring a pan of salted water to the boil. Add the pasta and the remaining oil and cook for 8–10 minutes or until tender. Drain and transfer to a serving dish. Remove the casserole from the oven and cool for 3 minutes. Pour the meatballs and sauce on to the pasta, garnish and serve.

Pork Chops with Sage

The fresh taste of sage is the perfect ingredient to counteract the richness of pork.

NUTRITIONAL INFORMATION

Calories	364	Sugars	........5g
Protein	........34g	Fat	..........19g
Carbohydrate	...14g	Saturates	.......7g

 10 MINS   15 MINS

SERVES 4

I N G R E D I E N T S

2 tbsp flour

1 tbsp chopped fresh sage or 1 tsp dried

4 lean boneless pork chops, trimmed of
    excess fat

2 tbsp olive oil

15 g/½ oz/1 tbsp butter

2 red onions, sliced into rings

1 tbsp lemon juice

2 tsp caster (superfine) sugar

4 plum tomatoes, quartered

salt and pepper

1 Mix the flour, sage and salt and pepper to taste on a plate. Lightly dust the pork chops on both sides with the seasoned flour.

2 Heat the oil and butter in a frying pan (skillet), add the chops and cook them for 6–7 minutes on each side until cooked through. Drain the chops, reserving the pan juices, and keep warm.

3 Toss the onion in the lemon juice and fry along with the sugar and tomatoes for 5 minutes until tender.

4 Serve the pork with the tomato and onion mixture and a green salad.

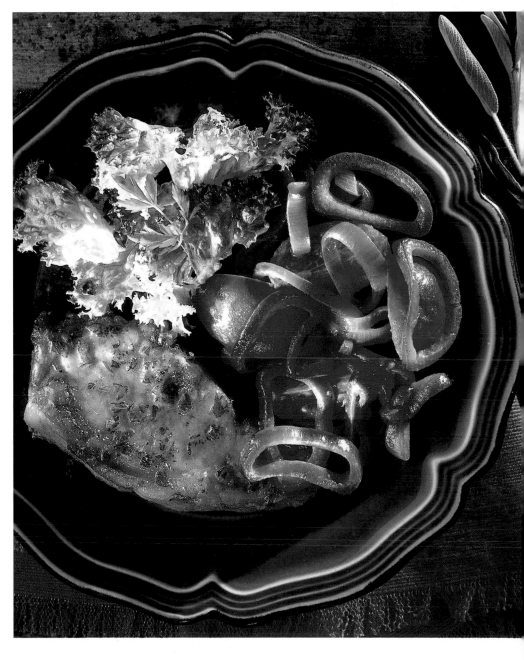

Pasta & Pork in Cream Sauce

This unusual and attractive dish is extremely delicious. Make the Italian Red Wine Sauce well in advance to reduce the preparation time.

NUTRITIONAL INFORMATION

Calories 735	Sugars 4g
Protein 31g	Fat 52g
Carbohydrate . . .37g	Saturates 19g

 15 MINS 🕐 35 MINS

SERVES 4

I N G R E D I E N T S

450 g/1 lb pork fillet (tenderloin),
  thinly sliced

4 tbsp olive oil

225 g/8 oz button mushrooms, sliced

200 ml/7 fl oz/⅞ cup Italian Red Wine Sauce
  (see page 15)

1 tbsp lemon juice

pinch of saffron

350 g/12 oz/3 cups dried orecchioni

4 tbsp double (heavy) cream

12 quail eggs (see Cook's Tip)

salt

1 Pound the slices of pork between 2 sheets of cling film until wafer thin, then cut into strips.

2 Heat the olive oil in a large frying pan (skillet), add the pork and stir-fry for 5 minutes. Add the mushrooms to the pan and stir-fry for a further 2 minutes.

3 Pour over the Italian Red Wine Sauce, lower the heat and simmer gently for 20 minutes.

4 Meanwhile, bring a large saucepan of lightly salted water to the boil. Add the lemon juice, saffron and orecchioni and cook for 8–10 minutes, until tender but still firm to the bite. Drain the pasta and keep warm.

5 Stir the cream into the pan with the pork and heat gently for a few minutes.

6 Boil the quail eggs for 3 minutes, cool them in cold water and remove the shells.

7 Transfer the pasta to a large, warm serving plate, top with the pork and the sauce and garnish with the eggs. Serve immediately.

COOK'S TIP

In this recipe, the quail eggs are soft-boiled (soft-cooked). As they are extremely difficult to shell when warm, it is important that they are thoroughly cooled first. Otherwise, they will break up unattractively.

Pork with Fennel & Juniper

The addition of juniper and fennel to the pork chops gives an unusual and delicate flavour to this dish.

NUTRITIONAL INFORMATION

Calories 277	Sugars 0.4g
Protein 32g	Fat 16g
Carbohydrate ...0.4g	Saturates 5g

2¼ HOURS   15 MINS

SERVES 4

INGREDIENTS

½ fennel bulb

1 tbsp juniper berries

about 2 tbsp olive oil

finely grated rind and juice of 1 orange

4 pork chops, each about 150 g/5½ oz

fresh bread and a crisp salad, to serve

1 Finely chop the fennel bulb, discarding the green parts.

2 Grind the juniper berries in a pestle and mortar. Mix the crushed juniper berries with the fennel flesh, olive oil and orange rind.

3 Using a sharp knife, score a few cuts all over each chop.

4 Place the pork chops in a roasting tin (pan) or an ovenproof dish. Spoon the fennel and juniper mixture over the chops.

5 Pour the orange juice over the top of each chop, cover and marinate in the refrigerator for about 2 hours.

6 Cook the pork chops, under a preheated grill (broiler), for 10–15 minutes, depending on the thickness of the meat, or until the meat is tender and cooked through, turning occasionally.

7 Transfer the pork chops to serving plates and serve with a crisp, fresh salad and plenty of fresh bread to mop up the cooking juices.

COOK'S TIP

Juniper berries are most commonly associated with gin, but they are often added to meat dishes in Italy for a delicate citrus flavour. They can be bought dried from most health food shops and some larger supermarkets.

Pork Cooked in Milk

This traditional dish of boned pork cooked with garlic and milk can be served hot or cold.

NUTRITIONAL INFORMATION

Calories 498	Sugars 15g
Protein 50g	Fat 27g
Carbohydrate ...15g	Saturates 9g

 20 MINS 1¾ HOURS

SERVES 4

I N G R E D I E N T S

800 g/1 lb 12 oz leg of pork, boned

1 tbsp oil

25 g/1 oz/2 tbsp butter

1 onion, chopped

2 garlic cloves, chopped

75 g/2¾ oz pancetta, diced

1.2 litres/2 pints/5 cups milk

1 tbsp green peppercorns, crushed

2 fresh bay leaves

2 tbsp marjoram

2 tbsp thyme

1 Using a sharp knife, remove the fat from the pork. Shape the meat into a neat form, tying it in place with a length of string.

2 Heat the oil and butter in a large pan. Add the onion, garlic and pancetta to the pan and cook for 2–3 minutes.

3 Add the pork to the pan and cook, turning occasionally, until it is browned all over.

4 Pour over the milk, add the peppercorns, bay leaves, marjoram and thyme and cook over a low heat for 1¼–1½ hours or until tender. Watch the

liquid carefully for the last 15 minutes of cooking time because it tends to reduce very quickly and will then burn. If the liquid reduces and the pork is still not tender, add another 100 ml/3½ fl oz milk and continue cooking. Reserve the cooking liquid (as the milk reduces naturally in this dish, it forms a thick and creamy sauce, which curdles slightly but tastes very delicious).

5 Remove the pork from the saucepan. Using a sharp knife, cut the meat into slices. Transfer the pork slices to serving plates and serve immediately with the reserved cooking liquid.

Pork with Lemon & Garlic

This is a simplified version of a traditional dish from the Marche region of Italy. Pork fillet pockets are stuffed with ham (prosciutto) and herbs.

NUTRITIONAL INFORMATION

Calories 428	Sugars 2g	
Protein 31g	Fat 32g	
Carbohydrate 4g	Saturates 4g	

 25 MINS 1 HOUR

SERVES 4

INGREDIENTS

450 g/1 lb pork fillet

50 g/1¾ oz chopped almonds

2 tbsp olive oil

100 g/3½ oz raw Parma ham (prosciutto), finely chopped

2 garlic cloves, chopped

1 tbsp fresh oregano, chopped

finely grated rind of 2 lemons

4 shallots, finely chopped

200 ml/7 fl oz/¾ cup ham or chicken stock

1 tsp sugar

1 Using a sharp knife, cut the pork fillet into 4 equal pieces. Place the pork between sheets of greaseproof paper and pound each piece with a meat mallet or the end of a rolling pin to flatten it.

2 Cut a horizontal slit in each piece of pork to make a pocket.

3 Place the almonds on a baking tray (cookie sheet). Lightly toast the almonds under a medium-hot grill (broiler) for 2–3 minutes or until golden.

4 Mix the almonds with 1 tbsp oil, ham (prosciutto), garlic, oregano and the finely grated rind from 1 lemon. Spoon the mixture into the pockets of the pork.

5 Heat the remaining oil in a large frying pan (skillet). Add the shallots and cook for 2 minutes.

6 Add the pork to the frying pan (skillet) and cook for 2 minutes on each side or until browned all over.

7 Add the ham or chicken stock to the pan, bring to the boil, cover and leave to simmer for 45 minutes or until the pork is tender. Remove the meat from the pan, set aside and keep warm.

8 Add the lemon rind and sugar to the pan, boil for 3–4 minutes or until reduced and syrupy. Pour the lemon sauce over the pork fillets and serve immediately.

Neapolitan Pork Steaks

An Italian version of grilled pork steaks, this dish is easy to make and delicious to eat.

NUTRITIONAL INFORMATION

Calories	353	Sugars	.........3g
Protein	........39g	Fat	..........20g
Carbohydrate	....4g	Saturates	.......5g

 10 MINS 25 MINS

SERVES 4

I N G R E D I E N T S

2 tbsp olive oil

1 garlic clove, chopped

1 large onion, sliced

400 g/14 oz can tomatoes

2 tsp yeast extract

4 pork loin steaks, each about 125 g/4½ oz

75 g/2¾ oz black olives, pitted

2 tbsp fresh basil, shredded

freshly grated Parmesan cheese, to serve

1 Heat the oil in a large frying pan (skillet). Add the onions and garlic and cook, stirring, for 3–4 minutes or until they just begin to soften.

2 Add the tomatoes and yeast extract to the frying pan (skillet) and leave to simmer for about 5 minutes or until the sauce starts to thicken.

COOK'S TIP

Parmesan is a mature and exceptionally hard cheese produced in Italy. You only need to add a little as it has a very strong flavour.

3 Cook the pork steaks, under a preheated grill (broiler), for 5 minutes on both sides, until the the meat is cooked through. Set the pork aside and keep warm.

4 Add the olives and fresh shredded basil to the sauce in the frying pan (skillet) and stir quickly to combine.

5 Transfer the steaks to warm serving plates. Top the steaks with the sauce, sprinkle with freshly grated Parmesan cheese and serve immediately.

Roman Pan-Fried Lamb

Chunks of tender lamb, pan-fried with garlic and stewed in red wine are a real Roman dish.

NUTRITIONAL INFORMATION

Calories	299	Sugars	.........1g	
Protein	........31g	Fat	..........16g	
Carbohydrate	....1g	Saturates	.......7g	

15 MINS   50 MINS

SERVES 4

I N G R E D I E N T S

1 tbsp oil

15 g/½ oz/1 tbsp butter

600 g/1 lb 5 oz lamb (shoulder or leg),
  cut into 2.5 cm/1 inch chunks

4 garlic cloves, peeled

3 sprigs thyme, stalks removed

6 canned anchovy fillets

150 ml/¼ pint/⅔ cup red wine

150 ml/¼ pint/⅔ cup lamb or
  vegetable stock

1 tsp sugar

50 g/1¾ oz black olives, pitted and halved

2 tbsp chopped parsley, to garnish

mashed potato, to serve

1 Heat the oil and butter in a large frying pan (skillet). Add the lamb and cook for 4–5 minutes, stirring, until the meat is browned all over.

2 Using a pestle and mortar, grind together the garlic, thyme and anchovies to make a smooth paste.

3 Add the wine and lamb or vegetable stock to the frying pan (skillet). Stir in the garlic and anchovy paste together with the sugar.

4 Bring the mixture to the boil, reduce the heat, cover and simmer for 30–40 minutes or until the lamb is tender. For the last 10 minutes of the cooking time, remove the lid to allow the sauce to reduce slightly.

5 Stir the olives into the sauce and mix to combine.

6 Transfer the lamb and the sauce to a serving bowl and garnish. Serve with creamy mashed potatoes.

COOK'S TIP

Rome is the capital of both the region of Lazio and Italy and thus has become a focal point for specialities from all over Italy. Food from this region tends to be fairly simple and quick to prepare, all with plenty of herbs and seasonings giving really robust flavours.

Lamb Cutlets with Rosemary

A classic combination of flavours, this dish would make a perfect Sunday lunch. Serve with tomato and onion salad and jacket potatoes.

NUTRITIONAL INFORMATION

Calories .... .560 Sugars 1g
Protein ....48g Fat .... .40g
Carbohydrate ....1g Saturates ...... .13g

1¼ HOURS   15 MINS

SERVES 4

INGREDIENTS

8 lamb cutlets

5 tbsp olive oil

2 tbsp lemon juice

1 clove garlic, crushed

½ tsp lemon pepper

salt

8 sprigs rosemary

jacket potatoes, to serve

SALAD

4 tomatoes, sliced

4 spring onions (scallion), sliced diagonally

DRESSING

2 tbsp olive oil

1 tbsp lemon juice

1 clove garlic, chopped

¼ tsp fresh rosemary, chopped finely

 1 Trim the lamb chops by cutting away the flesh with a sharp knife to expose the tips of the bones.

2 Place the oil, lemon juice, garlic, lemon pepper and salt in a shallow, non-metallic dish and whisk with a fork to combine.

3 Lay the sprigs of rosemary in the dish and place the lamb on top. Leave to marinate for at least 1 hour, turning the lamb cutlets once.

4 Remove the chops from the marinade and wrap a little kitchen foil around the bones to stop them from burning.

5 Place the rosemary sprigs on the rack and place the lamb on top. Barbecue (grill) for 10–15 minutes, turning once.

6 Meanwhile make the salad and dressing. Arrange the tomatoes on a serving dish and scatter the spring onions (scallions) on top. Place all the ingredients for the dressing in a screw-top jar, shake well and pour over the salad. Serve with the lamb cutlets and jacket potatoes.

COOK'S TIP

Choose medium to small baking potatoes if you want to cook jacket potatoes on the barbecue (grill). Scrub them well, prick with a fork and wrap in buttered kitchen foil. Bury them in the hot coals and barbecue (grill) for 50–60 minutes.

Lamb with Olives

This is a very simple dish, and the chilli adds a bit of spiciness. It is quick to prepare and makes an ideal supper dish.

NUTRITIONAL INFORMATION

Calories 577	Sugars 1g	
Protein 62g	Fat 33g	
Carbohydrate 1g	Saturates 10g	

🥩 15 MINS 🕐 1½ HOURS

SERVES 4

I N G R E D I E N T S

1.25 kg/2 lb 12 oz boned leg of lamb

90 ml/3 fl oz/⅓ cup olive oil

2 garlic cloves, crushed

1 onion, sliced

1 small red chilli, cored, deseeded and
  chopped finely

175 ml/6 fl oz/¾ cup dry white wine

175 g/6 oz/1 cup pitted black olives

salt

chopped fresh parsley, to garnish

1 Using a sharp knife, cut the lamb into 2.5 cm/1 inch cubes.

2 Heat the oil in a frying pan (skillet) and fry the garlic, onion and chilli for 5 minutes.

3 Add the meat and wine and cook for a further 5 minutes.

4 Stir in the olives, then transfer the mixture to a casserole. Place in a preheated oven, 180°C/350°F/Gas Mark 4, and cook for 1 hour 20 minutes or until the meat is tender. Season with salt to taste, and serve garnished with chopped fresh parsley.

Lamb with Bay & Lemon

These lamb chops quickly become more elegant when the bone is removed to make noisettes.

NUTRITIONAL INFORMATION

Calories . . . . . . .268 Sugars 0.2g
Protein . . . . .24g Fat 16g
Carbohydrate . . .0.2g Saturates 7g

10 MINS   35 MINS

SERVES 4

INGREDIENTS

4 lamb chops

1 tbsp oil

15 g/½ oz/1 tbsp butter

150 ml/¼ pint/⅔ cup white wine

150 ml/¼ pint/⅔ cup lamb or
 vegetable stock

2 bay leaves

pared rind of 1 lemon

salt and pepper

1 Using a sharp knife, carefully remove the bone from each lamb chop, keeping the meat intact. Alternatively, ask the butcher to prepare the lamb noisettes for you.

2 Shape the meat into rounds and secure with a length of string.

3 In a large frying pan (skillet), heat together the oil and butter until the mixture starts to froth.

4 Add the lamb noisettes to the frying pan (skillet) and cook for 2–3 minutes on each side or until browned all over.

5 Remove the frying pan (skillet) fom the heat, drain off all of the excess fat and discard.

6 Return the frying pan (skillet) to the heat. Add the wine, stock, bay leaves and lemon rind to the frying pan (skillet) and cook for 20–25 minutes or until the lamb is tender. Season the lamb noisettes and sauce to taste with a little salt and pepper.

7 Transfer to serving plates. Remove the string from each noisette and serve with the sauce.

COOK'S TIP

Your local butcher will offer you good advice on how to prepare the lamb noisettes, if you are wary of preparing them yourself.

Barbecued Butterfly Lamb

The appearance of the lamb as it is opened out to cook on the barbecue gives this dish its name. Marinate the lamb in advance if possible.

NUTRITIONAL INFORMATION

Calories 733   Sugars 6g
Protein . . . . .69g   Fat 48g
Carbohydrate . . . .6g   Saturates 13g

6¼ HOURS   1 HOUR

SERVES 4

I N G R E D I E N T S

boned leg of lamb, about 1.8 kg/4 lb

8 tbsp balsamic vinegar

grated rind and juice of 1 lemon

150 ml/¼ pint/⅔ cup sunflower oil

4 tbsp chopped, fresh mint

2 cloves garlic, crushed

2 tbsp light muscovado sugar

salt and pepper

TO SERVE

grilled (broiled) vegetables

green salad leaves

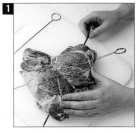

1 Open out the boned leg of lamb so that its shape resembles a butterfly. Thread 2–3 skewers through the meat in order to make it easier to turn on the barbecue (grill).

2 Combine the balsamic vinegar, lemon rind and juice, oil, mint, garlic, sugar and salt and pepper to taste in a non-metallic dish that is large enough to hold the lamb.

3 Place the lamb in the dish and turn it over a few times so that the meat is coated on both sides with the marinade. Leave to marinate for at least 6 hours or preferably overnight, turning occasionally.

4 Remove the lamb from the marinade and reserve the liquid for basting.

5 Place the rack about 15 cm/6 inches above the coals and barbecue (grill) the lamb for about 30 minutes on each side, turning once and basting frequently with the marinade.

6 Transfer the lamb to a chopping board and remove the skewers. Cut the lamb into slices across the grain and serve.

COOK'S TIP

If you prefer, cook the lamb for half the cooking time in a preheated oven at 180°C/350°F/ Gas Mark 4, then finish off on the barbecue (grill).

Veal in a Rose Petal Sauce

This truly spectacular dish is equally delicious whether you use veal or pork fillet. Make sure the roses are free of blemishes and pesticides.

NUTRITIONAL INFORMATION

Calories	.810	Sugars	.2g
Protein	.31g	Fat	.56g
Carbohydrate	.49g	Saturates	.28g

 10 MINS   35 MINS

SERVES 4

INGREDIENTS

450 g/1 lb dried fettuccine

7 tbsp olive oil

1 tsp chopped fresh oregano

1 tsp chopped fresh marjoram

175 g/6 oz/¾ cup butter

450 g/1 lb veal fillet, thinly sliced

150 ml/¼ pint/⅔ cup rose petal vinegar
   (see Cook's Tip)

150 ml/¼ pint/⅔ cup fish stock

50 ml/2 fl oz/¼ cup grapefruit juice

50 ml/2 fl oz/¼ cup double
   (heavy) cream

salt

TO GARNISH

12 pink grapefruit segments

12 pink peppercorns

rose petals

fresh herb leaves

1 Bring a large saucepan of lightly salted water to the boil. Add the fettuccine and 1 tablespoon of the oil and cook for 8–10 minutes or until tender, but still firm to the bite. Drain and transfer to a warm serving dish, sprinkle over 2 tablespoons of the olive oil, the oregano and marjoram.

2 Heat 50 g/2 oz/4 tbsp of the butter with the remaining oil in a large frying pan (skillet). Add the veal and cook over a low heat for 6 minutes. Remove the veal from the pan and place on top of the pasta.

3 Add the vinegar and fish stock to the pan and bring to the boil. Boil vigorously until reduced by two thirds. Add the grapefruit juice and cream and simmer over a low heat for 4 minutes. Dice the remaining butter and add to the pan, one piece at a time, whisking constantly until it has been completely incorporated.

4 Pour the sauce around the veal, garnish with grapefruit segments, pink peppercorns, the rose petals (washed) and your favourite herb leaves.

COOK'S TIP

To make rose petal vinegar, infuse the petals of 8 pesticide-free roses in 150 ml/¼ pint/⅔ cup white wine vinegar for 48 hours. Prepare well in advance to reduce the preparation time.

Vitello Tonnato

Veal dishes are the speciality of Lombardy, with this dish being one of the more sophisticated. Serve cold with seasonal salads.

NUTRITIONAL INFORMATION

Calories	654	Sugars	.........1g
Protein	........49g	Fat	..........47g
Carbohydrate	....1g	Saturates	.......8g

 30 MINS   1¼ HOURS

SERVES 4

INGREDIENTS

750 g/1 lb 10 oz boned leg of veal, rolled

2 bay leaves

10 black peppercorns

2–3 cloves

½ tsp salt

2 carrots, sliced

1 onion, sliced

2 celery stalks, sliced

about 700 ml/1¼ pints/3 cups stock
   or water

150 ml/¼ pint/⅔ cup dry white wine
   (optional)

90 g/3 oz canned tuna fish, well drained

50 g/1½ oz can anchovy fillets, drained

150 ml/¼ pint/⅔ cup olive oil

2 tsp bottled capers, drained

2 egg yolks

1 tbsp lemon juice

salt and pepper

TO GARNISH

capers

lemon wedges

fresh herbs

1 Put the veal in a saucepan with the bay leaves, peppercorns, cloves, salt and vegetables. Add sufficient stock or water and the wine (if using) to barely cover the veal. Bring to the boil, remove any scum from the surface, then cover the pan and simmer gently for about 1 hour or until tender. Leave in the water until cold, then drain thoroughly. If time allows, chill the veal to make it easier to carve.

2 For the tuna sauce: thoroughly mash the tuna with 4 anchovy fillets, 1 tablespoon of oil and the capers. Add the egg yolks and press through a sieve (strainer) or purée in a food processor or liquidizer until smooth.

3 Stir in the lemon juice then gradually whisk in the rest of the oil a few drops at a time until the sauce is smooth and has the consistency of thick cream. Season with salt and pepper to taste.

4 Slice the veal thinly and arrange on a platter in overlapping slices. Spoon the sauce over the veal to cover. Then cover the dish and chill overnight.

5 Before serving, uncover the veal carefully. Arrange the remaining anchovy fillets and the capers in a decorative pattern on top, and then garnish with lemon wedges and sprigs of fresh herbs.

Neapolitan Veal Cutlets

The delicious combination of apple, onion and mushroom perfectly complements the delicate flavour of veal.

NUTRITIONAL INFORMATION

Calories . . . . . . .1071 Sugars 13g
Protein . . . . .74g Fat 59g
Carbohydrate . . .66g Saturates 16g

  20 MINS   45 MINS

SERVES 4

INGREDIENTS

200 g/7 oz/⅞ cup butter

4 x 250 g/9 oz veal cutlets, trimmed

1 large onion, sliced

2 apples, peeled, cored and sliced

175 g/6 oz button mushrooms

1 tbsp chopped fresh tarragon

8 black peppercorns

1 tbsp sesame seeds

400 g/14 oz dried marille

100 ml/3½ fl oz/scant ½ cup extra virgin
    olive oil

175 g/6 oz/¾ cup mascarpone cheese,
    broken into small pieces

2 large beef tomatoes, cut in half

leaves of 1 fresh basil sprig

salt and pepper

fresh basil leaves, to garnish

1 Melt 60 g/2 oz/4 tbsp of the butter in a frying pan (skillet). Fry the veal over a low heat for 5 minutes on each side. Transfer to a dish and keep warm.

2 Fry the onion and apples in the pan until lightly browned. Transfer to a dish, place the veal on top and keep warm.

3 Melt the remaining butter in the frying pan (skillet). Gently fry the mushrooms, tarragon and peppercorns over a low heat for 3 minutes. Sprinkle over the sesame seeds.

4 Bring a pan of salted water to the boil. Add the pasta and 1 tbsp of oil. Cook for 8–10 minutes or until tender, but still firm to the bite. Drain; transfer to a plate.

5 Grill (broil) or fry the tomatoes and basil for 2–3 minutes.

6 Top the pasta with the mascarpone cheese and sprinkle over the remaining olive oil. Place the onions, apples and veal cutlets on top of the pasta. Spoon the mushrooms, peppercorns and pan juices on to the cutlets, place the tomatoes and basil leaves around the edge and place in a preheated oven at 150°C/300°F/Gas Mark 2 for 5 minutes.

7 Season to taste with salt and pepper, garnish with fresh basil leaves and serve immediately.

Veal Italienne

This dish is really superb if made with tender veal. However, if veal is unavailable, use pork or turkey escalopes instead.

NUTRITIONAL INFORMATION

Calories 592   Sugars 5g
Protein . . . . .44g   Fat 23g
Carbohydrate . . .48g   Saturates 9g

25 MINS   1 HR 20 MINS

SERVES 4

I N G R E D I E N T S

60 g/2 oz/¼ cup butter

1 tbsp olive oil

675 g/1½ lb potatoes, cubed

4 veal escalopes, weighing 175 g/6 oz each

1 onion, cut into 8 wedges

2 garlic cloves, crushed

2 tbsp plain (all-purpose) flour

2 tbsp tomato purée (paste)

150 ml/¼ pint/⅔ cup red wine

300 ml/½ pint/1¼ cups chicken stock

8 ripe tomatoes, peeled, seeded and diced

25 g/1 oz stoned (pitted) black olives,
  halved

2 tbsp chopped fresh basil

salt and pepper

fresh basil leaves, to garnish

1 Heat the butter and oil in a large frying pan (skillet). Add the potato cubes and cook for 5-7 minutes, stirring frequently, until they begin to brown.

2 Remove the potatoes from the pan (skillet) with a perforated spoon and set aside.

3 Place the veal in the frying pan (skillet) and cook for 2-3 minutes on each side until sealed. Remove from the pan and set aside.

4 Stir the onion and garlic into the pan (skillet) and cook for 2-3 minutes.

5 Add the flour and tomato purée (paste) and cook for 1 minute, stirring. Gradually blend in the red wine and chicken stock, stirring to make a smooth sauce.

6 Return the potatoes and veal to the pan (skillet). Stir in the tomatoes, olives and chopped basil and season with salt and pepper.

7 Transfer to a casserole dish and cook in a preheated oven, 180°C/350°F/Gas Mark 4, for 1 hour or until the potatoes and veal are cooked through. Garnish with basil leaves and serve.

COOK'S TIP

For a quicker cooking time and really tender meat, pound the meat with a meat mallet to flatten it slightly before cooking.

Escalopes & Italian Sausage

Anchovies are often used to enhance flavour, particularly in meat dishes. Either veal or turkey escalopes can be used for this pan-fried dish.

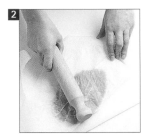

NUTRITIONAL INFORMATION

Calories 233	Sugars 1g
Protein 28g	Fat 13g
Carbohydrate 1g	Saturates 1g

 10 MINS   20 MINS

SERVES 4

INGREDIENTS

1 tbsp olive oil

6 canned anchovy fillets, drained

1 tbsp capers, drained

1 tbsp fresh rosemary, stalks removed

finely grated rind and juice of 1 orange

75 g/2¾ oz Italian sausage, diced

3 tomatoes, skinned and chopped

4 turkey or veal escalopes, each about
  125 g/4½ oz

salt and pepper

crusty bread or cooked polenta, to serve

1 Heat the oil in a large frying pan (skillet). Add the anchovies, capers, fresh rosemary, orange rind and juice, Italian sausage and tomatoes to the pan and cook for 5–6 minutes, stirring occasionally.

2 Meanwhile, place the turkey or veal escalopes between sheets of greasproof paper. Pound the meat with a meat mallet or the end of a rolling pin to flatten it.

3 Add the meat to the mixture in the frying pan (skillet). Season to taste with salt and pepper, cover and cook for 3–5 minutes on each side, slightly longer if the meat is thicker.

4 Transfer to serving plates and serve with fresh crusty bread or cooked polenta, if you prefer.

VARIATION

Try using 4-minute steaks, slightly flattened, instead of the turkey or veal. Cook them for 4–5 minutes on top of the sauce in the pan.

Liver with Wine Sauce

Liver is popular in Italy and is served in many ways. Tender calf's liver is the best type to use for this recipe, but you could use lamb's liver.

NUTRITIONAL INFORMATION

Calories ....435 Sugars 2g
Protein ....30g Fat 31g
Carbohydrate ....4g Saturates 12g

  25 MINS    20 MINS

SERVES 4

I N G R E D I E N T S

4 slices calf's liver or 8 slices lamb's liver, about 500 g/1 lb 2 oz

flour, for coating

1 tbsp olive oil

25 g/1 oz/2 tbsp butter

125 g/4½ oz lean bacon rashers, rinded and cut into narrow strips

1 garlic clove, crushed

1 onion, chopped

1 celery stick, sliced thinly

150 ml/¼ pint/⅔ cup red wine

150 ml/¼ pint/⅔ cup beef stock

good pinch of ground allspice

1 tsp Worcestershire sauce

1 tsp chopped fresh sage or ½ tsp dried sage

3–4 tomatoes, peeled, quartered and deseeded

salt and pepper

fresh sage leaves, to garnish

new potatoes or sauté potatoes, to serve

1 Wipe the liver with kitchen paper (paper towels), season with salt and pepper to taste and then coat lightly in flour, shaking off any excess.

2 Heat the oil and butter in a pan and fry the liver until well sealed on both sides and just cooked through – take care not to overcook. Remove the liver from the pan, cover and keep warm, but do not allow to dry out.

3 Add the bacon to the fat left in the pan, with the garlic, onion and celery. Fry gently until soft.

4 Add the red wine, beef stock, allspice, Worcestershire sauce, sage and salt and pepper to taste. Bring to the boil and simmer for 3–4 minutes.

5 Cut each tomato segment in half. Add to the sauce and continue to cook for 2–3 minutes.

6 Serve the liver on a little of the sauce, with the remainder spooned over. Garnish with fresh sage leaves and serve with tiny new potatoes or sauté potatoes.

Chicken & Poultry

For the poultry-lover there are pasta dishes, risottos and bakes in this chapter, incorporating a variety of healthy and colourful ingredients. For those who enjoy Asian cuisine,

there are a number of spicy dishes; alternatively there are rich Italian sauces and old favourites such as more traditional casseroles. All of these recipes are mouth-watering and quick and easy to prepare. All of the recipes are extremely wholesome, offering a comprehensive range of tastes. Those on a low-fat diet should choose lean cuts of meat and look out for low-fat mince to enjoy the dishes featured here.

Garlic & Herb Chicken

There is a delicious surprise of creamy herb and garlic soft cheese hidden inside these chicken parcels!

NUTRITIONAL INFORMATION

Calories ....272 Sugars 4g
Protein ....29g Fat 13g
Carbohydrate ....4g Saturates 6g

 20 MINS   25 MINS

SERVES 4

INGREDIENTS

4 chicken breasts, skin removed

100 g/3½ oz full fat soft cheese, flavoured
  with herbs and garlic

8 slices Parma ham (prosciutto)

150 ml/¼ pint/⅔ cup red wine

150 ml/¼ pint/⅔ cup chicken stock

1 tbsp brown sugar

1 Using a sharp knife, make a horizontal slit along the length of each chicken breast to form a pocket.

2 Beat the cheese with a wooden spoon to soften it. Spoon the cheese into the pocket of the chicken breasts.

3 Wrap 2 slices of Parma ham (prosciutto) around each chicken breast and secure firmly in place with a length of string.

4 Pour the wine and chicken stock into a large frying pan (skillet) and bring to the boil. When the mixture is just starting to boil, add the sugar and stir well to dissolve.

5 Add the chicken breasts to the mixture in the frying pan (skillet). Leave to simmer for 12–15 minutes or until the chicken is tender and the juices run clear when a skewer is inserted into the thickest part of the meat.

6 Remove the chicken from the pan, set aside and keep warm.

7 Reheat the sauce and boil until reduced and thickened. Remove the string from the chicken and cut into slices. Pour the sauce over the chicken to serve.

VARIATION

Try adding 2 finely chopped sun-dried tomatoes to the soft cheese in step 2, if you prefer.

Chicken with Vegetables

This dish combines succulent chicken with tasty vegetables, flavoured with wine and olives.

NUTRITIONAL INFORMATION

Calories	.470	Sugars	.7g
Protein	.29g	Fat	.34g
Carbohydrate	.7g	Saturates	.16g

 20 MINS 1½ HOURS

SERVES 4

I N G R E D I E N T S

4 chicken breasts, part boned

25 g/1 oz/2 tbsp butter

2 tbsp olive oil

1 large onion, chopped finely

2 garlic cloves, crushed

2 (bell) peppers, red, yellow or green, cored, deseeded and cut into large pieces

225 g/8 oz large closed cup mushrooms, sliced or quartered

175 g/6 oz tomatoes, peeled and halved

150 ml/¼ pint/⅔ cup dry white wine

125–175 g/4–6 oz green olives, pitted

4–6 tbsp double (heavy) cream

salt and pepper

chopped flat-leaf parsley, to garnish

1 Season the chicken with salt and pepper to taste. Heat the oil and butter in a frying pan (skillet), add the chicken and fry until browned all over. Remove the chicken from the pan.

2 Add the onion and garlic to the frying pan (skillet) and fry gently until just beginning to soften. Add the (bell) peppers to the pan with the mushrooms and continue to cook for a few minutes longer, stirring occasionally.

3 Add the tomatoes and plenty of seasoning to the pan and then transfer the vegetable mixture to an ovenproof casserole. Place the chicken on the bed of vegetables.

4 Add the wine to the frying pan (skillet) and bring to the boil. Pour the wine over the chicken and cover the casserole tightly. Cook in a preheated oven, 180°C/350°F/Gas Mark 4, for 50 minutes.

5 Add the olives to the chicken, mix lightly then pour on the cream. Re-cover the casserole and return to the oven for 10–20 minutes or until the chicken is very tender.

6 Adjust the seasoning and serve the pieces of chicken, surrounded by the vegetables and sauce, with pasta or tiny new potatoes. Sprinkle with chopped parsley to garnish.

Rich Chicken Casserole

This casserole is packed with the sunshine flavours of Italy. Sun-dried tomatoes add a wonderful richness.

NUTRITIONAL INFORMATION

Calories 320	Sugars 8g
Protein 34g	Fat 17g
Carbohydrate 8g	Saturates 4g

 15 MINS   1¼ HOURS

SERVES 4

INGREDIENTS

8 chicken thighs

2 tbsp olive oil

1 medium red onion, sliced

2 garlic cloves, crushed

1 large red (bell) pepper, sliced thickly

thinly pared rind and juice of 1 small orange

125 ml/4 fl oz/½ cup chicken stock

400 g/14 oz can chopped tomatoes

25 g/1 oz/½ cup sun-dried tomatoes, thinly sliced

1 tbsp chopped fresh thyme

50 g/1¾ oz/½ cup pitted black olives

salt and pepper

orange rind and thyme sprigs, to garnish

crusty fresh bread, to serve

1 In a heavy or non-stick large frying pan (skillet), fry the chicken without fat over a fairly high heat, turning occasionally until golden brown. Using a slotted spoon, drain off any excess fat from the chicken and transfer to a flameproof casserole.

2 Add the oil to the pan and fry the onion, garlic and (bell) pepper over a moderate heat for 3–4 minutes. Transfer the vegetables to the casserole.

3 Add the orange rind and juice, chicken stock, canned tomatoes and sun-dried tomatoes to the casserole and stir to combine.

4 Bring to the boil then cover the casserole with a lid and simmer very gently over a low heat for about 1 hour, stirring occasionally. Add the chopped fresh thyme and pitted black olives, then adjust the seasoning with salt and pepper to taste.

5 Scatter orange rind and thyme over the casserole to garnish, and serve with crusty bread.

COOK'S TIP

Sun-dried tomatoes have a dense texture and concentrated taste, and add intense flavour to slow-cooking casseroles.

Pasta & Chicken Medley

Strips of cooked chicken are tossed with coloured pasta, grapes and carrot sticks in a pesto-flavoured dressing.

NUTRITIONAL INFORMATION

Calories 609	Sugars 11g	
Protein 26g	Fat 38g	
Carbohydrate ...45g	Saturates 6g	

30 MINS   10 MINS

SERVES 2

I N G R E D I E N T S

125–150 g/4½–5½ oz dried pasta shapes,
    such as twists or bows

1 tbsp oil

2 tbsp mayonnaise

2 tsp bottled pesto sauce

1 tbsp soured cream or natural
    fromage frais

175 g/6 oz cooked skinless, boneless
    chicken meat

1–2 celery stalks

125 g/4½ oz/1 cup black grapes
    (preferably seedless)

1 large carrot, trimmed

salt and pepper

celery leaves, to garnish

FRENCH DRESSING

1 tbsp wine vinegar

3 tbsp extra-virgin olive oil

salt and pepper

1 To make the French dressing, whisk all the ingredients together until smooth.

2 Cook the pasta with the oil for 8–10 minutes in plenty of boiling salted water until just tender. Drain thoroughly, rinse and drain again. Transfer to a bowl and mix in 1 tablespoon of the French dressing while hot; set aside until cold.

3 Combine the mayonnaise, pesto sauce and soured cream or fromage frais in a bowl, and season to taste.

4 Cut the chicken into narrow strips. Cut the celery diagonally into narrow slices. Reserve a few grapes for garnish, halve the rest and remove any pips (seeds). Cut the carrot into narrow julienne strips.

5 Add the chicken, the celery, the halved grapes, the carrot and the mayonnaise mixture to the pasta, and toss thoroughly. Check the seasoning, adding more salt and pepper if necessary.

6 Arrange the pasta mixture on two plates and garnish with the reserved black grapes and the celery leaves.

Pasta with Chicken Sauce

Spinach ribbon noodles, topped with a rich tomato sauce and creamy chicken, make a very appetizing dish.

 15 MINS   45 MINS

SERVES 4

INGREDIENTS

250 g/9 oz fresh green tagliatelle

1 tbsp olive oil

salt

fresh basil leaves, to garnish

TOMATO SAUCE

2 tbsp olive oil

1 small onion, chopped

1 garlic clove, chopped

400 g/14 oz can chopped tomatoes

2 tbsp chopped fresh parsley

1 tsp dried oregano

2 bay leaves

2 tbsp tomato purée (paste)

1 tsp sugar

salt and pepper

CHICKEN SAUCE

60 g/2 oz/4 tbsp unsalted butter

400 g/14 oz boned chicken breasts,
   skinned and cut into thin strips

90 g/3 oz/¾ cup blanched almonds

300 ml/½ pint/1¼ cups double
   (heavy) cream

salt and pepper

1 To make the tomato sauce, heat the oil in a pan over a medium heat. Add the onion and fry until translucent. Add the garlic and fry for 1 minute. Stir in the tomatoes, parsley, oregano, bay leaves, tomato purée (paste), sugar and salt and pepper to taste, bring to the boil and simmer, uncovered, for 15–20 minutes, until reduced by half. Remove the pan from the heat and discard the bay leaves.

2 To make the chicken sauce, melt the butter in a frying pan (skillet) over a medium heat. Add the chicken and almonds and stir-fry for 5–6 minutes, or until the chicken is cooked through.

3 Meanwhile, bring the cream to the boil in a small pan over a low heat and boil for about 10 minutes, until reduced by almost half. Pour the cream over the chicken and almonds, stir and season to taste with salt and pepper. Set aside and keep warm.

4 Bring a large pan of lightly salted water to the boil. Add the tagliatelle and olive oil and cook for 8–10 minutes until tender, but still firm to the bite. Drain and transfer to a warm serving dish. Spoon over the tomato sauce and arrange the chicken sauce down the centre. Garnish with the basil leaves and serve immediately.

Chicken Pepperonata

All the sunshine colours and flavours of Italy are combined in this easy dish.

NUTRITIONAL INFORMATION

Calories 328	Sugars 7g	
Protein 35g	Fat 15g	
Carbohydrate ...13g	Saturates 4g	

15 MINS   40 MINS

SERVES 4

INGREDIENTS

8 skinless chicken thighs

2 tbsp wholemeal (whole wheat) flour

2 tbsp olive oil

1 small onion, sliced thinly

1 garlic clove, crushed

1 each large red, yellow and green (bell)
   peppers, sliced thinly

400 g/14 oz can chopped tomatoes

1 tbsp chopped oregano

salt and pepper

fresh oregano, to garnish

crusty wholemeal (whole wheat) bread,
   to serve

1 Remove the skin from the chicken thighs and toss in the flour.

2 Heat the oil in a wide frying pan (skillet) and fry the chicken quickly until sealed and lightly browned, then remove from the pan.

3 Add the onion to the pan and gently fry until soft. Add the garlic, (bell) peppers, tomatoes and oregano, then bring to the boil, stirring.

4 Arrange the chicken over the vegetables, season well with salt and pepper, then cover the pan tightly and simmer for 20–25 minutes or until the chicken is completely cooked and tender.

5 Season with salt and pepper to taste, garnish with oregano and serve with crusty wholemeal (whole wheat) bread.

COOK'S TIP

For extra flavour, halve the (bell) peppers and grill (broil) under a preheated grill (broiler) until the skins are charred. Leave to cool then remove the skins and seeds. Slice the (bell) peppers thinly and use in the recipe.

Chicken with Orange Sauce

The refreshing combination of chicken and orange sauce makes this a perfect dish for a warm summer evening.

NUTRITIONAL INFORMATION

Calories	797	Sugars	........28g
Protein	........59g	Fat	.........25g
Carbohydrate	...77g	Saturates	.......6g

 15 MINS 25 MINS

SERVES 4

INGREDIENTS

30 ml/1 fl oz/⅛ cup rapeseed oil

3 tbsp olive oil

4 x 225 g/8 oz chicken suprêmes

150 ml/¼ pint/⅔ cup orange brandy

15 g/½ oz/2 tbsp plain (all-purpose) flour

150 ml/¼ pint/⅔ cup freshly squeezed
   orange juice

25 g/1 oz courgette (zucchini), cut into
   matchstick strips

25 g/1 oz red (bell) pepper, cut into
   matchstick strips

25 g/1 oz leek, finely shredded

400 g/14 oz dried wholemeal
   (whole-wheat) spaghetti

3 large oranges, peeled and cut into
   segments

rind of 1 orange, cut into very fine strips

2 tbsp chopped fresh tarragon

150 ml/¼ pint/⅔ cup fromage frais or
   ricotta cheese

salt and pepper

fresh tarragon leaves, to garnish

1 Heat the rapeseed oil and 1 tablespoon of the olive oil in a frying pan (skillet). Add the chicken and cook quickly until golden brown. Add the orange brandy and cook for 3 minutes. Sprinkle over the flour and cook for 2 minutes.

2 Lower the heat and add the orange juice, courgette (zucchini), (bell) pepper and leek and season. Simmer for 5 minutes until the sauce has thickened.

3 Meanwhile, bring a pan of salted water to the boil. Add the spaghetti and 1 tablespoon of the olive oil and cook for 10 minutes. Drain the spaghetti, transfer to a serving dish and drizzle over the remaining oil.

4 Add half of the orange segments, half of the orange rind, the tarragon and fromage frais or ricotta cheese to the sauce in the pan and cook for 3 minutes.

5 Place the chicken on top of the pasta, pour over a little sauce, garnish with orange segments, rind and tarragon. Serve immediately.

Skewered Chicken Spirals

These unusual chicken kebabs (kabobs) have a wonderful Italian flavour, and the bacon helps keep them moist during cooking.

NUTRITIONAL INFORMATION

Calories . . . . .231 Sugars 1g

Protein . . . . .29g Fat 13g

Carbohydrate . . . .1g Saturates 5g

15 MINS   10 MINS

SERVES 4

I N G R E D I E N T S

4 skinless, boneless chicken breasts

1 garlic clove, crushed

2 tbsp tomato purée (paste)

4 slices smoked back bacon

large handful of fresh basil leaves

oil for brushing

salt and pepper

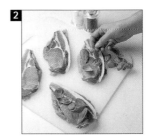
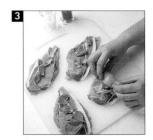

1 Spread out a piece of chicken between two sheets of cling film (plastic wrap) and beat firmly with a rolling pin to flatten the chicken to an even thickness. Repeat with the remaining chicken breasts.

2 Mix the garlic and tomato purée (paste) and spread over the chicken. Lay a bacon slice over each, then scatter with the basil. Season with salt and pepper.

3 Roll up each piece of chicken firmly, then cut into thick slices.

4 Thread the slices on to 4 skewers, making sure the skewer holds the chicken in a spiral shape.

5 Brush lightly with oil and cook on a preheated hot barbecue (grill) or grill (broiler) for about 10 minutes, turning once. Serve hot with a green salad.

Chicken Scallops

Served in scallop shells, this makes a stylish presentation for a starter or a light lunch.

NUTRITIONAL INFORMATION

Calories 532	Sugars 3g	
Protein 25g	Fat 34g	
Carbohydrate ...33g	Saturates 14g	

🍳 20 MINS   🕐 25 MINS

SERVES 4

INGREDIENTS

175 g/6 oz short-cut macaroni, or other short pasta shapes

3 tbsp vegetable oil, plus extra for brushing

1 onion, chopped finely

3 rashers unsmoked collar or back bacon, rind removed, chopped

125 g/4½ oz button mushrooms, sliced thinly or chopped

175 g/6 oz/¾ cup cooked chicken, diced

175 ml/6 fl oz/¾ cup crème fraîche

4 tbsp dry breadcrumbs

60 g/2 oz/½ cup mature (sharp) Cheddar, grated

salt and pepper

flat-leaf parsley sprigs, to garnish

1 Cook the pasta in a large pan of boiling salted water, to which you have added 1 tablespoon of the oil, for 8–10 minutes or until tender. Drain the pasta, return to the pan and cover.

2 Heat the grill (broiler) to medium. Heat the remaining oil in a pan over medium heat and fry the onion until it is translucent. Add the chopped bacon and mushrooms and cook for 3–4 minutes, stirring once or twice.

3 Stir in the pasta, chicken and crème fraîche and season to taste with salt and pepper.

4 Brush four large scallop shells with oil. Spoon in the chicken mixture and smooth to make neat mounds.

5 Mix together the breadcrumbs and cheese, and sprinkle over the top of the shells. Press the topping lightly into the chicken mixture, and grill (broil) for 4–5 minutes, until golden brown and bubbling. Garnish with sprigs of flat-leaf parsley, and serve hot.

Chicken & Balsamic Vinegar

A rich caramelized sauce, flavoured with balsamic vinegar and wine, adds a piquant flavour. The chicken needs to be marinated overnight.

NUTRITIONAL INFORMATION

Calories	148	Sugars	.......0.2g
Protein	........11g	Fat	...........8g
Carbohydrate	...0.2g	Saturates	.......3g

 10 MINS 35 MINS

SERVES 4

I N G R E D I E N T S

4 chicken thighs, boned

2 garlic cloves, crushed

200 ml/7 fl oz/¾ cup red wine

3 tbsp white wine vinegar

1 tbsp oil

15 g/½ oz/1 tbsp butter

6 shallots

3 tbsp balsamic vinegar

2 tbsp fresh thyme

salt and pepper

cooked polenta or rice, to serve

1 Using a sharp knife, make a few slashes in the skin of the chicken. Brush the chicken with the crushed garlic and place in a non-metallic dish.

2 Pour the wine and white wine vinegar over the chicken and season with salt and pepper to taste. Cover and leave to marinate in the refrigerator overnight.

3 Remove the chicken pieces with a perforated spoon, draining well, and reserve the marinade.

4 Heat the oil and butter in a frying pan (skillet). Add the shallots and cook for 2–3 minutes or until they begin to soften.

5 Add the chicken pieces to the pan and cook for 3–4 minutes, turning, until browned all over. Reduce the heat and add half of the reserved marinade. Cover and cook for 15–20 minutes, adding more marinade when necessary.

6 Once the chicken is tender, add the balsamic vinegar and thyme and cook for a further 4 minutes.

7 Transfer the chicken and marinade to serving plates and serve with polenta or rice.

COOK'S TIP

To make the chicken pieces look a little neater, use wooden skewers to hold them together or secure them with a length of string.

Chicken with Green Olives

Olives are a popular flavouring for poultry and game in the Apulia region of Italy, where this recipe originates.

NUTRITIONAL INFORMATION

Calories	.614	Sugars	.6g
Protein	.34g	Fat	.30g
Carbohydrate	.49g	Saturates	.11g

 15 MINS   1½ HOURS

SERVES 4

INGREDIENTS

3 tbsp olive oil

25 g/1 oz/2 tbsp butter

4 chicken breasts, part boned

1 large onion, finely chopped

2 garlic cloves, crushed

2 red, yellow or green (bell) peppers, cored,
   seeded and cut into large pieces

250 g/9 oz button mushrooms, sliced
   or quartered

175 g/6 oz tomatoes, skinned and halved

150 ml/¼ pint/⅔ cup dry white wine

175 g/6 oz/1½ cups stoned (pitted)
   green olives

4–6 tbsp double (heavy) cream

400 g/14 oz dried pasta

salt and pepper

chopped flat leaf parsley, to garnish

1 Heat 2 tbsp of the oil and the butter in a frying pan (skillet). Add the chicken breasts and fry until golden brown all over. Remove the chicken from the pan.

2 Add the onion and garlic to the pan and fry over a medium heat until beginning to soften. Add the (bell) peppers and mushrooms and cook for 2–3 minutes.

3 Add the tomatoes and season to taste with salt and pepper. Transfer the vegetables to a casserole and arrange the chicken on top.

4 Add the wine to the pan and bring to the boil. Pour the wine over the chicken. Cover and cook in a preheated oven at 180°C/350°F/Gas Mark 4 for 50 minutes.

5 Add the olives to the casserole and mix in. Pour in the cream, cover and return to the oven for 10–20 minutes.

6 Meanwhile, bring a large pan of lightly salted water to the boil. Add the pasta and the remaining oil and cook for 8–10 minutes or until tender, but still firm to the bite. Drain the pasta well and transfer to a serving dish.

7 Arrange the chicken on top of the pasta, spoon over the sauce, garnish with the parsley and serve immediately. Alternatively, place the pasta in a large serving bowl and serve separately.

Grilled (Broiled) Chicken

This Italian-style dish is richly flavoured with pesto, which is a mixture of basil, olive oil, pine nuts and Parmesan cheese.

NUTRITIONAL INFORMATION

Calories 787	Sugars 6g	
Protein 45g	Fat 38g	
Carbohydrate ...70g	Saturates 9g	

 10 MINS   25 MINS

SERVES 4

I N G R E D I E N T S

8 part-boned chicken thighs

olive oil, for brushing

400 ml/14 fl oz/1⅔ cups passata
(sieved tomatoes)

125 ml/4 fl oz/½ cup green or
red pesto sauce

12 slices French bread

90 g/3 oz/1 cup freshly grated
Parmesan cheese

60 g/2 oz/½ cup pine nuts or flaked
(slivered) almonds

salad leaves, to serve

1 Arrange the chicken in a single layer in a wide flameproof dish and brush lightly with oil. Place under a preheated grill (broiler) for about 15 minutes, turning occasionally, until golden brown.

COOK'S TIP

Although leaving the skin on the chicken means that it will have a higher fat content, many people like the rich taste and crispy skin especially when it is blackened by the barbecue (grill). The skin also keeps in the cooking juices.

2 Pierce the chicken with a skewer to test if it is cooked through – the juices will run clear, not pink, when it is ready.

3 Pour off any excess fat. Warm the passata (sieved tomatoes) and half the pesto sauce in a small pan and pour over the chicken. Grill (broil) for a few more minutes, turning until coated.

4 Meanwhile, spread the remaining pesto on to the slices of bread. Arrange the bread over the chicken and sprinkle with the Parmesan cheese. Scatter the pine nuts over the cheese. Grill (broil) for 2–3 minutes, or until browned and bubbling. Serve with salad leaves.

Chicken Cacciatora

This is a popular Italian classic in which browned chicken quarters are cooked in a tomato and (bell) pepper sauce.

NUTRITIONAL INFORMATION

Calories	397	Sugars	........4g
Protein	........37g	Fat	..........17g
Carbohydrate	...22g	Saturates	.......4g

 20 MINS 1 HOUR

SERVES 4

INGREDIENTS

1 roasting chicken, about 1.5 kg/ 3 lb 5 oz,
  cut into 6 or 8 serving pieces

125 g/4½ oz/1 cup plain (all-purpose) flour

3 tbsp olive oil

150 ml/¼ pint/⅔ cup dry white wine

1 green (bell) pepper, deseeded and sliced

1 red (bell) pepper, deseeded and sliced

1 carrot, chopped finely

1 celery stalk, chopped finely

1 garlic clove, crushed

200 g/7 oz can of chopped tomatoes

salt and pepper

1 Rinse and pat dry the chicken pieces with paper towels. Lightly dust them with seasoned flour.

2 Heat the oil in a large frying pan (skillet). Add the chicken and fry over a medium heat until browned all over. Remove from the pan and set aside.

3 Drain off all but 2 tablespoons of the fat in the pan. Add the wine and stir for a few minutes. Then add the (bell) peppers, carrots, celery and garlic, season with salt and pepper to taste and simmer together for about 15 minutes.

4 Add the chopped tomatoes to the pan. Cover and simmer for 30 minutes, stirring often, until the chicken is completely cooked through.

5 Check the seasoning before serving piping hot.

Pan-Cooked Chicken

Artichokes are a familiar ingredient in Italian cookery. In this dish, they are used to delicately flavour chicken.

NUTRITIONAL INFORMATION

Calories 296	Sugars 2g	
Protein 27g	Fat 15g	
Carbohydrate 7g	Saturates 6g	

 15 MINS 55 MINS

SERVES 4

INGREDIENTS

4 chicken breasts, part boned

25 g/1 oz/2 tbsp butter

2 tbsp olive oil

2 red onions, cut into wedges

2 tbsp lemon juice

150 ml/¼ pt/⅔ cup dry white wine

150 ml/¼ pt/⅔ cup chicken stock

2 tsp plain (all-purpose) flour

400 g/14 oz can artichoke halves,
   drained and halved

salt and pepper

chopped fresh parsley, to garnish

1 Season the chicken with salt and pepper to taste. Heat the oil and 15 g/½ oz/1 tablespoon of the butter in a large frying pan (skillet). Add the chicken and fry for 4–5 minutes on each side until lightly golden. Remove from the pan using a slotted spoon.

2 Toss the onion in the lemon juice, and add to the frying pan (skillet). Gently fry, stirring, for 3–4 minutes until just beginning to soften.

3 Return the chicken to the pan. Pour in the wine and stock, bring to the boil, cover and simmer gently for 30 minutes.

4 Remove the chicken from the pan, reserving the cooking juices, and keep warm. Bring the juices to the boil, and boil rapidly for 5 minutes.

5 Blend the remaining butter with the flour to form a paste. Reduce the juices to a simmer and spoon the paste into the frying pan (skillet), stirring until thickened.

6 Adjust the seasoning according to taste, stir in the artichoke hearts and cook for a further 2 minutes. Pour the mixture over the chicken and garnish with chopped parsley.

Mustard-Baked Chicken

Chicken pieces are cooked in a succulent, mild mustard sauce, then coated in poppy seeds and served on a bed of fresh pasta shells.

NUTRITIONAL INFORMATION

Calories	652	Sugars	.........5g
Protein	........51g	Fat	..........31g
Carbohydrate	...46g	Saturates	......12g

10 MINS   35 MINS

SERVES 4

I N G R E D I E N T S

8 chicken pieces (about 115 g/4 oz each)

60g/2 oz/4 tbsp butter, melted

4 tbsp mild mustard (see Cook's Tip)

2 tbsp lemon juice

1 tbsp brown sugar

1 tsp paprika

3 tbsp poppy seeds

400 g/14 oz fresh pasta shells

1 tbsp olive oil

salt and pepper

1 Arrange the chicken pieces in a single layer in a large ovenproof dish.

2 Mix together the butter, mustard, lemon juice, sugar and paprika in a bowl and season with salt and pepper to taste. Brush the mixture over the upper

COOK'S TIP

Dijon is the type of mustard most often used in cooking, as it has a clean and only mildly spicy flavour. German mustard has a sweet-sour taste, with Bavarian mustard being slightly sweeter. American mustard is mild and sweet.

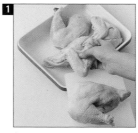  

surfaces of the chicken pieces and bake in a preheated oven at 200°C/400°F/Gas Mark 6 for 15 minutes.

3 Remove the dish from the oven and carefully turn over the chicken pieces. Coat the upper surfaces of the chicken with the remaining mustard mixture, sprinkle the chicken pieces with poppy seeds and return to the oven for a further 15 minutes.

4 Meanwhile, bring a large saucepan of lightly salted water to the boil. Add the pasta shells and olive oil and cook for 8–10 minutes or until tender, but still firm to the bite.

5 Drain the pasta thoroughly and arrange on a warmed serving dish. Top the pasta with the chicken, pour over the sauce and serve immediately.

Chicken & Lobster on Penne

While this is certainly a treat to get the taste buds tingling,
it is not as extravagant as it sounds.

NUTRITIONAL INFORMATION

Calories	696	Sugars	.........4g
Protein	........59g	Fat	..........32g
Carbohydrate	...45g	Saturates	.......9g

20 MINS   30 MINS

SERVES 6

INGREDIENTS

butter, for greasing

6 chicken suprêmes

450 g/1 lb dried penne rigate

6 tbsp extra virgin olive oil

90 g/3 oz/1 cup freshly grated
   Parmesan cheese

salt

FILLING

115 g/4 oz lobster meat, chopped

2 shallots, very finely chopped

2 figs, chopped

1 tbsp Marsala

2 tbsp breadcrumbs

1 large egg, beaten

salt and pepper

COOK'S TIP

The cut of chicken known as
suprême consists of the breast
and wing. It is always skinned.

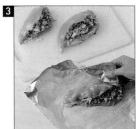

1 Grease 6 pieces of foil large enough to enclose each chicken suprême and lightly grease a baking tray (cookie sheet).

2 Place all of the filling ingredients into a mixing bowl and blend together thoroughly with a spoon.

3 Cut a pocket in each chicken suprême with a sharp knife and fill with the lobster mixture. Wrap each chicken suprême in foil, place the parcels on the greased baking tray (cookie sheet) and bake in a preheated oven at 200°C/400°F/Gas Mark 6 for 30 minutes.

4 Meanwhile, bring a large pan of lightly salted water to the boil. Add the pasta and 1 tablespoon of the olive oil and cook for about 10 minutes, or until tender but still firm to the bite. Drain the pasta thoroughly and transfer to a large serving plate. Sprinkle over the remaining olive oil and the grated Parmesan cheese, set aside and keep warm.

5 Carefully remove the foil from around the chicken suprêmes. Slice the suprêmes very thinly, arrange over the pasta and serve immediately.

Chicken Marengo

Napoleon's chef was ordered to cook a sumptuous meal on the eve of the battle of Marengo – this feast of flavours was the result.

NUTRITIONAL INFORMATION

Calories	.521	Sugars	.6g
Protein	.47g	Fat	.19g
Carbohydrate	.34g	Saturates	.8g

  20 MINS   50 MINS

SERVES 4

INGREDIENTS

8 chicken pieces

2 tbsp olive oil

300 g/10½ oz passata (sieved tomatoes)

200 ml/7 fl oz/¾ cup white wine

2 tsp dried mixed herbs

40 g/1½ oz butter, melted

2 garlic cloves, crushed

8 slices white bread

100 g/3½ oz mixed mushrooms
  (such as button, oyster and ceps)

40 g/1½ oz black olives, chopped

1 tsp sugar

fresh basil, to garnish

1 Using a sharp knife, remove the bone from each of the chicken pieces.

2 Heat 1 tbsp of oil in a large frying pan (skillet). Add the chicken pieces and cook for about 4–5 minutes, turning occassionally, or until browned all over.

3 Add the passata (sieved tomatoes), wine and mixed herbs to the frying pan (skillet). Bring to the boil and then leave to simmer for 30 minutes or until the chicken is tender and the juices run clear when a skewer is inserted into the thickest part of the meat.

4 Mix the melted butter and crushed garlic together. Lightly toast the slices of bread and brush with the garlic butter.

5 Add the remaining oil to a separate frying pan (skillet) and cook the mushrooms for 2–3 minutes or until just browned.

6 Add the olives and sugar to the chicken mixture and warm through.

7 Transfer the chicken and sauce to serving plates. Serve with the bruschetta (fried bread) and fried mushrooms.

Italian Chicken Spirals

These little foil parcels retain all the natural juices of the chicken while cooking conveniently over the pasta while it boils.

NUTRITIONAL INFORMATION

Calories .... .367	Sugars 1g	
Protein .... .33g	Fat .... .12g	
Carbohydrate ...35g	Saturates 2g	

 20 MINS   🕐 20 MINS

SERVES 4

I N G R E D I E N T S

4 skinless, boneless chicken breasts

25 g/1 oz/1 cup fresh basil leaves

15 g/½ oz/2 tbsp hazelnuts

1 garlic clove, crushed

250 g/9 oz/2 cups wholemeal (whole wheat) pasta spirals

2 sun-dried tomatoes or fresh tomatoes

1 tbsp lemon juice

1 tbsp olive oil

1 tbsp capers

60 g/2 oz/½ cup black olives

1 Beat the chicken breasts with a rolling pin to flatten evenly.

2 Place the basil and hazelnuts in a food processor and process until finely chopped. Mix with the garlic and salt and pepper to taste.

3 Spread the basil mixture over the chicken breasts and roll up from one short end to enclose the filling. Wrap the chicken roll tightly in foil so that they hold their shape, then seal the ends well.

4 Bring a pan of lightly salted water to the boil and cook the pasta for 8–10 minutes or until tender, but still firm to the bite. Meanwhile, place the chicken parcels in a steamer or colander set over the pan, cover tightly, and steam for 10 minutes.

5 Using a sharp knife, dice the tomatoes.

6 Drain the pasta and return to the pan with the lemon juice, olive oil, tomatoes, capers and olives. Heat through.

7 Pierce the chicken with a skewer to make sure that the juices run clear and not pink (this shows that the chicken is cooked through). Slice the chicken, arrange over the pasta and serve.

COOK'S TIP

Sun-dried tomatoes have a wonderful, rich flavour but if they're unavailable, use fresh tomatoes instead.

Slices of Duckling with Pasta

A raspberry and honey sauce superbly counterbalances the richness of the duckling.

NUTRITIONAL INFORMATION

Calories	686	Sugars	........15g
Protein	........62g	Fat	..........20g
Carbohydrate	...70g	Saturates	.......7g

  15 MINS   25 MINS

SERVES 4

INGREDIENTS

4 x 275 g/9 oz boned breasts of duckling

25 g/1 oz/2 tbsp butter

50 g/1¾ oz/⅜ cup finely chopped carrots

50 g/1¾ oz/4 tbsp finely chopped shallots

1 tbsp lemon juice

150 ml/¼ pint/⅔ cup meat stock

4 tbsp clear honey

115 g/4 oz/¾ cup fresh or thawed frozen raspberries

25 g/1 oz/¼ cup plain (all-purpose) flour

1 tbsp Worcestershire sauce

400 g/14 oz fresh linguine

1 tbsp olive oil

salt and pepper

TO GARNISH

fresh raspberries

fresh sprig of flat-leaf parsley

1 Trim and score the duck breasts with a sharp knife and season well all over. Melt the butter in a frying pan (skillet), add the duck breasts and fry all over until lightly coloured.

2 Add the carrots, shallots, lemon juice and half the meat stock and simmer over a low heat for 1 minute. Stir in half of the honey and half of the raspberries.

Sprinkle over half of the flour and cook, stirring constantly for 3 minutes. Season with pepper to taste and add the Worcestershire sauce.

3 Stir in the remaining stock and cook for 1 minute. Stir in the remaining honey and remaining raspberries and sprinkle over the remaining flour. Cook for a further 3 minutes.

4 Remove the duck breasts from the pan, but leave the sauce to continue simmering over a very low heat.

5 Meanwhile, bring a large saucepan of lightly salted water to the boil. Add the linguine and olive oil and cook for 8–10 minutes or until tender, but still firm to the bite. Drain and divide between 4 individual plates.

6 Slice the duck breast lengthways into 5 mm/¼ inch thick pieces. Pour a little sauce over the pasta and arrange the sliced duck in a fan shape on top of it. Garnish with raspberries and flat-leaf parsley and serve immediately.

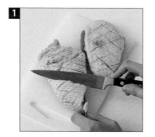

Pesto-Baked Partridge

Partridge has a more delicate flavour than many game birds and this subtle sauce perfectly complements it.

NUTRITIONAL INFORMATION

Calories 895	Sugars 5g	
Protein 79g	Fat 45g	
Carbohydrate ...45g	Saturates 18g	

🕐 15 MINS 🕐 40 MINS

SERVES 4

I N G R E D I E N T S

8 partridge pieces (about 115 g/4 oz each)

60 g/2 oz/4 tbsp butter, melted

4 tbsp Dijon mustard

2 tbsp lime juice

1 tbsp brown sugar

6 tbsp pesto sauce (see page 223)

450 g/1 lb dried rigatoni

1 tbsp olive oil

115 g/4 oz/1⅓ cups freshly grated
   Parmesan cheese

salt and pepper

1 Arrange the partridge pieces, smooth side down, in a single layer in a large, ovenproof dish.

2 Mix together the butter, Dijon mustard, lime juice and brown sugar in a bowl. Season to taste. Brush this mixture over the partridge pieces and bake in a preheated oven at 200°C/400°F/Gas Mark 6 for 15 minutes.

3 Remove the dish from the oven and coat the partridge pieces with 3 tbsp of the Pesto Sauce. Return to the oven and bake for a further 12 minutes.

4 Remove the dish from the oven and carefully turn over the partridge

pieces. Coat the top of the partridges with the remaining mustard mixture and return to the oven for a further 10 minutes.

5 Meanwhile, bring a large pan of lightly salted water to the boil. Add the rigatoni and olive oil and cook for 8–10 minutes until tender, but still firm to the bite. Drain and transfer to a serving dish. Toss the pasta with the remaining Pesto Sauce and the Parmesan cheese.

6 Serve the partridge with the pasta, pouring over the cooking juices.

VARIATION
You could also prepare young pheasant in the same way.

Pasta & Rice

Pasta and rice are quick and easy to cook and, when combined with a variety of ingredients, can produce an enormous variety of dishes. To cook pasta, bring a pan of lightly salted water to the boil, add the pasta and 1 tbsp

olive oil. Do not cover but bring the water to a rolling boil. When the pasta is tender but firm to the bite, drain and toss with butter, olive oil or sauce. As a rough guide, fresh unfilled pasta will take three minutes, filled fresh 10 minutes to cook. Dried pasta will take approximately 10–15 minutes. To cook a good quality rice like basmati, soak it for about 20–30 minutes to prevent the grains from sticking to each other. Add it to gently boiling, lightly salted water, stir once and cook until tender but firm to the bite. This will take up to 20 minutes. Allow 75 g/2¾ oz per person.

Spaghetti Bolognese

The original recipe takes about 4 hours to cook and should be left over night to allow the flavours to mingle. This version is much quicker.

NUTRITIONAL INFORMATION

Calories 591	Sugars 7g
Protein 29g	Fat 24g
Carbohydrate . . .64g	Saturates 9g

20 MINS   1 HR 5 MINS

SERVES 4

I N G R E D I E N T S

1 tbsp olive oil

1 onion, finely chopped

2 garlic cloves, chopped

1 carrot, scraped and chopped

1 stick celery, chopped

50 g/1¾ oz pancetta or streaky bacon, diced

350 g/12 oz lean minced beef

400 g/14 oz can chopped tomatoes

2 tsp dried oregano

125 ml/4 fl oz/scant ½ cup red wine

2 tbsp tomato purée (paste)

salt and pepper

675 g/1½ lb fresh spaghetti or 350 g/12 oz
   dried spaghetti

1 Heat the oil in a large frying pan (skillet). Add the onions and cook for 3 minutes.

2 Add the garlic, carrot, celery and pancetta or bacon and sauté for 3–4 minutes or until just beginning to brown.

3 Add the beef and cook over a high heat for another 3 minutes or until all of the meat is brown.

4 Stir in the tomatoes, oregano and red wine and bring to the boil. Reduce the heat and leave to simmer for about 45 minutes.

5 Stir in the tomato purée (paste) and season with salt and pepper.

6 Cook the spaghetti in a pan of boiling water for 8–10 minutes until tender, but still has 'bite'. Drain thoroughly.

7 Transfer the spaghetti to a serving plate and pour over the bolognese sauce. Toss to mix well and serve hot.

VARIATION

Try adding 25 g/1 oz dried porcini, soaked for 10 minutes in 2 tablespoons of warm water, to the bolognese sauce in step 4, if you wish.

Pasta Carbonara

Lightly cooked eggs and pancetta are combined with cheese to make this rich, classic sauce.

NUTRITIONAL INFORMATION

Calories 547	Sugars 1g	
Protein 21g	Fat 31g	
Carbohydrate ...49g	Saturates 14g	

15 MINS   20 MINS

SERVES 4

I N G R E D I E N T S

1 tbsp olive oil

40 g/1½ oz/3 tbsp butter

100 g/3½ oz pancetta or
   unsmoked bacon, diced

3 eggs, beaten

2 tbsp milk

1 tbsp thyme, stalks removed

675 g/1½ lb fresh or 350 g/12 oz dried
   conchigoni rigati

50 g/1¾ oz Parmesan cheese, grated

salt and pepper

1 Heat the oil and butter in a frying pan (skillet) until the mixture is just beginning to froth.

2 Add the pancetta or bacon to the pan and cook for 5 minutes or until browned all over.

3 Mix together the eggs and milk in a small bowl. Stir in the thyme and season to taste with salt and pepper.

4 Cook the pasta in a saucepan of boiling water for 8–10 minutes until tender, but still has 'bite'. Drain thoroughly.

5 Add the cooked, drained pasta to the frying pan (skillet) with the eggs and cook over a high heat for about 30 seconds or until the eggs just begin to cook and set. Do not overcook the eggs or they will become rubbery.

6 Add half of the grated Parmesan cheese, stirring to combine.

7 Transfer the pasta to a serving plate, pour over the sauce and toss to mix well.

8 Sprinkle the rest of the grated Parmesan over the top and serve immediately.

VARIATION

For an extra rich Carbonara sauce, stir in 4 tablespoons of double (heavy) cream with the eggs and milk in step 3. Follow exactly the same cooking method.

Three-Cheese Macaroni

Based on a traditional family favourite, this pasta bake has plenty of flavour. Serve with a crisp salad for a quick, tasty supper.

NUTRITIONAL INFORMATION

Calories 672	Sugars 10g	
Protein 31g	Fat 44g	
Carbohydrate ...40g	Saturates 23g	

 30 MINS   45 MINS

SERVES 4

I N G R E D I E N T S

600 ml/1 pint/2½ cups Béchamel Sauce (see page 14)

225 g/8 oz/2 cups macaroni

1 egg, beaten

125 g/4½ oz/1 cup grated mature (sharp) Cheddar

1 tbsp wholegrain mustard

2 tbsp chopped fresh chives

4 tomatoes, sliced

125 g/4½ oz/1 cup grated Red Leicester (brick) cheese

60 g/2 oz/½ cup grated blue cheese

2 tbsp sunflower seeds

salt and pepper

snipped fresh chives, to garnish

1 Make the Béchamel Sauce, put into a bowl and cover with cling film (plastic wrap) to prevent a skin forming. Set aside.

2 Bring a saucepan of salted water to the boil and cook the macaroni for 8–10 minutes or until just tender. Drain well and place in an ovenproof dish.

3 Stir the beaten egg, Cheddar, mustard, chives and seasoning into the Béchamel Sauce and spoon over the macaroni, making sure it is well covered. Top with a layer of sliced tomatoes.

4 Sprinkle over the Red Leicester (brick) and blue cheeses, and sunflower seeds. Put on a baking tray (cookie sheet) and bake in a preheated oven, 190°C/375°F/Gas Mark 5, for 25–30 minutes or until bubbling and golden. Garnish with chives and serve immediately.

Macaroni & Corn Pancakes

This vegetable pancake can be filled with your favourite vegetables – a favourite alternative is shredded parsnips with 1 tbsp mustard.

NUTRITIONAL INFORMATION

Calories 702   Sugars 4g
Protein . . . . .13g   Fat 50g
Carbohydrate . . .55g   Saturates 23g

 15 MINS   40 MINS

SERVES 4

INGREDIENTS

2 corn cobs

60 g/2 oz/4 tbsp butter

115 g/4 oz red (bell) peppers, cored, seeded
  and finely diced

285 g/10 oz/2½ cups dried
  short-cut macaroni

150 ml/¼ pint/⅔ cup double (heavy) cream

25 g/1 oz/¼ cup plain (all-purpose) flour

4 egg yolks

4 tbsp olive oil

salt and pepper

TO SERVE

oyster mushrooms

fried leeks

1 Bring a saucepan of water to the boil, add the corn cobs and cook for about 8 minutes. Drain thoroughly and refresh under cold running water for 3 minutes. Carefully cut away the kernels on to kitchen paper (towels) and set aside to dry.

2 Melt 25 g/1 oz/2 tbsp of the butter in a frying pan (skillet). Add the (bell) peppers and cook over a low heat for 4 minutes. Drain and pat dry with kitchen paper (towels).

3 Bring a large saucepan of lightly salted water to the boil. Add the macaroni and cook for about 12 minutes, or until tender but still firm to the bite. Drain the macaroni thoroughly and leave to cool in cold water until required.

4 Beat together the cream, flour, a pinch of salt and the egg yolks in a bowl until smooth. Add the corn and (bell) peppers to the cream and egg mixture. Drain the macaroni and then toss into the

corn and cream mixture. Season with pepper to taste.

5 Heat the remaining butter with the oil in a large frying pan (skillet). Drop spoonfuls of the mixture into the pan and press down until the mixture forms a flat pancake. Fry until golden on both sides, and all the mixture is used up. Serve immediately with oyster mushrooms and fried leeks.

Italian Tomato Sauce & Pasta

Fresh tomatoes make a delicious Italian-style sauce which goes particularly well with pasta.

NUTRITIONAL INFORMATION

Calories ....304 Sugars 8g
Protein ....15g Fat 14g
Carbohydrate ...31g Saturates 5g

 10 MINS   25 MINS

SERVES 2

I N G R E D I E N T S

1 tbsp olive oil

1 small onion, chopped finely

1–2 cloves garlic, crushed

350 g/12 oz tomatoes, peeled and chopped

2 tsp tomato purée (paste)

2 tbsp water

300–350 g/10½–12 oz dried pasta shapes

90 g/3 oz/¾ cup lean bacon,
   derinded and diced

40 g/1½ oz/½ cup mushrooms, sliced

1 tbsp chopped fresh parsley or 1 tsp
   chopped fresh coriander (cilantro)

2 tbsp soured cream or natural fromage
   frais (optional)

salt and pepper

COOK'S TIP

Sour cream contains
18–20% fat, so if you are
following a low fat diet you can leave
it out of this recipe or substitute a
low-fat alternative.

1 To make the tomato sauce, heat the oil in a saucepan and fry the onion and garlic gently until soft.

2 Add the tomatoes, tomato purée (paste), water and salt and pepper to taste to the mixture in the pan and bring to the boil. Cover and simmer gently for 10 minutes.

3 Meanwhile, cook the pasta in a saucepan of boiling salted water for 8–10 minutes, or until just tender. Drain the pasta thoroughly and transfer to warm serving dishes.

4 Heat the bacon gently in a frying pan (skillet) until the fat runs, then add the mushrooms and continue cooking for 3–4 minutes. Drain off any excess oil.

5 Add the bacon and mushrooms to the tomato mixture, together with the parsley or coriander (cilantro) and the soured cream or fromage frais, if using. Reheat and serve with the pasta.

Pasta with Green Vegetables

The different shapes and textures of the vegetables make a mouthwatering presentation in this light and summery dish.

NUTRITIONAL INFORMATION

Calories	.517	Sugars	.5g
Protein	.17g	Fat	.32g
Carbohydrate	.42g	Saturates	.18g

10 MINS   25 MINS

SERVES 4

INGREDIENTS

225 g/8 oz gemelli or other pasta shapes

1 tbsp olive oil

2 tbsp chopped fresh parsley

2 tbsp freshly grated Parmesan

salt and pepper

SAUCE

1 head of green broccoli, cut into florets

2 courgettes (zucchini), sliced

225 g/8 oz asparagus spears, trimmed

125 g/4½ oz mangetout (snow peas), trimmed

125 g/4½ oz frozen peas

25 g/1 oz/2 tbsp butter

3 tbsp vegetable stock

5 tbsp double (heavy) cream

large pinch of freshly grated nutmeg

1 Cook the pasta in a large pan of salted boiling water, adding the olive oil, for 8–10 minutes or until tender. Drain the pasta in a colander, return to the pan, cover and keep warm.

2 Steam the broccoli, courgettes (zucchini), asparagus spears and mangetout (snow peas) over a pan of boiling, salted water until just beginning to soften. Remove from the heat and plunge into cold water to prevent further cooking. Drain and set aside.

3 Cook the peas in boiling, salted water for 3 minutes, then drain. Refresh in cold water and drain again.

4 Put the butter and vegetable stock in a pan over a medium heat. Add all of the vegetables except for the asparagus spears and toss carefully with a wooden spoon to heat through, taking care not to break them up. Stir in the cream, allow the sauce to heat through and season with salt, pepper and nutmeg.

5 Transfer the pasta to a warmed serving dish and stir in the chopped parsley. Spoon the sauce over, and sprinkle on the freshly grated Parmesan. Arrange the asparagus spears in a pattern on top. Serve hot.

Pasta with Garlic & Broccoli

Broccoli coated in a garlic-flavoured cream sauce, served on herb tagliatelle. Try sprinkling with toasted pine nuts to add extra crunch.

NUTRITIONAL INFORMATION

Calories	538	Sugars	.........4g
Protein	........23g	Fat	..........29g
Carbohydrate	...50g	Saturates	......17g

 5 MINS   5 MINS

SERVES 4

INGREDIENTS

500 g/1 lb 2 oz broccoli

300 g/10½ oz/1¼ cups garlic & herb
  cream cheese

4 tbsp milk

350 g/12 oz fresh herb tagliatelle

25 g/1 oz/¼ cup grated Parmesan cheese

chopped fresh chives, to garnish

1 Cut the broccoli into even-sized florets. Cook the broccoli in a saucepan of boiling salted water for 3 minutes and drain thoroughly.

2 Put the soft cheese into a saucepan and heat gently, stirring, until melted. Add the milk and stir until well combined.

3 Add the broccoli to the cheese mixture and stir to coat.

4 Meanwhile, bring a large saucepan of salted water to the boil and add the tagliatelle. Stir and bring back to the boil. Reduce the heat slightly and cook the tagliatelle, uncovered, for 3–4 minutes until just tender.

5 Drain the tagliatelle thoroughly and divide among 4 warmed serving plates. Spoon the broccoli and cheese sauce on top. Sprinkle with grated Parmesan cheese, garnish with chopped chives and serve.

COOK'S TIP

A herb flavoured pasta goes particularly well with the broccoli sauce, but failing this, a tagliatelle verde or 'paglia e fieno' (literally 'straw and hay' – thin green and yellow noodles) will fit the bill.

Pasta & Bean Casserole

A satisfying winter dish, this is a slow-cooked, one-pot meal. The beans need to be soaked overnight so prepare well in advance.

NUTRITIONAL INFORMATION

Calories ....377 Sugars 5g
Protein ....10g Fat 18g
Carbohydrate ...43g Saturates 5g

30 MINS 3½ HOURS

SERVES 6

INGREDIENTS

225 g/8 oz/1¼ cups dried haricot (navy)
   beans, soaked overnight and drained

225 g/8 oz dried penne

6 tbsp olive oil

850 ml/1½ pints /3½ cups vegetable stock

2 large onions, sliced

2 garlic cloves, chopped

2 bay leaves

1 tsp dried oregano

1 tsp dried thyme

5 tbsp red wine

2 tbsp tomato purée (paste)

2 celery sticks (stalks), sliced

1 fennel bulb, sliced

115 g/4 oz/1⅝ cups sliced mushrooms

225 g/8 oz tomatoes, sliced

1 tsp dark muscovado sugar

4 tbsp dry white breadcrumbs

salt and pepper

salad leaves (greens) and crusty bread,
   to serve

1 Put the haricot (navy) beans in a large saucepan and add sufficient cold water to cover. Bring to the boil and continue to boil vigorously for 20 minutes. Drain, set aside and keep warm.

2 Bring a large saucepan of lightly salted water to the boil. Add the penne and 1 tbsp of the olive oil and cook for about 3 minutes. Drain the pasta thoroughly, set aside and keep warm.

3 Put the beans in a large, flameproof casserole. Add the vegetable stock and stir in the remaining olive oil, the onions, garlic, bay leaves, oregano, thyme, wine and tomato purée (paste). Bring to the boil, then cover and cook in a preheated oven at 180°C/350°°F/Gas Mark 4 for 2 hours.

4 Add the penne, celery, fennel, mushrooms and tomatoes to the casserole and season to taste with salt and pepper. Stir in the muscovado sugar and sprinkle over the breadcrumbs. Cover the dish and cook in the oven for 1 hour.

5 Serve the pasta and bean casserole hot with salad leaves (greens) and crusty bread.

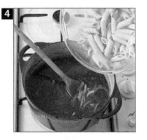

Pasta & Vegetable Sauce

A Mediterranean mixture of red (bell) peppers, garlic and courgettes (zucchini) cooked in olive oil and tossed with pasta.

NUTRITIONAL INFORMATION

Calories 341	Sugars 8g
Protein 13g	Fat 20g
Carbohydrate . . .30g	Saturates 8g

15 MINS   20 MINS

SERVES 4

I N G R E D I E N T S

3 tbsp olive oil

1 onion, sliced

2 garlic cloves, chopped

3 red (bell) peppers, deseeded and cut
    into strips

3 courgettes (zucchini), sliced

400 g/14 oz can chopped tomatoes

3 tbsp sun-dried tomato paste

2 tbsp chopped fresh basil

225 g/8 oz fresh pasta spirals

125 g/4½ oz/1 cup grated Gruyère
    (Swiss) cheese

salt and pepper

fresh basil sprigs, to garnish

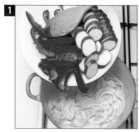  

1 Heat the oil in a heavy-based saucepan or flameproof casserole. Add the onion and garlic and cook, stirring occasionally, until softened. Add the (bell) peppers and courgettes (zucchini) and fry for 5 minutes, stirring occasionally.

2 Add the tomatoes, sun-dried tomato paste, basil and seasoning, cover and cook for 5 minutes.

3 Meanwhile, bring a large saucepan of salted water to the boil and add the pasta. Stir and bring back to the boil.

Reduce the heat slightly and cook, uncovered, for 3 minutes, or until just tender. Drain thoroughly and add to the vegetables. Toss gently to mix well.

4 Put the mixture into a shallow ovenproof dish and sprinkle over the cheese.

5 Cook under a preheated grill (broiler) for 5 minutes until the cheese is golden. Garnish with basil sprigs and serve.

COOK'S TIP

Be careful not to overcook fresh pasta – it should be 'al dente' (retaining some 'bite'). It takes only a few minutes to cook as it is still full of moisture.

Basil & Pine Nut Pesto

Delicious stirred into pasta, soups and salad dressings, pesto is available in most supermarkets, but making your own gives a concentrated flavour.

NUTRITIONAL INFORMATION

Calories	321	Sugars	.........1g
Protein	........11g	Fat	..........17g
Carbohydrate	...32g	Saturates	.......4g

 15 MINS 10 MINS

SERVES 4

INGREDIENTS

about 40 fresh basil leaves,
    washed and dried

3 garlic cloves, crushed

25 g/1 oz pine nuts

50 g/1¾ oz Parmesan cheese, finely grated

2–3 tbsp extra virgin olive oil

salt and pepper

675 g/1½ lb fresh pasta or
    350 g/12 oz dried pasta

1 Rinse the basil leaves and pat them dry with paper towels.

2 Put the basil leaves, garlic, pine nuts and grated Parmesan into a food processor and blend for about 30 seconds or until smooth. Alternatively, pound all of the ingredients by hand, using a mortar and pestle.

3 If you are using a food processor, keep the motor running and slowly add the olive oil. Alternatively, add the oil drop by drop while stirring briskly. Season with salt and pepper to taste.

4 Cook the pasta in a saucepan of boiling water allowing 3–4 minutes for fresh pasta or 8–10 minutes for dried, or until it is cooked through, but still has

'bite'. Drain the pasta thoroughly in a colander.

5 Transfer the pasta to a serving plate and serve with the pesto. Toss to mix well and serve hot.

COOK'S TIP

You can store pesto in the refrigerator for about 4 weeks. Cover the surface of the pesto with olive oil before sealing the container or bottle, to prevent the basil from oxidising and turning black.

Spaghetti Olio e Aglio

This easy and satisfying Roman dish originated as a cheap meal for poor people, but has now become a favourite in restaurants and trattorias.

NUTRITIONAL INFORMATION

Calories	.515	Sugars	.1g
Protein	.8g	Fat	.33g
Carbohydrate	.50g	Saturates	.5g

5 MINS 5 MINS

SERVES 4

INGREDIENTS

125 ml/4 fl oz/½ cup olive oil

3 garlic cloves, crushed

450 g/1 lb fresh spaghetti

3 tbsp roughly chopped fresh parsley

salt and pepper

1 Reserve 1 tablespoon of the olive oil and heat the remainder in a medium saucepan. Add the garlic and a pinch of salt and cook over a low heat, stirring constantly, until golden brown, then remove the pan from the heat. Do not allow the garlic to burn as it will taint its flavour. (If it does burn, you will have to start all over again!)

2 Meanwhile, bring a large saucepan of lightly salted water to the boil. Add the spaghetti and remaining olive oil to the pan and cook for 2–3 minutes, or until tender, but still firm to the bite. Drain the spaghetti thoroughly and return to the pan.

3 Add the oil and garlic mixture to the spaghetti and toss to coat thoroughly. Season with pepper, add the chopped fresh parsley and toss to coat again.

4 Transfer the spaghetti to a warm serving dish and serve immediately.

COOK'S TIP

Oils produced by different countries, mainly Italy, Spain and Greece, have their own characteristic flavours. Some produce an oil which has a hot, peppery taste while others have a 'green' flavour.

Vegetables & Tofu (Bean Curd)

This is a simple, clean-tasting dish of green vegetables, tofu (bean curd) and pasta, lightly tossed in olive oil.

NUTRITIONAL INFORMATION

Calories	400	Sugars	.........5g
Protein	........19g	Fat	..........17g
Carbohydrate	...46g	Saturates	.......5g

25 MINS   20 MINS

SERVES 4

I N G R E D I E N T S

225 g/8 oz asparagus

125 g/4½ oz mangetout (snow peas)

225 g/8 oz French (green) beans

1 leek

225 g/8 oz shelled small broad (fava) beans

300 g/10½ oz dried fusilli

2 tbsp olive oil

25 g/1 oz/2 tbsp butter or margarine

1 garlic clove, crushed

225 g/8 oz tofu (bean curd), cut into
2.5 cm/1 inch cubes

60 g/2 oz/⅓ cup pitted green olives in
brine, drained

salt and pepper

freshly grated Parmesan, to serve

1 Cut the asparagus into 5 cm/2 inch lengths. Finely slice the mangetout (snow peas) diagonally and slice the French (green) beans into 2.5 cm/1 inch pieces. Finely slice the leek.

2 Bring a large saucepan of water to the boil and add the asparagus, green beans and broad (fava) beans. Bring back to the boil and cook for 4 minutes until just tender. Drain well and rinse in cold water. Set aside.

3 Bring a large saucepan of salted water to the boil and cook the fusilli for 8–9 minutes until just tender. Drain well. Toss in 1 tablespoon of the oil and season well.

4 Meanwhile, in a wok or large frying pan (skillet), heat the remaining oil and the butter or margarine and gently fry the leek, garlic and tofu (bean curd) for 1–2 minutes until the vegetables have just softened.

5 Stir in the mangetout (snow peas) and cook for 1 minute.

6 Add the boiled vegetables and olives to the pan and heat through for 1 minute. Carefully stir in the pasta and seasoning. Cook for 1 minute and pile into a warmed serving dish. Serve sprinkled with Parmesan.

Tagliatelle with Pumpkin

This unusual pasta dish comes from the Emilia Romagna region of Italy.

NUTRITIONAL INFORMATION

Calories 454   Sugars 4g
Protein ....9g   Fat 33g
Carbohydrate ...33g   Saturates 12g

15 MINS   35 MINS

SERVES 4

INGREDIENTS

500 g/1 lb 2 oz pumpkin or butternut
  squash

2 tbsp olive oil

1 onion, chopped finely

2 garlic cloves, crushed

4–6 tbsp chopped fresh parsley

good pinch of ground or freshly grated
  nutmeg

about 250 ml/9 fl oz/1 cup chicken or
  vegetable stock

125 g/4½ oz Parma ham (prosciutto), cut
  into narrow strips

275 g/9 oz tagliatelle, green or white (fresh
  or dried)

150 ml/¼ pint/⅔ cup double (heavy) cream

salt and pepper

freshly grated Parmesan, to serve

1 Peel the pumpkin or squash and scoop out the seeds and membrane. Cut the flesh into 1 cm/½ inch dice.

2 Heat the olive oil in a pan and gently fry the onion and garlic until softened. Add half of the parsley and fry for 1–2 minutes.

3 Add the pumpkin or squash and continue to cook for 2–3 minutes. Season well with salt, pepper and nutmeg.

4 Add half of the stock, bring to the boil, cover and simmer for about 10 minutes or until the pumpkin is tender, adding more stock as necessary. Add the Parma ham (prosciutto) and continue to cook for 2 minutes, stirring frequently.

5 Meanwhile, cook the tagliatelle in a large saucepan of boiling salted water, allowing 3–4 minutes for fresh pasta or 8–10 minutes for dried. Drain thoroughly and turn into a warmed dish.

6 Add the cream to the ham mixture and heat gently. Season and spoon over the pasta. Sprinkle with the remaining parsley and grated Parmesan separately.

Pasta with Cheese & Broccoli

Some of the simplest and most satisfying dishes are made with pasta, such as this delicious combination of tagliatelle with two-cheese sauce.

NUTRITIONAL INFORMATION

Calories	624	Sugars	.........2g
Protein	........22g	Fat	..........45g
Carbohydrate	...34g	Saturates	......28g

 5 MINS   15 MINS

SERVES 4

INGREDIENTS

300 g/10½ oz dried tagliatelle tricolore
  (plain, spinach- and tomato-flavoured
  noodles)

225 g/8 oz/2½ cups broccoli, broken into
  small florets

350g/12 oz/1½ cups Mascarpone cheese

125 g/4½ oz/1 cup blue cheese, chopped

1 tbsp chopped fresh oregano

25 g/1 oz/2 tbsp butter

salt and pepper

sprigs of fresh oregano, to garnish

freshly grated Parmesan, to serve

1 Cook the tagliatelle in plenty of boiling salted water for 8–10 minutes or until just tender.

2 Meanwhile, cook the broccoli florets in a small amount of lightly salted, boiling water. Avoid overcooking the broccoli, so that it retains much of its colour and texture.

3 Heat the Mascarpone and blue cheeses together gently in a large saucepan until they are melted. Stir in the oregano and season with salt and pepper to taste.

4 Drain the pasta thoroughly. Return it to the saucepan and add the butter, tossing the tagliatelle to coat it. Drain the broccoli well and add to the pasta with the sauce, tossing gently to mix.

5 Divide the pasta between 4 warmed serving plates. Garnish with sprigs of fresh oregano and serve with freshly grated Parmesan.

Spicy Tomato Tagliatelle

A deliciously fresh and slightly spicy tomato sauce which is excellent for lunch or a light supper.

NUTRITIONAL INFORMATION

Calories 306	Sugars 7g
Protein 8g	Fat 12g
Carbohydrate ...45g	Saturates 7g

 15 MINS   🕐 35 MINS

SERVES 4

I N G R E D I E N T S

50 g/1¾ oz/3 tbsp butter

1 onion, finely chopped

1 garlic clove, crushed

2 small red chillies,
    deseeded and diced

450 g/1 lb fresh tomatoes, skinned,
    deseeded and diced

200 ml/7 fl oz/¾ cup vegetable stock

2 tbsp tomato purée (paste)

1 tsp sugar

salt and pepper

675 g/1½ lb fresh green and white
    tagliatelle, or 350 g/12 oz dried

VARIATION

Try topping your pasta dish
with 50 g/1¾ oz pancetta or
unsmoked bacon, diced and
dry-fried for 5 minutes until crispy.

1 Melt the butter in a large saucepan. Add the onion and garlic and cook for 3–4 minutes or until softened.

2 Add the chillies to the pan and continue cooking for about 2 minutes.

3 Add the tomatoes and stock, reduce the heat and leave to simmer for 10 minutes, stirring.

4 Pour the sauce into a food processor and blend for 1 minute until smooth.

Alternatively, push the sauce through a sieve.

5 Return the sauce to the pan and add the tomato purée (paste) sugar, and salt and pepper to taste. Gently reheat over a low heat, until piping hot.

6 Cook the tagliatelle in a pan of boiling water for 8–10 minutes or until it is tender, but still has 'bite'. Drain the tagliatelle, transfer to serving plates and serve with the tomato sauce.

Pasta & Cheese Puddings

These delicious pasta puddings are served with a tasty tomato and bay-leaf sauce.

🕐 45 MINS   🕓 50 MINS

SERVES 4

I N G R E D I E N T S

15 g/½ oz/1 tbsp butter or margarine, softened

60 g/2 oz/½ cup dried white breadcrumbs

175 g/6 oz tricolour spaghetti

300 ml/½ pint/1¼ cups Béchamel Sauce (see page 14)

1 egg yolk

125 g/4½ oz/1 cup Gruyère (Swiss) cheese, grated

salt and pepper

fresh flat-leaf parsley, to garnish

T O M A T O   S A U C E

2 tsp olive oil

1 onion, chopped finely

1 bay leaf

150 ml/¼ pint/⅔ cup dry white wine

150 ml/¼ pint/⅔ cup passatta (sieved tomatoes)

1 tbsp tomato purée (paste)

1 Grease four 180 ml/6 fl oz/¾ cup moulds (molds) or ramekins with the butter or margarine. Evenly coat the insides with half of the breadcrumbs.

2 Break the spaghetti into 5 cm/2 inch lengths. Bring a saucepan of lightly salted water to the boil and cook the spaghetti for 5–6 minutes or until just tender. Drain well and put in a bowl.

3 Mix the Béchamel Sauce, egg yolk, cheese and seasoning into the cooked pasta and pack into the moulds (molds).

4 Sprinkle with the remaining breadcrumbs and place the moulds (molds) on a baking tray (cookie sheet). Bake in a preheated oven, 220°C/425°F/Gas Mark 7, for 20 minutes until golden. Leave to stand for 10 minutes.

5 Meanwhile, make the sauce. Heat the oil in a pan and fry the onion and bay leaf for 2–3 minutes or until just softened.

6 Stir in the wine, passata (sieved tomatoes), tomato purée (paste) and seasoning. Bring to the boil and simmer for 20 minutes or until thickened. Discard the bay leaf.

7 Run a palette knife (spatula) around the inside of the moulds (molds). Turn on to serving plates, garnish and serve with the tomato sauce.

Tagliatelle with Garlic Butter

Pasta is not difficult to make yourself, just a little time consuming. The resulting pasta only takes a couple of minutes to cook and tastes wonderful.

NUTRITIONAL INFORMATION

Calories ....642 Sugars 2g
Protein ....16g Fat 29g
Carbohydrate ...84g Saturates 13g

45 MINS   5 MINS

SERVES 4

INGREDIENTS

450 g/1 lb strong white flour,
    plus extra for dredging

2 tsp salt

4 eggs, beaten

3 tbsp olive oil

75 g/2¾ oz/5 tbsp butter, melted

3 garlic cloves, finely chopped

2 tbsp chopped, fresh parsley

pepper

1 Sift the flour into a large bowl and stir in the salt.

2 Make a well in the middle of the dry ingredients and add the eggs and 2 tablespoons of oil. Using a wooden spoon, stir in the eggs, gradually drawing in the flour. After a few minutes the dough will be too stiff to use a spoon and you will need to use your fingers.

3 Once all of the flour has been incorporated, turn the dough out on to a floured surface and knead for about 5 minutes, or until smooth and elastic. If you find the dough is too wet, add a little more flour and continue kneading. Cover with cling film (plastic wrap) and leave to rest for at least 15 minutes.

4 The basic dough is now ready; roll out the pasta thinly and create the pasta shapes required. This can be done by hand or using a pasta machine. Results from a machine are usually neater and thinner, but not necessarily better.

5 To make the tagliatelle by hand, fold the thinly rolled pasta sheets into 3 and cut out long, thin stips, about 1 cm/ ½ inch wide.

6 To cook, bring a pan of water to the boil, add 1 tbsp of oil and the pasta. It will take 2–3 minutes to cook, and the texture should have a slight bite to it. Drain.

7 Mix together the butter, garlic and parsley. Stir into the pasta, season with a little pepper to taste and serve immediately.

COOK'S TIP

Generally allow about 150 g/5½ oz fresh pasta or about 100 g/3½ oz dried pasta per person.

Fettuccine & Walnut Sauce

This mouthwatering dish would make an excellent light, vegetarian lunch for four or a good starter for six.

NUTRITIONAL INFORMATION

Calories 833	Sugars 5g
Protein 20g	Fat 66g
Carbohydrate ...44g	Saturates 15g

 15 MINS 🕐 10 MINS

SERVES 6

I N G R E D I E N T S

2 thick slices wholemeal (whole-wheat)
  bread, crusts removed

300 ml/½ pint/1¼ cups milk

275 g/9½ oz/2½ cups shelled walnuts

2 garlic cloves, crushed

115 g/4 oz/1 cup stoned (pitted)
  black olives

60 g/2 oz/⅔ cup freshly grated
  Parmesan cheese

8 tbsp extra virgin olive oil

150 ml/¼ pint/⅔ cup double (heavy) cream

450 g/1 lb fresh fettuccine

salt and pepper

2–3 tbsp chopped fresh parsley

COOK'S TIP

Parmesan quickly loses its pungency and 'bite'. It is better to buy small quantities and grate it yourself. Wrapped in foil, it will keep in the refrigerator for several months.

1 Put the bread in a shallow dish, pour over the milk and set aside to soak until the liquid has been absorbed.

2 Spread the walnuts out on a baking tray (cookie sheet) and toast in a preheated oven, at 190°C/375°F/Gas Mark 5, for about 5 minutes, or until golden. Set aside to cool.

3 Put the soaked bread, walnuts, garlic, olives, Parmesan cheese and 6 tablespoons of the olive oil in a food processor and work to make a purée. Season to taste with salt and pepper and stir in the cream.

4 Bring a large pan of lightly salted water to the boil. Add the fettuccine and 1 tablespoon of the remaining oil and cook for 2–3 minutes, or until tender but still firm to the bite. Drain the fettuccine thoroughly and toss with the remaining olive oil.

5 Divide the fettuccine between individual serving plates and spoon the olive, garlic and walnut sauce on top. Sprinkle over the fresh parsley and serve.

Fettuccine all'Alfredo

This simple, traditional dish can be made with any long pasta, but is especially good with flat noodles, such as fettuccine or tagliatelle.

NUTRITIONAL INFORMATION

Calories	627	Sugars	.........2g
Protein	........18g	Fat	..........41g
Carbohydrate	...51g	Saturates	......23g

 5 MINS   10 MINS

SERVES 4

INGREDIENTS

25 g/1 oz/2 tbsp butter

200 ml/7 fl oz/⅞ cup double (heavy) cream

450 g/1 lb fresh fettuccine

1 tbsp olive oil

90 g/3 oz/1 cup freshly grated Parmesan cheese, plus extra to serve

pinch of freshly grated nutmeg

salt and pepper

fresh parsley sprigs, to garnish

1 Put the butter and 150 ml/ ¼ pint/⅔ cup of the cream in a large saucepan and bring the mixture to the boil over a medium heat. Reduce the heat and then simmer gently for about 1½ minutes, or until slightly thickened.

2 Meanwhile, bring a large pan of lightly salted water to the boil. Add

VARIATION

This classic Roman dish is often served with the addition of strips of ham and fresh peas. Add 225 g/8 oz/2 cups shelled cooked peas and 175 g/6 oz ham strips with the Parmesan cheese in step 4.

the fettuccine and olive oil and cook for 2–3 minutes, until tender but still firm to the bite. Drain the fettuccine thoroughly and then pour over the cream sauce.

3 Toss the fettuccine in the sauce over a low heat until thoroughly coated.

4 Add the remaining cream, the Parmesan cheese and nutmeg to the fettuccine mixture and season to taste

with salt and pepper. Toss thoroughly to coat while gently heating through.

5 Transfer the fettucine mixture to a warm serving plate and garnish with the fresh sprig of parsley. Serve immediately, handing out extra grated Parmesan cheese separately.

Spaghetti with Ricotta Sauce

This makes a quick and easy starter, and is particularly ideal for the summer.

NUTRITIONAL INFORMATION

Calories 688   Sugars 5g
Protein . . . . .17g   Fat 51g
Carbohydrate . . .43g   Saturates 16g

 15 MINS   20 MINS

SERVES 4

I N G R E D I E N T S

350 g/12 oz spaghetti

3 tbsp olive oil

45 g/1½ oz/3 tbsp butter, cut into small
    pieces

2 tbsp chopped parsley

S A U C E

125 g/4½ oz/1 cup freshly ground almonds

125 g/4½ oz/½ cup Ricotta

large pinch of grated nutmeg

large pinch of ground cinnamon

150 ml/¼ pint/⅔ cup crème fraîche

125 ml/4 fl oz/½ cup hot chicken stock

1 tbsp pine kernels

pepper

coriander (cilantro) leaves, to garnish

COOK'S TIP

To toss spaghetti and coat it with a sauce or dressing, use the 2 largest forks you can find. Holding one fork in each hand, ease the prongs under the spaghetti from each side and lift them towards the centre. Repeat evenly until the pasta is well coated.

1 Cook the spaghetti in a large pan of boiling salted water, to which you have added 1 tablespoon of the oil, for 8–10 minutes or until tender. Drain the pasta in a colander, return to the pan and toss with the butter and parsley. Cover the pan and keep warm.

2 To make the sauce, mix together the ground almonds, Ricotta, nutmeg, cinnamon and crème fraîche to make a

thick paste. Gradually pour on the remaining oil, stirring constantly until it is well blended. Gradually pour on the hot stock, stirring all the time, until the sauce is smooth.

3 Transfer the spaghetti to warmed serving dishes, pour on the sauce and toss well. Sprinkle each serving with pine kernels (nuts) and garnish with coriander (cilantro) leaves. Serve warm.

Artichoke & Olive Spaghetti

The tasty flavours of artichoke hearts and black olives are a winning combination.

NUTRITIONAL INFORMATION

Calories 393	Sugars 11g
Protein 14g	Fat 11g
Carbohydrate ...63g	Saturates 2g

20 MINS   35 MINS

SERVES 4

INGREDIENTS

2 tbsp olive oil

1 large red onion, chopped

2 garlic cloves, crushed

1 tbsp lemon juice

4 baby aubergines (eggplant), quartered

600 ml/1 pint/2½ cups passata (sieved tomatoes)

2 tsp caster (superfine) sugar

2 tbsp tomato purée (paste)

400 g/14 oz can artichoke hearts, drained and halved

125 g/4½ oz/¾ cup pitted black olives

350 g/12 oz wholewheat dried spaghetti

salt and pepper

sprigs of fresh basil, to garnish

olive bread, to serve

1 Heat 1 tablespoon of the oil in a large frying pan (skillet) and gently fry the onion, garlic, lemon juice and aubergines (eggplant) for 4–5 minutes or until lightly browned.

2 Pour in the passata (sieved tomatoes), season with salt and pepper to taste and add the sugar and tomato purée (paste). Bring to the boil, reduce the heat and simmer for 20 minutes.

3 Gently stir in the artichoke halves and olives and cook for 5 minutes.

4 Meanwhile, bring a large saucepan of lightly salted water to the boil, and cook the spaghetti for 8–10 minutes or until just tender. Drain well, toss in the remaining olive oil and season with salt and pepper to taste.

5 Transfer the spaghetti to a warmed serving bowl and top with the vegetable sauce. Garnish with basil sprigs and serve with olive bread.

Chilli & (Bell) Pepper Pasta

This roasted (bell) pepper and chilli sauce is sweet and spicy – the perfect combination!

NUTRITIONAL INFORMATION

Calories 423	Sugars 5g	
Protein 9g	Fat 27g	
Carbohydrate ...38g	Saturates 4g	

25 MINS   30 MINS

SERVES 4

INGREDIENTS

2 red (bell) peppers, halved and deseeded

1 small red chilli

4 tomatoes, halved

2 garlic cloves

50 g/1¾ oz ground almonds

7 tbsp olive oil

675 g/1½ lb fresh pasta or 350 g/12 oz
   dried pasta

fresh oregano leaves, to garnish

   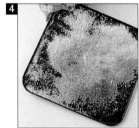

1 Place the (bell) peppers, skin-side up, on a baking tray (cookie sheet) with the chilli and tomatoes. Cook under a preheated grill (broiler) for 15 minutes or until charred. After 10 minutes turn the tomatoes skin-side up. Place the (bell) peppers and chillies in a polythene bag and leave to sweat for 10 minutes.

2 Remove the skin from the (bell) peppers and chillies and slice the flesh into strips, using a sharp knife.

3 Peel the garlic, and peel and deseed the tomatoes.

4 Place the almonds on a baking tray (cookie sheet) and place under the grill (broiler) for 2–3 minutes until golden.

5 Using a food processor, blend the (bell) pepper, chilli, garlic and tomatoes to make a purée. Keep the motor running and slowly add the olive oil to form a thick sauce. Alternatively, mash the mixture with a fork and beat in the olive oil, drop by drop.

6 Stir the toasted ground almonds into the mixture.

7 Warm the sauce in a saucepan until it is heated through.

8 Cook the pasta in a saucepan of boiling water for 8–10 minutes if using dried, or 3–5 minutes if using fresh. Drain the pasta thoroughly and transfer to a serving dish. Pour over the sauce and toss to mix. Garnish with the fresh oregano leaves.

VARIATION

Add 2 tablespoons of red wine vinegar to the sauce and use as a dressing for a cold pasta salad, if you wish.

Tagliatelle & Garlic Sauce

This pasta dish can be prepared in a moment – the intense flavours are sure to make this a popular recipe.

NUTRITIONAL INFORMATION

Calories 501	Sugars 3g	
Protein 15g	Fat 31g	
Carbohydrate . . .43g	Saturates 11g	

 15 MINS   20 MINS

SERVES 4

INGREDIENTS

2 tbsp walnut oil

1 bunch spring onions (scallions), sliced

2 garlic cloves, sliced thinly

225 g/8 oz mushrooms, sliced

500 g/1 lb 2 oz fresh green and white
    tagliatelle

225 g/8 oz frozen chopped leaf spinach,
    thawed and drained

125 g/4½ oz/½ cup full-fat soft cheese with
    garlic and herbs

4 tbsp single (light) cream

60 g/2 oz/½ cup chopped, unsalted
    pistachio nuts

2 tbsp shredded fresh basil

salt and pepper

sprigs of fresh basil, to garnish

Italian bread, to serve

1 Gently heat the oil in a wok or frying pan (skillet) and fry the spring onions (scallions) and garlic for 1 minute or until just softened. Add the mushrooms, stir well, cover and cook gently for 5 minutes or until softened.

2 Meanwhile, bring a large saucepan of lightly salted water to the boil and cook the pasta for 3–5 minutes or until just tender. Drain the pasta thoroughly and return to the saucepan.

3 Add the spinach to the mushrooms and heat through for 1–2 minutes. Add the cheese and allow to melt slightly. Stir in the cream and continue to heat without allowing to boil.

4 Pour the mixture over the pasta, season to taste and mix well. Heat gently, stirring, for 2–3 minutes.

5 Pile into a warmed serving bowl and sprinkle over the pistachio nuts and shredded basil. Garnish with basil sprigs and serve with Italian bread.

Pasta with Nuts & Cheese

Simple and inexpensive, this tasty pasta dish can be prepared very quickly.

NUTRITIONAL INFORMATION

Calories	.531	Sugars	.4g
Protein	.20g	Fat	.35g
Carbohydrate	.35g	Saturates	.16g

 10 MINS   30 MINS

SERVES 4

INGREDIENTS

60 g/2 oz/1 cup pine kernels (nuts)

350 g/12 oz dried pasta shapes

2 courgettes (zucchini), sliced

125 g/4½ oz/1¼ cups broccoli,
   broken into florets

200 g/7 oz/1 cup full-fat soft cheese

150 ml/¼ pint/⅔ cup milk

1 tbsp chopped fresh basil

125 g/4½ oz button mushrooms, sliced

90 g/3 oz blue cheese, crumbled

salt and pepper

sprigs of fresh basil, to garnish

green salad, to serve

1 Scatter the pine kernels (nuts) on to a baking tray (cookie sheet) and grill (broil), turning occasionally, until lightly browned all over. Set aside.

2 Cook the pasta in plenty of boiling salted water for 8–10 minutes or until just tender.

3 Meanwhile, cook the courgettes (zucchini) and broccoli in a small amount of boiling, lightly salted water for about 5 minutes or until just tender.

4 Put the soft cheese into a pan and heat gently, stirring constantly. Add the milk and stir to mix. Add the basil and mushrooms and cook gently for 2–3 minutes. Stir in the blue cheese and season to taste.

5 Drain the pasta and the vegetables and mix together. Pour over the cheese and mushroom sauce and add the pine kernels (nuts). Toss gently to mix. Garnish with basil sprigs and serve with a green salad.

Macaroni & Tuna Fish Layer

A layer of tuna fish with garlic, mushroom and red (bell) pepper is sandwiched between two layers of macaroni with a crunchy topping.

NUTRITIONAL INFORMATION

Calories 691   Sugars 10g
Protein . . . . .41g   Fat 33g
Carbohydrate . . .62g   Saturates 15g

20 MINS   50 MINS

SERVES 2

INGREDIENTS

125–150 g/4½–5½ oz/1¼ cup dried
   macaroni

2 tbsp oil

1 garlic clove, crushed

60 g/2 oz/¾ cup button mushrooms, sliced

½ red (bell) pepper, thinly sliced

200 g/7 oz can of tuna fish in brine,
   drained and flaked

½ tsp dried oregano

salt and pepper

SAUCE

25 g/1 oz/2 tbsp butter or margarine

1 tbsp plain (all-purpose) flour

250 ml/9 fl oz/1 cup milk

2 tomatoes, sliced

2 tbsp dried breadcrumbs

25 g/1 oz/¼ cup mature (sharp) Cheddar or
   Parmesan cheese, grated

VARIATION

Replace the tuna fish with chopped cooked chicken, beef, pork or ham or with 3–4 sliced hard-boiled (hard-cooked) eggs.

1 Cook the macaroni in boiling salted water, with 1 tablespoon of the oil added, for 10–12 minutes or until tender. Drain, rinse and drain thoroughly.

2 Heat the remaining oil in a saucepan or frying pan (skillet) and fry the garlic, mushrooms and (bell) pepper until soft. Add the tuna fish, oregano and seasoning, and heat through.

3 Grease an ovenproof dish (about 1 litre/1¾ pint/4 cup capacity), and add half of the cooked macaroni. Cover with the tuna mixture and then add the remaining macaroni.

4 To make the sauce, melt the butter or margarine in a saucepan, stir in the flour and cook for 1 minute. Add the milk gradually and bring to the boil. Simmer for 1–2 minutes, stirring continuously, until thickened. Season to taste. Pour the sauce over the macaroni.

5 Lay the sliced tomatoes over the sauce and sprinkle with the breadcrumbs and cheese.

6 Place in a preheated oven, at 200°C/400°F/Gas Mark 6, for about 25 minutes, or until piping hot and the top is well browned.

Pasta & Chilli Tomatoes

The pappardelle and vegetables are tossed in a delicious chilli and tomato sauce for a quick and economical meal.

NUTRITIONAL INFORMATION

Calories 353	Sugars 7g	
Protein 10g	Fat 24g	
Carbohydrate ...26g	Saturates 4g	

 15 MINS   20 MINS

SERVES 4

INGREDIENTS

275 g/9½ oz pappardelle

3 tbsp groundnut oil

2 cloves garlic, crushed

2 shallots, sliced

225 g/8 oz green beans, sliced

100 g/3½ oz cherry tomatoes, halved

1 tsp chilli flakes

4 tbsp crunchy peanut butter

150 ml/¼ pint/⅔ cup coconut milk

1 tbsp tomato purée (paste)

sliced spring onions (scallions), to garnish

1 Cook the pappardelle in a large saucepan of boiling, lightly salted water for 5-6 minutes.

2 Heat the groundnut oil in a large pan or preheated wok.

3 Add the garlic and shallots and stir-fry for 1 minute.

4 Drain the pappardelle thoroughly and set aside.

5 Add the green beans and drained pasta to the wok and stir-fry for 5 minutes.

6 Add the cherry tomatoes to the wok and mix well.

7 Mix together the chilli flakes, peanut butter, coconut milk and tomato purée (paste).

8 Pour the chilli mixture over the noodles, toss well to combine and heat through.

9 Transfer to warm serving dishes and garnish. Serve immediately.

VARIATION

Add slices of chicken or beef to the recipe and stir-fry with the beans and pasta in step 5 for a more substantial main meal.

Vermicelli & Clam Sauce

This recipe is quick to prepare and cook – it's so delicious that it will be devoured even faster!

NUTRITIONAL INFORMATION

Calories	502	Sugars	.........2g
Protein	........27g	Fat	..........17g
Carbohydrate	...58g	Saturates	.......7g

 15 MINS 25 MINS

SERVES 4

INGREDIENTS

400 g/14 oz vermicelli, spaghetti, or other
   long pasta

1 tbsp olive oil

25 g/1 oz/2 tbsp butter

2 tbsp Parmesan shavings, to garnish

sprig of basil, to garnish

SAUCE

1 tbsp olive oil

2 onions, chopped

2 garlic cloves, chopped

2 x 200 g/7 oz jars clams in brine

125 ml/4 fl oz/½ cup white wine

4 tbsp chopped fresh parsley

½ tsp dried oregano

pinch of freshly grated nutmeg

salt and pepper

1 Cook the pasta in a large pan of boiling salted water, adding the olive oil, for 8–10 minutes or until tender. Drain the pasta in a colander and return to the pan. Add the butter, cover and shake the pan. Keep warm until required.

2 To make the clam sauce, heat the oil in a pan over a medium heat and fry the onion until it is translucent. Stir in the garlic and cook for 1 minute.

3 Strain the liquid from one jar of clams, pour into the pan and add the wine. Stir well, bring to simmering point and simmer for 3 minutes. Drain the brine from the second jar of clams and discard.

4 Add the shellfish and herbs to the pan, and season with pepper to taste

and the nutmeg. Lower the heat and cook until the sauce is heated through.

5 Transfer the pasta to a warmed serving dish and pour on the sauce.

6 Sprinkle with the Parmesan and garnish with the basil sprig. Serve hot.

Macaroni & Squid Casserole

This pasta dish is easy to make and is a very hearty meal for a large number of guests.

NUTRITIONAL INFORMATION

Calories	237	Sugars	.........4g
Protein	........12g	Fat	...........11g
Carbohydrate	...19g	Saturates	.......2g

15 MINS   35 MINS

SERVES 6

INGREDIENTS

225 g/8 oz short-cut macaroni, or other
   short pasta shapes

1 tbsp olive oil

2 tbsp chopped fresh parsley

salt and pepper

SAUCE

350 g/12 oz cleaned squid,
   cut into 4 cm/½ in strips

6 tbsp olive oil

2 onions, sliced

250 ml/9 fl oz/1 cup fish stock

150 ml/¼ pint/⅔ cup red wine

350 g/12 oz tomatoes, peeled
   and thinly sliced

2 tbsp tomato purée (paste)

1 tsp dried oregano

2 bay leaves

1 Cook the pasta for only 3 minutes in a large pan of boiling salted water, adding the oil. Drain in a colander, return to the pan, cover and keep warm.

2 To make the sauce, heat the oil in a pan over medium heat and fry the onion until translucent. Add the squid and stock and simmer for 5 minutes. Pour on the wine and add the tomatoes, tomato purée (paste), oregano and bay leaves. Bring the sauce to the boil, season with salt and pepper to taste and cook, uncovered, for 5 minutes.

3 Add the pasta, stir well, cover the pan and continue simmering for 10 minutes, or until the macaroni and squid are almost tender. By this time the sauce should be thick and syrupy. If it is too liquid, uncover the pan and continue cooking for a few minutes. Taste the sauce and adjust the seasoning if necessary.

4 Remove the bay leaves and stir in most of the parsley, reserving a little to garnish. Transfer to a warmed serving dish. Sprinkle on the remaining parsley and serve hot. Serve with warm, crusty bread, such as ciabatta.

Spaghetti & Salmon Sauce

The smoked salmon ideally complements the spaghetti to give a very luxurious dish.

NUTRITIONAL INFORMATION

Calories	782	Sugars	.........3g
Protein	........20g	Fat	..........48g
Carbohydrate	...48g	Saturates	......27g

 10 MINS   15 MINS

SERVES 4

INGREDIENTS

500 g/1 lb 2 oz buckwheat spaghetti

2 tbsp olive oil

90 g/3 oz/½ cup feta cheese, crumbled

coriander (cilantro) or parsley, to garnish

SAUCE

300 ml/½ pint/1¼ cups double (heavy) cream

150 ml/¼ pint/⅔ cup whisky or brandy

125 g/4½ oz smoked salmon

large pinch of cayenne pepper

2 tbsp chopped coriander (cilantro) or parsley

salt and pepper

1 Cook the spaghetti in a large saucepan of salted boiling water, adding 1 tablespoon of the olive oil, for 8–10 minutes or until tender. Drain the pasta in a colander. Return the pasta to the pan, sprinkle over the remaining oil, cover and shake the pan. Set aside and keep warm until required.

2 In separate small saucepans, heat the cream and the whisky or brandy to simmering point. Do not let them boil.

3 Combine the cream with the whisky or brandy.

4 Cut the smoked salmon into thin strips and add to the cream mixture. Season with a little black pepper and cayenne pepper to taste, and then stir in the chopped coriander (cilantro) or parsley.

5 Transfer the spaghetti to a warmed serving dish, pour on the sauce and toss thoroughly using two large forks. Scatter the crumbled cheese over the pasta and garnish with the coriander (cilantro) or parsley. Serve at once.

Pasta & Mussel Sauce

Serve this aromatic seafood dish with plenty of fresh, crusty bread to soak up the delicious sauce.

NUTRITIONAL INFORMATION

Calories 735	Sugars 3g	
Protein 37g	Fat 46g	
Carbohydrate ...41g	Saturates 26g	

25 MINS   25 MINS

SERVES 6

INGREDIENTS

400 g/14 oz pasta shells

1 tbsp olive oil

SAUCE

3.5 litres/6 pints mussels, scrubbed

250 ml/9 fl oz/1 cup dry white wine

2 large onions, chopped

125 g/4½ oz/½ cup unsalted butter

6 large garlic cloves, chopped finely

5 tbsp chopped fresh parsley

300 ml/½ pint/1¼ cups double
    (heavy) cream

salt and pepper

crusty bread, to serve

1 Pull off the 'beards' from the mussels and rinse well in several changes of water. Discard any mussels that refuse to close when tapped. Put the mussels in a large pan with the white wine and half of the onions. Cover the pan, shake and cook over a medium heat for 2–3 minutes until the mussels open.

2 Remove the pan from the heat, lift out the mussels with a slotted spoon, reserving the liquor, and set aside until they are cool enough to handle. Discard any mussels that have not opened.

3 Melt the butter in a pan over medium heat and fry the remaining onion for 3–4 minutes or until translucent. Stir in the garlic and cook for 1 minute. Gradually pour on the reserved cooking liquor, stirring to blend thoroughly. Stir in the parsley and cream. Season to taste and bring to simmering point. Taste and adjust the seasoning if necessary.

4 Cook the pasta in a large pan of salted boiling water, adding the oil, for 8–10 minutes or until tender. Drain the pasta in a colander, return to the pan, cover and keep warm.

5 Remove the mussels from their shells, reserving a few shells for garnish. Stir the mussels into the cream sauce. Tip the pasta into a warmed serving dish, pour on the sauce and, using 2 large spoons, toss it together well. Garnish with a few of the reserved mussel shells. Serve hot, with warm, crusty bread.

Pasta & Sicilian Sauce

This Sicilian recipe of anchovies mixed with pine nuts and sultanas in a tomato sauce is delicious with all types of pasta.

NUTRITIONAL INFORMATION

Calories 286   Sugars 14g
Protein ....11g   Fat 8g
Carbohydrate ...46g   Saturates 1g

25 MINS   30 MINS

SERVES 4

INGREDIENTS

450 g/1 lb tomatoes, halved

25 g/1 oz pine nuts

50 g/1¾ oz sultanas

50 g/1¾ oz can anchovies, drained and
　halved lengthways

2 tbsp concentrated tomato purée (paste)

675 g/1½ lb fresh or
　350 g/12 oz dried penne

1 Cook the tomatoes under a preheated grill (broiler) for about 10 minutes. Leave to cool slightly, then once cool enough to handle, peel off the skin and dice the flesh.

2 Place the pine nuts on a baking tray (cookie sheet) and lightly toast under the grill (broiler) for 2–3 minutes or until golden brown.

VARIATION

Add 100 g/3½ oz bacon, grilled (broiled) for 5 minutes until crispy, then chopped, instead of the anchovies, if you prefer.

3 Soak the sultanas in a bowl of warm water for about 20 minutes. Drain the sultanas thoroughly.

4 Place the tomatoes, pine nuts and sultanas in a small saucepan and gently heat.

5 Add the anchovies and tomato purée, heating the sauce for a further 2–3 minutes or until hot.

6 Cook the pasta in a saucepan of boiling water for 8–10 minutes or until it is cooked through, but still has 'bite'. Drain thoroughly.

7 Transfer the pasta to a serving plate and serve with the hot Sicilian sauce.

Spaghetti & Shellfish

Frozen shelled prawns (shrimp) from the freezer can become the star ingredient in this colourful and tasty dish.

NUTRITIONAL INFORMATION

Calories	.510	Sugars	.38g
Protein	.33g	Fat	.24g
Carbohydrate	.44g	Saturates	.11g

35 MINS   30 MINS

SERVES 4

INGREDIENTS

225 g/8 oz short-cut spaghetti, or long
   spaghetti broken into 15 cm/6 inch
   lengths

2 tbsp olive oil

300 ml/½ pint/1¼ cups chicken stock

1 tsp lemon juice

1 small cauliflower, cut into florets

2 carrots, sliced thinly

125 g/4½ oz mangetout (snow peas),
   trimmed

60 g/2 oz/¼ cup butter

1 onion, sliced

225 g/8 oz courgettes (zucchini),
   sliced thinly

1 garlic clove, chopped

350 g/12 oz frozen shelled prawns
   (shrimp), defrosted

2 tbsp chopped fresh parsley

25 g/1 oz/¼ cup Parmesan, grated

salt and pepper

½ tsp paprika, to sprinkle

4 unshelled prawns (shrimp),
   to garnish (optional)

1 Cook the spaghetti in a large pan of boiling salted water, adding 1 tbsp of the oil, for 8–10 minutes or until tender. Drain, then return to the pan and stir in the remaining oil. Cover and keep warm.

2 Bring the chicken stock and lemon juice to the boil. Add the cauliflower and carrots and cook for 3–4 minutes until they are barely tender. Remove with a slotted spoon and set aside. Add the mangetout (snow peas) and cook for 1–2 minutes, until they begin to soften. Remove with a slotted spoon and add to the other vegetables. Reserve the stock for future use.

3 Melt half of the butter in a frying pan (skillet) over a medium heat and fry the onion and courgettes (zucchini) for about 3 minutes. Add the garlic and prawns (shrimp) and cook for a further 2–3 minutes until thoroughly heated through.

4 Stir in the reserved vegetables and heat through. Season with salt and pepper, then stir in the remaining butter.

5 Transfer the spaghetti to a warmed serving dish. Pour on the sauce and parsley. Toss well using 2 forks, until thoroughly coated. Sprinkle on the grated cheese and paprika, and garnish with unshelled prawns (shrimp), if using. Serve immediately.

Pasta Vongole

Fresh clams are available from most good fishmongers. If you prefer, used canned clams, which are less messy to eat but not as attractive.

NUTRITIONAL INFORMATION

Calories 410	Sugars 1g	
Protein 39g	Fat 9g	
Carbohydrate . . .39g	Saturates 1g	

 20 MINS 20 MINS

SERVES 4

I N G R E D I E N T S

675 g/1½ lb fresh clams or 1 x 290 g/10 oz
   can clams, drained

400 g/14 oz mixed seafood, such as
   prawns (shrimps), squid and mussels,
   defrosted if frozen

2 tbsp olive oil

2 cloves garlic, finely chopped

150 ml/¼ pint/⅔ cup white wine

150 ml/¼ pint/⅔ cup fish stock

2 tbsp chopped tarragon

salt and pepper

675 g/1½ lb fresh pasta or
   350 g/12 oz dried pasta

1 If you are using fresh clams, scrub them clean and discard any that are already open.

2 Heat the oil in a large frying pan (skillet). Add the garlic and the clams to the pan and cook for 2 minutes, shaking the pan to ensure that all of the clams are coated in the oil.

3 Add the remaining seafood mixture to the pan and cook for a further 2 minutes.

4 Pour the wine and stock over the mixed seafood and garlic and bring to the boil. Cover the pan, reduce the heat and leave to simmer for 8–10 minutes or until the shells open. Discard any clams or mussels that do not open.

5 Meanwhile, cook the pasta in a saucepan of boiling water for 8–10 minutes or until it is cooked through, but still has 'bite'. Drain the pasta thoroughly.

6 Stir the tarragon into the sauce and season with salt and pepper to taste.

7 Transfer the pasta to a serving plate and pour over the sauce. Serve immediately.

VARIATION

Red clam sauce can be made by adding 8 tablespoons of passata (sieved tomatoes) to the sauce along with the stock in step 4. Follow the same cooking method.

Spaghetti, Tuna & Parsley

This is a recipe to look forward to when parsley is at its most prolific, in the growing season.

NUTRITIONAL INFORMATION

Calories 970	Sugars 2g	
Protein 23g	Fat 80g	
Carbohydrate . . .42g	Saturates 18g	

10 MINS   15 MINS

SERVES 4

INGREDIENTS

500 g/1 lb 2 oz spaghetti

1 tbsp olive oil

25 g/1 oz/2 tbsp butter

black olives, to serve (optional)

SAUCE

200 g/7 oz can tuna, drained

60 g/2 oz can anchovies, drained

250 ml/9 fl oz/1 cup olive oil

250 ml/9 fl oz/1 cup roughly chopped fresh, flat-leaf parsley

150 ml/¼ pint/⅔ cup crème fraîche

salt and pepper

1 Cook the spaghetti in a large saucepan of salted boiling water, adding the olive oil, for 8–10 minutes or until tender. Drain the spaghetti in a colander and return to the pan. Add the butter, toss thoroughly to coat and keep warm until required.

2 Remove any bones from the tuna and flake into smaller pieces, using 2 forks. Put the tuna in a blender or food processor with the anchovies, olive oil and parsley and process until the sauce is smooth. Pour in the crème fraîche and process for a few seconds to blend. Taste the sauce and season with salt and pepper.

3 Warm 4 plates. Shake the saucepan of spaghetti over a medium heat for a few minutes or until it is thoroughly warmed through.

4 Pour the sauce over the spaghetti and toss quickly, using 2 forks. Serve immediately with a small dish of black olives, if liked.

Penne & Butternut Squash

The creamy, nutty flavour of squash complements the 'al dente' texture of the pasta perfectly. This recipe has been adapted for the microwave.

NUTRITIONAL INFORMATION

Calories	499	Sugars	.........4g
Protein	........20g	Fat	..........26g
Carbohydrate	...49g	Saturates	......13g

 15 MINS   30 MINS

SERVES 4

INGREDIENTS

2 tbsp olive oil

1 garlic clove, crushed

60 g/2 oz/1 cup fresh white breadcrumbs

500 g/1 lb 2 oz peeled and deseeded
   butternut squash

8 tbsp water

500 g/1 lb 2 oz fresh penne,
   or other pasta shape

15 g/½ oz/1 tbsp butter

1 onion, sliced

125 g/4½ oz/½ cup ham, cut into strips

200 ml/7 fl oz/scant cup single (light) cream

60 g/2 oz/½ cup Cheddar cheese, grated

2 tbsp chopped fresh parsley

salt and pepper

COOK'S TIP

If the squash weighs more than is needed for this recipe, blanch the excess for 3–4 minutes on HIGH power in a covered bowl with a little water. Drain, cool and place in a freezer bag. Store in the freezer for up to 3 months.

1 Mix together the oil, garlic and breadcrumbs and spread out on a large plate. Cook on HIGH power for 4–5 minutes, stirring every minute, until crisp and beginning to brown. Set aside.

2 Dice the squash. Place in a large bowl with half of the water. Cover and cook on HIGH power for 8–9 minutes, stirring occasionally. Leave to stand for 2 minutes.

3 Place the pasta in a large bowl, add a little salt and pour over boiling water to cover by 2.5 cm/1 inch. Cover and cook on HIGH power for 5 minutes, stirring once, until the pasta is just tender but still firm to the bite. Leave to stand, covered, for 1 minute before draining.

4 Place the butter and onion in a large bowl. Cover and cook on HIGH power for 3 minutes.

5 Coarsely mash the squash, using a fork. Add to the onion with the pasta, ham, cream, cheese, parsley and remaining water. Season generously and mix well. Cover and cook on HIGH power for 4 minutes until heated through.

6 Serve the pasta sprinkled with the crisp garlic crumbs.

Sicilian Spaghetti Cake

Any variety of long pasta could be used for this very tasty dish from Sicily.

30 MINS   50 MINS

SERVES 4

I N G R E D I E N T S

2 aubergines (eggplant), about 650 g/
  1 lb 7 oz

150 ml/¼ pint/⅔ cup olive oil

350 g/12 oz finely minced (ground)
  lean beef

1 onion, chopped

2 garlic cloves, crushed

2 tbsp tomato purée (paste)

400 g/14 oz can chopped tomatoes

1 tsp Worcestershire sauce

1 tsp chopped fresh oregano or marjoram
  or ½ tsp dried oregano or marjoram

45 g/1½ oz stoned black olives, sliced

1 green, red or yellow (bell) pepper, cored,
  deseeded and chopped

175 g/6 oz spaghetti

125 g/4½ oz/1 cup Parmesan, grated

1 Brush a 20 cm/8 inch loose-based round cake tin (pan) with olive oil, place a disc of baking parchment in the base and brush with oil. Trim the aubergines (eggplants) and cut into slanting slices, 5 mm/¼ inch thick. Heat some of the oil in a frying pan (skillet). Fry a few slices of aubergine (eggplant) at a time until lightly browned, turning once, and adding more oil as necessary. Drain on kitchen paper.

2 Put the minced (ground) beef, onion and garlic into a saucepan and cook, stirring frequently, until browned all over. Add the tomato purée (paste), tomatoes, Worcestershire sauce, herbs and seasoning. Simmer for 10 minutes, stirring occasionally, then add the olives and (bell) pepper and cook for 10 minutes.

3 Bring a large saucepan of salted water to the boil. Cook the spaghetti for 8–10 minutes or until just tender. Drain the spaghetti thoroughly. Turn the spaghetti into a bowl and mix in the meat mixture and Parmesan, tossing together with 2 forks.

4 Lay overlapping slices of aubergine (eggplant) over the base of the cake tin (pan) and up the sides. Add the meat mixture, pressing it down, and cover with the remaining aubergine (eggplant) slices.

5 Stand the cake tin (pan) in a baking tin (pan) and cook in a preheated oven, 200°C/400°F/Gas Mark 6, for 40 minutes. Leave to stand for 5 minutes then loosen around the edges and invert on to a warmed serving dish, releasing the tin (pan) clip. Remove the baking parchment. Serve immediately.

Vegetable Pasta Nests

These large pasta nests look impressive when presented filled with grilled (broiled) mixed vegetables, and taste delicious.

NUTRITIONAL INFORMATION

Calories	392	Sugars	.........1g
Protein	.........6g	Fat	..........28g
Carbohydrate	...32g	Saturates	.......9g

 25 MINS  40 MINS

SERVES 4

I N G R E D I E N T S

175 g/6 oz spaghetti

1 aubergine (eggplant), halved and sliced

1 courgette (zucchini), diced

1 red (bell) pepper, seeded and chopped
   diagonally

6 tbsp olive oil

2 garlic cloves, crushed

50 g/1¾ oz/4 tbsp butter or margarine,
   melted

15 g/½ oz/1 tbsp dry white breadcrumbs

salt and pepper

fresh parsley sprigs, to garnish

1 Bring a large saucepan of water to the boil and cook the spaghetti for 8–10 minutes or until 'al dente'. Drain the spaghetti in a colander and set aside until required.

2 Place the aubergine (eggplant), courgette (zucchini) and (bell) pepper on a baking tray (cookie sheet).

3 Mix the oil and garlic together and pour over the vegetables, tossing to coat all over.

4 Cook under a preheated hot grill (broiler) for about 10 minutes, turning, until tender and lightly charred. Set aside and keep warm.

5 Divide the spaghetti among 4 lightly greased Yorkshire pudding tins (pans). Using 2 forks, curl the spaghetti to form nests.

6 Brush the pasta nests with melted butter or margarine and sprinkle with the breadcrumbs. Bake in a preheated oven, at 200°C/400°F/ Gas Mark 6, for 15 minutes or until lightly golden. Remove the pasta nests from the tins (pans) and transfer to serving plates. Divide the grilled (broiled) vegetables between the pasta nests, season and garnish.

COOK'S TIP

'Al dente' means 'to the bite' and describes cooked pasta that is not too soft, but still has a 'bite' to it.

Pasticcio

A recipe that has both Italian and Greek origins, this dish may be served hot or cold, cut into thick, satisfying squares.

NUTRITIONAL INFORMATION

Calories 590	Sugars 8g
Protein 34g	Fat 39g
Carbohydrate ...23g	Saturates 16g

35 MINS   1¼ HOURS

SERVES 6

INGREDIENTS

225 g/8 oz fusilli, or other short
   pasta shapes

1 tbsp olive oil

4 tbsp double (heavy) cream

salt

rosemary sprigs, to garnish

SAUCE

2 tbsp olive oil, plus extra for brushing

1 onion, sliced thinly

1 red (bell) pepper, cored, deseeded
   and chopped

2 cloves garlic, chopped

625 g/1 lb 6 oz minced (ground) lean beef

400 g/14 oz can chopped tomatoes

125 ml/4 fl oz/½ cup dry white wine

2 tbsp chopped fresh parsley

50 g/1¾ oz can anchovies, drained
   and chopped

salt and pepper

TOPPING

300 ml/½ pint/1¼ cups natural
(unsweetened) yogurt

3 eggs

pinch of freshly grated nutmeg

40 g/1½ oz/⅓ cup Parmesan, grated

1 To make the sauce, heat the oil in a large frying pan (skillet) and fry the onion and red (bell) pepper for 3 minutes. Stir in the garlic and cook for 1 minute more. Stir in the beef and cook, stirring frequently, until no longer pink.

2 Add the tomatoes and wine, stir well and bring to the boil. Simmer, uncovered, for 20 minutes, or until the sauce is fairly thick. Stir in the parsley and anchovies, and season to taste.

3 Cook the pasta in a large pan of boiling salted water, adding the oil, for 8–10 minutes or until tender. Drain the pasta in a colander, then transfer to a bowl. Stir in the cream and set aside.

4 To make the topping, beat together the yogurt and eggs and season with nutmeg, and salt and pepper to taste.

5 Brush a shallow baking dish with oil. Spoon in half of the pasta and cover with half of the meat sauce. Repeat these layers, then spread the topping evenly over the final layer. Sprinkle the cheese on top.

6 Bake in a preheated oven, 190°C/375°F/Gas Mark 5, for 25 minutes, or until the topping is golden brown and bubbling. Garnish with sprigs of rosemary and serve with a selection of raw vegetable crudités.

Tagliatelle with Meatballs

There is an appetizing contrast of textures and flavours in this satisfying family dish.

NUTRITIONAL INFORMATION

Calories 910   Sugars 13g

Protein . . . . .40g   Fat 54g

Carbohydrate . . .65g   Saturates 19g

45 MINS   1 HR 5 MINS

SERVES 4

I N G R E D I E N T S

500 g/1 lb 2 oz minced (ground) lean beef

60 g/2 oz/1 cup soft white breadcrumbs

1 garlic clove, crushed

2 tbsp chopped fresh parsley

1 tsp dried oregano

large pinch of freshly grated nutmeg

¼ tsp ground coriander

60 g/2 oz/½ cup Parmesan, grated

2–3 tbsp milk

flour, for dusting

4 tbsp olive oil

400 g/14 oz tagliatelle

25 g/1 oz/2 tbsp butter, diced

salt and pepper

S A U C E

3 tbsp olive oil

2 large onions, sliced

2 celery sticks, sliced thinly

2 garlic cloves, chopped

400 g/14 oz can chopped tomatoes

125 g/4½ oz bottled sun-dried tomatoes, drained and chopped

2 tbsp tomato purée (paste)

1 tbsp dark muscovado sugar

150 ml/¼ pint/⅔ cup white wine, or water

1 To make the sauce, heat the oil in a frying pan (skillet) and fry the onions and celery until translucent. Add the garlic and cook for 1 minute. Stir in the tomatoes, tomato purée (paste), sugar and wine, and season. Bring to the boil and simmer for 10 minutes.

2 Meanwhile, break up the meat in a bowl with a wooden spoon until it becomes a sticky paste. Stir in the breadcrumbs, garlic, herbs and spices. Stir in the cheese and enough milk to make a firm paste. Flour your hands, take large spoonfuls of the mixture and shape it into 12 balls. Heat 3 tbsp of the oil in a frying pan (skillet) and fry the meatballs for 5–6 minutes until browned.

3 Pour the tomato sauce over the meatballs. Lower the heat, cover the pan and simmer for 30 minutes, turning once or twice. Add a little extra water if the sauce begins to dry.

4 Cook the pasta in a large saucepan of boiling salted water, adding the remaining oil, for 8–10 minutes or until tender. Drain the pasta, then turn into a warmed serving dish, dot with the butter and toss with two forks. Spoon the meatballs and sauce over the pasta and serve.

Tortelloni

These tasty little squares of pasta stuffed with mushrooms and cheese are surprisingly filling. This recipe makes 36 tortelloni.

NUTRITIONAL INFORMATION

Calories	360	Sugars	.........1g
Protein	.........9g	Fat	..........21g
Carbohydrate	...36g	Saturates	......12g

1¼ HOURS   25 MINS

SERVES 4

INGREDIENTS

about 300 g/10½ oz fresh pasta, rolled out
to thin sheets

75 g/2¾ oz/5 tbsp butter

50 g/1¾ oz shallots, finely chopped

3 garlic clove, crushed

50 g/1¾ oz mushrooms, wiped and
   finely chopped

½ stick celery, finely chopped

25 g/1 oz Pecorino cheese, finely grated,
   plus extra to garnish

1 tbsp oil

salt and pepper

1 Using a serrated pasta cutter, cut 5 cm/2 inch squares from the sheets of fresh pasta. To make 36 tortelloni you will need 72 squares. Once the pasta is cut, cover the squares with cling film (plastic wrap) to stop them drying out.

2 Heat 25 g/1 oz/3 tbsp of the butter in a frying pan (skillet). Add the shallots, 1 crushed garlic clove, the mushrooms and celery and cook for 4–5 minutes.

3 Remove the pan from the heat, stir in the cheese and season with salt and pepper to taste.

4 Spoon ½ teaspoon of the mixture on to the middle of 36 pasta squares. Brush the edges of the squares with water and top with the remaining 36 squares. Press the edges together to seal. Leave to rest for 5 minutes.

5 Bring a large pan of water to the boil, add the oil and cook the tortelloni, in batches, for 2–3 minutes. The tortelloni will rise to the surface when cooked and the pasta should be tender with a slight 'bite'. Remove from the pan with a perforated spoon and drain thoroughly.

6 Meanwhile, melt the remaining butter in a pan. Add the remaining garlic and plenty of pepper and cook for 1–2 minutes. Transfer the tortelloni to serving plates and pour over the garlic butter. Garnish with grated pecorino cheese and serve immediately.

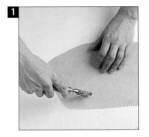

Tagliatelle & Chicken Sauce

Spinach ribbon noodles covered with a rich tomato sauce and topped with creamy chicken makes a very appetizing dish.

NUTRITIONAL INFORMATION

Calories 853	Sugars 6g
Protein 32g	Fat 71g
Carbohydrate . . .23g	Saturates 34g

30 MINS   25 MINS

SERVES 4

INGREDIENTS

Basic Tomato Sauce (see page 14)

225 g/8 oz fresh green ribbon noodles

1 tbsp olive oil

salt

basil leaves, to garnish

CHICKEN SAUCE

60 g/2 oz/¼ cup unsalted butter

400 g/14 oz boned, skinned chicken
   breast, thinly sliced

90 g/3 oz/¾ cup blanched almonds

300 ml/½ pint/1¼ cups double
   (heavy) cream

salt and pepper

basil leaves, to garnish

1 Make the tomato sauce, and keep warm.

2 To make the chicken sauce, melt the butter in a pan over a medium heat and fry the chicken strips and almonds for 5–6 minutes, stirring frequently, until the chicken is cooked through.

3 Meanwhile, pour the cream into a small pan over a low heat, bring it to the boil and boil for about 10 minutes, until reduced by almost half. Pour the cream over the chicken and almonds, stir well, and season with salt and pepper to taste. Set aside and keep warm.

4 Cook the pasta in a pan of boiling salted water, to which you have added the oil, for 8–10 minutes or until tender. Drain, then return to the pan, cover and keep warm.

5 Turn the pasta into a warmed serving dish and spoon the tomato sauce over it. Spoon the chicken and cream over the centre, scatter over the basil leaves and serve at once.

Sun-Dried Tomato Risotto

A Milanese risotto can be cooked in a variety of ways – but always with saffron. This version with sun-dried tomatoes has a lovely tangy flavour.

NUTRITIONAL INFORMATION

Calories	558	Sugars	.........2g
Protein	.........16g	Fat	..........19g
Carbohydrate	...80g	Saturates	.......9g

 10 MINS 30 MINS

SERVES 4

I N G R E D I E N T S

1 tbsp olive oil

25 g/1 oz/2 tbsp butter

1 large onion, finely chopped

350 g/12 oz arborio (risotto) rice, washed

about 15 strands of saffron

150 ml/¼ pint/⅔ cup white wine

850 ml/1½ pints/3¾ cup hot vegetable or chicken stock

8 sun-dried tomatoes, cut into strips

100 g/3½ oz frozen peas, defrosted

50 g/1¾ oz Parma ham (prosciutto), shredded

75 g/2¾ oz Parmesan cheese, grated

1 Heat the oil and butter in a large frying pan (skillet). Add the onion and cook for 4–5 minutes or until softened.

2 Add the rice and saffron to the frying pan (skillet), stirring well to coat the rice in the oil, and cook for 1 minute.

3 Add the wine and stock slowly to the rice mixture in the pan, a ladleful at a time, stirring and making sure that all the liquid is absorbed before adding the next ladleful of liquid.

4 About half-way through adding the stock, stir in the sun-dried tomatoes.

5 When all of the wine and stock has been absorbed, the rice should be cooked. Test by tasting a grain – if it is still crunchy, add a little more water and continue cooking. It should take 15–20 minutes to cook.

6 Stir in the peas, Parma ham (prosciutto) and cheese. Cook for 2–3 minutes, stirring, until hot. Serve with extra Parmesan.

COOK'S TIP

The finished risotto should have moist but separate grains. This is achieved by adding the hot stock a little at a time, only adding more when the last addition has been absorbed. Don't leave the risotto to cook by itself: it needs constant checking to see when more liquid is required.

Golden Chicken Risotto

Long-grain rice can be used instead of risotto rice, but it won't give you the traditional, creamy texture that is typical of Italian risottos.

NUTRITIONAL INFORMATION

Calories	.701	Sugars	.7g
Protein	.35g	Fat	.26g
Carbohydrate	.88g	Saturates	.8g

 10 MINS 30 MINS

SERVES 4

I N G R E D I E N T S

2 tbsp sunflower oil

15 g/ ½ oz/1 tbsp butter or margarine

1 medium leek, thinly sliced

1 large yellow (bell) pepper, diced

3 skinless, boneless chicken breasts, diced

350 g/12 oz arborio (risotto) rice

a few strands of saffron

1.5 litres/2 ¾ pints/6 ¼ cups chicken stock

200 g/7 oz can sweetcorn
   (corn-on-the-cob)

60 g/2 oz/ ½ cup toasted unsalted peanuts

60 g/2 oz/ ½ cup grated Parmesan cheese

salt and pepper

COOK'S TIP

Risottos can be frozen, before adding the Parmesan cheese, for up to 1 month, but remember to reheat this risotto thoroughly as it contains chicken.

1 Heat the sunflower oil and butter or margarine in a large saucepan. Fry the leek and (bell) pepper for 1 minute, then stir in the chicken and cook, stirring until golden brown.

2 Stir in the arborio (risotto) rice and cook for 2–3 minutes.

3 Stir in the saffron strands and salt and pepper to taste. Add the chicken stock, a little at a time, cover and cook over a low heat, stirring occasionally, for about 20 minutes, or until the rice is tender and most of the liquid has been absorbed. Do not let the risotto dry out – add more stock if necessary.

4 Stir in the sweetcorn (corn-on-the-cob), peanuts and Parmesan cheese, then season with salt and pepper to taste. Serve hot.

Milanese Risotto

Italian rice is a round, short-grained variety with a nutty flavour, which is essential for a good risotto. Arborio is a good one to use.

NUTRITIONAL INFORMATION

Calories 631	Sugars 1g
Protein 16g	Fat 29g
Carbohydrate . . .77g	Saturates 17g

10 MINS   35 MINS

SERVES 4

INGREDIENTS

2 good pinches of saffron threads

1 large onion, chopped finely

1–2 garlic cloves, crushed

90 g/3 oz/6 tbsp butter

350 g/12 oz/1²⁄₃ cups arborio (risotto) rice

150 ml/¼ pint/²⁄₃ cup dry white wine

1.2 litres/2 pints/5 cups boiling stock
   (chicken, beef or vegetable)

90 g/3 oz/³⁄₄ cup Parmesan, grated

salt and pepper

1 Put the saffron in a small bowl, cover with 3–4 tablespoons of boiling water and leave to soak while cooking the risotto.

2 Fry the onion and garlic in 60 g/2 oz of the butter until soft but not coloured. Add the rice and continue to cook for 2–3 minutes or until all of the grains are coated in oil and just beginning to colour lightly.

3 Add the wine to the rice and simmer gently, stirring from time to time, until it is all absorbed.

4 Add the boiling stock a little at a time, about 150 ml/¼ pint/²⁄₃ cup, cooking until the liquid is fully absorbed before adding more, and stirring frequently.

5 When all the stock has been absorbed (this should take about 20 minutes), the rice should be tender but not soft and soggy. Add the saffron liquid, Parmesan, remaining butter and salt and pepper to taste. Leave to simmer for 2 minutes until piping hot and thoroughly mixed.

6 Cover the pan tightly and leave to stand for 5 minutes off the heat. Give a good stir and serve at once.

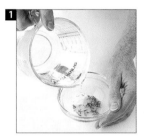

Green Risotto

A simple rice dish cooked with green vegetables and herbs. This recipe has been adapted for the microwave.

NUTRITIONAL INFORMATION

Calories	344	Sugars	........4g
Protein	........13g	Fat	..........10g
Carbohydrate	...54g	Saturates	.......4g

15 MINS — 20 MINS

SERVES 4

INGREDIENTS

1 onion, chopped

2 tbsp olive oil

225 g/8 oz/generous 1 cup risotto rice

700 ml/1¼ pints/3 cups hot
  vegetable stock

350 g/12 oz mixed green vegetables, such
  as asparagus, thin green beans,
  mangetout (snow peas), courgettes
  (zucchini), broccoli florets, frozen peas

2 tbsp chopped fresh parsley

60 g/2 oz/¼ cup fresh Parmesan cheese,
  shaved thinly

salt and pepper

1 Place the onion and oil in a large bowl. Cover and cook on HIGH power for 2 minutes.

2 Add the rice and stir until thoroughly coated in the oil. Pour in about 75 ml/ 3 fl oz/⅓ cup of the hot stock. Cook, uncovered, for 2 minutes, until the liquid has been absorbed. Pour in another 75 ml/ 3 fl oz/⅓ cup of the stock and cook, uncovered, on HIGH power for 2 minutes. Repeat once more.

3 Chop or slice the vegetables into even-sized pieces. Stir into the rice with the remaining stock. Cover and cook on HIGH power for 8 minutes, stirring occasionally, until most of the liquid has been absorbed and the rice is just tender.

4 Stir in the parsley and season generously. Leave to stand, covered, for almost 5 minutes. The rice should be tender and creamy.

5 Scatter the Parmesan cheese over the risotto before serving.

COOK'S TIP

For extra texture, stir in a few toasted pine kernels (nuts) or coarsely chopped cashew nuts at the end of the cooking time.

Genoese Seafood Risotto

This is cooked in a different way from any of the other risottos. First, you cook the rice, then you prepare a sauce, then you mix the two together.

NUTRITIONAL INFORMATION

Calories 424	Sugars 0g	
Protein 23g	Fat 17g	
Carbohydrate . . .46g	Saturates 10g	

🕙 10 MINS   🕐 25 MINS

SERVES 4

I N G R E D I E N T S

1.2 litres/2 pints/5 cups hot fish or
  chicken stock

350 g/12 oz arborio (risotto) rice, washed

50 g/1¾ oz/3 tbsp butter

2 garlic cloves, chopped

250 g/9 oz mixed seafood, preferably raw,
  such as prawns (shrimp), squid, mussels,
  clams and (small) shrimps

2 tbsp chopped oregano, plus extra
  for garnishing

50 g/1¾ oz Pecorino or Parmesan
  cheese, grated

1 In a large saucepan, bring the stock to the boil. Add the rice and cook for about 12 minutes, stirring, or until the rice is tender. Drain thoroughly, reserving any excess liquid.

2 Heat the butter in a large frying pan (skillet) and add the garlic, stirring.

3 Add the raw mixed seafood to the pan (skillet) and cook for 5 minutes. If you are using cooked seafood, fry for 2–3 minutes.

4 Stir the oregano into the seafood mixture in the frying pan (skillet).

5 Add the cooked rice to the pan and cook for 2–3 minutes, stirring, or until hot. Add the reserved stock if the mixture gets too sticky.

6 Add the pecorino or Parmesan cheese and mix well.

7 Transfer the risotto to warm serving dishes and serve immediately.

COOK'S TIP

The Genoese are excellent cooks, and they make particularly delicious fish dishes flavoured with the local olive oil.

Chicken Risotto Milanese

This famous dish is known throughout the world, and it is perhaps the best known of all Italian risottos, although there are many variations.

NUTRITIONAL INFORMATION

Calories ....857 Sugars 1g

Protein ....57g Fat 38g

Carbohydrate ...72g Saturates 21g

5 MINS   55 MINS

SERVES 4

I N G R E D I E N T S

125 g/4½ oz/½ cup butter

900 g/2 lb chicken meat, sliced thinly

1 large onion, chopped

500 g/1 lb 2 oz/2½ cups risotto rice

600 ml/1 pint/2½ cups chicken stock

150 ml/¼ pint/⅔ cup white wine

1 tsp crumbled saffron

salt and pepper

60 g/2 oz/½ cup grated Parmesan cheese, to serve

1 Heat 60 g/2 oz/4 tbsp of butter in a deep frying pan (skillet), and fry the chicken and onion until golden brown.

2 Add the rice, stir well, and cook for 15 minutes.

3 Heat the stock until boiling and gradually add to the rice. Add the white wine, saffron, salt and pepper to taste and mix well. Simmer gently for 20 minutes, stirring occasionally, and adding more stock if the risotto becomes too dry.

4 Leave to stand for 2–3 minutes and just before serving, add a little more stock and simmer for 10 minutes. Serve the risotto, sprinkled with the grated Parmesan cheese and the remaining butter.

Wild Mushroom Risotto

This creamy risotto is flavoured with a mixture of wild and cultivated mushrooms and thyme.

NUTRITIONAL INFORMATION

Calories	364	Sugars	.........1g
Protein	........15g	Fat	..........16g
Carbohydrate	...44g	Saturates	.......6g

🍽 15 MINS   🕐 25 MINS

SERVES 4

I N G R E D I E N T S

2 tbsp olive oil

1 large onion, finely chopped

1 garlic clove, crushed

200 g/7 oz mixed wild and cultivated
   mushrooms, such as ceps, oyster, porcini
   and button, wiped and sliced if large

250 g/9 oz arborio (risotto) rice, washed

pinch of saffron threads

700 ml/1¼ pints/scant 3 cups hot
   vegetable stock

200 ml/7 fl oz/¾ cup white wine

100 g/3½ oz Parmesan cheese, grated,
   plus extra for serving

2 tbsp chopped thyme

salt and pepper

COOK'S TIP

Wild mushrooms
each have their own
distinctive flavours and make
a change from button mushrooms.
However, they can be quite
expensive, so you can always use
a mixture with chestnut (crimini)
or button mushrooms instead.

1 Heat the oil in a large frying pan (skillet). Add the onions and garlic and sauté for 3–4 minutes or until just softened.

2 Add the mushrooms to the pan and cook for 3 minutes or until they are just beginning to brown.

3 Add the rice and saffron to the pan and stir to coat the rice in the oil.

4 Mix together the stock and the wine and add to the pan, a ladleful at a time. Stir the rice mixture and allow the liquid to be fully absorbed before adding more liquid, a ladleful at a time.

5 When all of the wine and stock is incorporated, the rice should be cooked. Test by tasting a grain – if it is still crunchy, add a little more water and continue cooking. It should take at least 15 minutes to cook.

6 Stir in the cheese and thyme, and season with pepper to taste.

7 Transfer the risotto to serving dishes and serve sprinkled with extra Parmesan cheese.

Rice & Peas

If you can get fresh peas (and willing helpers to shell them), do use them: you will need 1 kg/2 lb 4 oz. Add them to the pan with the stock.

NUTRITIONAL INFORMATION

Calories 409	Sugars 2g	
Protein 15g	Fat 23g	
Carbohydrate ...38g	Saturates 12g	

 10 MINS   50 MINS

SERVES 4

INGREDIENTS

1 tbsp olive oil

60 g/2 oz/¼ cup butter

60 g/2 oz/¼ cup pancetta
   (Italian unsmoked bacon), chopped

1 small onion, chopped

1.4 litres/2½ pints/6¼ cups hot
   chicken stock

200 g/7 oz/1 cup risotto rice

3 tbsp chopped fresh parsley

225 g/8 oz/1¼ cups frozen or
   canned petits pois

60 g/2 oz/½ cup Parmesan, grated

pepper

1 Heat the oil and half of the butter in a saucepan.

2 Add the pancetta (Italian unsmoked bacon) and onion to the pan and fry for 5 minutes.

3 Add the stock (and fresh peas if using) to the pan and bring to the boil.

4 Stir in the rice and season to taste with pepper. Cook until the rice is tender, about 20–30 minutes, stirring occasionally.

5 Add the parsley and frozen or canned petits pois and cook for 8 minutes until the peas are thoroughly heated.

6 Stir in the remaining butter and the Parmesan. Serve immediately, with freshly ground black pepper.

Pesto Rice with Garlic Bread

Try this combination of two types of rice with the richness of pine kernels (nuts), basil, and freshly grated Parmesan.

NUTRITIONAL INFORMATION

Calories	918	Sugars	. . . . .2g
Protein	. . . . .18g	Fat	. . . . .64g
Carbohydrate	. . .73g	Saturates	. . . . . .19g

🥔 20 MINS   🕐 40 MINS

SERVES 4

I N G R E D I E N T S

300 g/10½ oz/1½ cups mixed long-grain
   and wild rice

fresh basil sprigs, to garnish

tomato and orange salad, to serve

P E S T O   D R E S S I N G

15 g/½ oz fresh basil

125 g/4½ oz/1 cup pine kernels (nuts)

2 garlic cloves, crushed

6 tbsp olive oil

60 g/2 oz/½ cup freshly grated Parmesan

salt and pepper

G A R L I C   B R E A D

2 small granary or whole wheat
   French bread sticks

90 g/3 oz/½ cup butter or
   margarine, softened

2 garlic cloves, crushed

1 tsp dried mixed herbs

1 Place the rice in a saucepan and cover with water. Bring to the boil and cook for 15–20 minutes. Drain well and keep warm.

2 Meanwhile, make the pesto dressing. Remove the basil leaves from the stalks and finely chop the leaves. Reserve 25 g/1 oz/¼ cup of the pine kernels (nuts) and finely chop the remainder. Mix with the chopped basil and dressing ingredients. Alternatively, put all the ingredients in a food processor or blender and blend for a few seconds until smooth. Set aside.

3 To make the garlic bread, slice the bread at 2.5 cm/ 1 inch intervals, taking care not to slice all the way through. Mix the butter or margarine with the garlic, herbs and seasoning. Spread thickly between each slice.

4 Wrap the bread in foil and bake in a preheated oven, 200°C/400°F/Gas Mark 6, for 10–15 minutes.

5 To serve, toast the reserved pine kernels (nuts) under a preheated medium grill (broiler) for 2–3 minutes until golden. Toss the pesto dressing into the hot rice and pile into a warmed serving dish. Sprinkle with toasted pine kernels (nuts) and garnish with basil sprigs. Serve with the garlic bread and a tomato and orange salad.

Green Easter Pie

This traditional Easter risotto pie is from Piedmont in northern Italy. Serve it warm or chilled in slices.

NUTRITIONAL INFORMATION

Calories	392	Sugars	.........3g
Protein	........17g	Fat	..........17g
Carbohydrate	...41g	Saturates	.......5g

25 MINS   50 MINS

SERVES 4

INGREDIENTS

2 tbsp olive oil

1 onion, chopped

2 garlic cloves, chopped

200 g/7 oz arborio (risotto) rice

700 ml/1¼ pints/scant 3 cups hot chicken
    or vegetable stock

125 ml/4 fl oz/scant ½ cup white wine

50 g/1¾ oz Parmesan cheese, grated

100 g/3½ oz frozen peas, defrosted

80 g/3 oz rocket (arugula)

2 tomatoes, diced

4 eggs, beaten

3 tbsp fresh marjoram, chopped

50 g/1¾ oz breadcrumbs

salt and pepper

1 Lightly grease and then line the base of a 23 cm/9 inch deep cake tin (pan).

2 Using a sharp knife, roughly chop the rocket (arugula).

3 Heat the oil in a large frying pan (skillet). Add the onion and garlic and cook for 4–5 minutes or until softened.

4 Add the rice to the mixture in the frying pan (skillet), mix well to combine, then begin adding the stock a ladleful at a time. Wait until all of the stock has been absorbed before adding another ladleful of liquid.

5 Continue to cook the mixture, adding the wine, until the rice is tender. This will take at least 15 minutes.

6 Stir in the Parmesan cheese, peas, rocket (arugula), tomatoes, eggs and 2 tablespoons of the marjoram. Season to taste with salt and pepper.

7 Spoon the risotto into the tin (pan) and level the surface by pressing down with the back of a wooden spoon.

8 Top with the breadcrumbs and the remaining marjoram.

9 Bake in a preheated oven, at 180°C/350°F/Gas Mark 4, for 30 minutes or until set. Cut into slices and serve immediately.

Chilli Polenta Chips

Polenta is used in Italy in the same way as potatoes and rice. It has little flavour, but combined with butter, garlic and herbs, it is transformed.

NUTRITIONAL INFORMATION

Calories 365	Sugars 1g
Protein 8g	Fat 12g
Carbohydrate . . .54g	Saturates 5g

5 MINS   20 MINS

SERVES 4

I N G R E D I E N T S

350 g/12 oz instant polenta

2 tsp chilli powder

1 tbsp olive oil

150 ml/¼ pint/⅔ cup soured cream

1 tbsp chopped parsley

salt and pepper

1 Place 1.5 litres/2¾ pints/6¼ cups of water in a saucepan and bring to the boil. Add 2 teaspoons of salt and then add the polenta in a steady stream, stirring constantly.

2 Reduce the heat slightly and continue stirring for about 5 minutes. It is essential to stir the polenta, otherwise it will stick and burn. The polenta should have a thick consistency at this point and should be stiff enough to hold the spoon upright in the pan.

3 Add the chilli powder to the polenta mixture and stir well. Season to taste with a little salt and pepper.

4 Spread the polenta out on to a board or baking tray (cookie sheet) to about 4 cm/1½ inch thick. Leave to cool and set.

5 Cut the cooled polenta mixture into thin wedges.

6 Heat 1 tablespoon of oil in a pan. Add the polenta wedges and fry for 3–4 minutes on each side or until golden and crispy. Alternatively, brush with melted butter and grill (broil) for 6–7 minutes until golden. Drain the cooked polenta on paper towels.

7 Mix the soured cream with parsley and place in a bowl.

8 Serve the polenta with the soured cream and parsley dip.

COOK'S TIP

Easy-cook instant polenta is widely available in supermarkets and is quick to make. It will keep for up to 1 week in the refrigerator. The polenta can also be baked in a preheated oven, at 200°C/400°F/Gas Mark 6, for 20 minutes.

Polenta Kebabs (Kabobs)

Here, skewers of thyme-flavoured polenta, wrapped in Parma ham (prosciutto), are grilled (broiled) or barbecued (grilled).

NUTRITIONAL INFORMATION

Calories 212	Sugars 0g	
Protein 8g	Fat 6g	
Carbohydrate . . .32g	Saturates 1g	

 20 MINS   45 MINS

SERVES 4

INGREDIENTS

175 g/6 oz instant polenta

750 ml/1 pint 7 fl oz/scant 3¼ cups water

2 tbsp fresh thyme, stalks removed

8 slices Parma ham (prosciutto)
  (about 75 g/2¾ oz)

1 tbsp olive oil

salt and pepper

fresh green salad, to serve

1 Cook the polenta, using 750 ml/1 pint 7 fl oz/3¼ cups of water to 175 g/6 oz polenta, stirring occasionally, for 30–35 minutes. Alternatively, follow the instructions on the packet.

2 Add the fresh thyme to the polenta mixture and season to taste with salt and pepper.

COOK'S TIP

Try flavouring the polenta with chopped oregano, basil or marjoram instead of the thyme, if you prefer. You should use 3 tablespoons of chopped herbs to every 350 g/12 oz instant polenta.

3 Spread out the polenta, about 2.5 cm/ 1 inch thick, on to a board. Set aside to cool.

4 Using a sharp knife, cut the cooled polenta into 2.5 cm/1 inch cubes.

5 Cut the Parma ham (prosciutto) slices into 2 pieces lengthways. Wrap the Parma ham (prosciutto) around the polenta cubes.

6 Thread the Parma ham (prosciutto) wrapped polenta cubes on to skewers.

7 Brush the kebabs (kabobs) with a little oil and cook under a preheated grill (broiler), turning frequently, for 7–8 minutes. Alternatively, barbecue (grill) the kebabs (kabobs) until golden. Transfer to serving plates and serve with a salad.

Gnocchi with Herb Sauce

These little potato dumplings are a traditional Italian appetizer but, served with a salad and bread, they make a substantial main course.

NUTRITIONAL INFORMATION

Calories 619	Sugars 3g	
Protein 11g	Fat 30g	
Carbohydrate . . .81g	Saturates 9g	

30 MINS ⏲ 30 MINS

SERVES 6

I N G R E D I E N T S

1 kg/2 lb 4 oz old potatoes, cut into
   1 cm/½ inch pieces

60 g/2 oz/¼ cup butter or margarine

1 egg, beaten

300 g/10½ oz/2½ cups plain
   (all-purpose) flour

salt

S A U C E

125 ml/4 fl oz/½ cup olive oil

2 garlic cloves, very finely chopped

1 tbsp chopped fresh oregano

1 tbsp chopped fresh basil

salt and pepper

TO SERVE

freshly grated Parmesan (optional)

mixed salad (greens)

warm ciabatta

1 Cook the potatoes in a saucepan of boiling salted water for about 10 minutes or until tender. Drain well.

2 Press the hot potatoes through a sieve (strainer) into a large bowl. Add 1 teaspoon of salt, the butter or margarine, egg and 150 g/5½ oz/1¼ cups of the flour. Mix well to bind together.

3 Turn on to a lightly floured surface and knead, gradually adding the remaining flour, until a smooth, soft, slightly sticky dough is formed.

4 Flour the hands and roll the dough into 2 cm/¾ inch thick rolls. Cut into 1 cm/½ inch pieces. Press the top of each piece with the floured prongs of a fork and spread out on a floured tea towel (dish cloth).

5 Bring a large saucepan of salted water to a simmer. Add the gnocchi and cook in batches for 2–3 minutes or until they rise to the surface.

6 Remove the gnocchi with a perforated spoon and put in a warmed, greased serving dish. Cover and keep warm.

7 To make the sauce, put the oil, garlic and seasoning in a pan and cook, stirring, for 3–4 minutes until the garlic is golden. Remove from the heat and stir in the herbs. Pour over the gnocchi and serve, sprinkled with Parmesan, and accompanied by salad and warm ciabatta.

Spinach & Ricotta Gnocchi

Try not to handle the mixture too much when making gnocchi, as this will make the dough a little heavy.

NUTRITIONAL INFORMATION

Calories	712	Sugars	........15g
Protein	........29g	Fat	..........59g
Carbohydrate	...16g	Saturates	......33g

20 MINS 15 MINS

SERVES 4

INGREDIENTS

1 kg/2 lb 4 oz spinach

350 g/12 oz/1½ cups Ricotta

125 g/4½ oz/1 cup Pecorino, grated

3 eggs, beaten

¼ tsp freshly grated nutmeg

plain (all-purpose) flour, to mix

125 g/4½ oz/½cup unsalted butter

25 g/1 oz/¼ cup pine kernels (nuts)

50 g/2 oz/⅓ cup raisins

salt and pepper

1 Wash and drain the spinach well and cook in a covered saucepan without any extra liquid until softened, about 8 minutes. Place the spinach in a colander and press well to remove as much juice as possible. Either rub the spinach through a sieve (strainer) or purée in a blender.

2 Combine the spinach purée with the Ricotta, half of the Pecorino, the eggs, nutmeg and seasoning to taste, mixing lightly but thoroughly. Work in enough flour, lightly and quickly, to make the mixture easy to handle.

3 Shape the dough quickly into small lozenge shapes, and dust lightly with a little flour.

4 Add a dash of oil to a large saucepan of salted water and bring to the boil. Add the gnocchi carefully and boil for about 2 minutes or until they float to the surface. Using a perforated spoon, transfer the gnocchi to a buttered ovenproof dish. Keep warm.

5 Melt the butter in a frying pan (skillet). Add the pine kernels (nuts) and raisins and fry until the nuts start to brown slightly, but do not allow the butter to burn. Pour the mixture over the gnocchi and serve sprinkled with the remaining grated Pecorino.

Potato & Spinach Gnocchi

These small potato dumplings are flavoured with spinach, cooked in boiling water and served with a simple tomato sauce.

NUTRITIONAL INFORMATION

Calories 315	Sugars 7g	
Protein 8g	Fat 8g	
Carbohydrate . . .56g	Saturates 1g	

20 MINS   30 MINS

SERVES 4

I N G R E D I E N T S

300 g/10½ oz floury (mealy) potatoes, diced

175 g/6 oz spinach

1 egg yolk

1 tsp olive oil

125 g/4½ oz/1 cup plain (all-purpose) flour

salt and pepper

spinach leaves, to garnish

S A U C E

1 tbsp olive oil

2 shallots, chopped

1 garlic clove, crushed

300 ml/½ pint/1¼ cups passata (sieved
   tomatoes)

2 tsp soft light brown sugar

1 Cook the diced potatoes in a saucepan of boiling water for 10 minutes or until cooked through. Drain and mash the potatoes.

2 Meanwhile, in a separate pan, blanch the spinach in a little boiling water for 1-2 minutes. Drain the spinach and shred the leaves.

3 Transfer the mashed potato to a lightly floured chopping board and make a well in the centre. Add the egg yolk, olive oil, spinach and a little of the flour and quickly mix the ingredients into the potato, adding more flour as you go, until you have a firm dough. Divide the mixture into very small dumplings.

4 Cook the gnocchi, in batches, in a saucepan of boiling salted water for about 5 minutes or until they rise to the surface.

5 Meanwhile, make the sauce. Put the oil, shallots, garlic, passata (sieved tomatoes) and sugar into a saucepan and cook over a low heat for 10-15 minutes or until the sauce has thickened.

6 Drain the gnocchi using a perforated spoon and transfer to warm serving dishes. Spoon the sauce over the gnocchi and garnish with the fresh spinach leaves.

VARIATION

Add chopped fresh herbs and
cheese to the gnocchi dough
instead of the spinach,
if you prefer.

Baked Semolina Gnocchi

Semolina has a similar texture to polenta, but is slightly grainier. These gnocchi, which are flavoured with cheese and thyme, are easy to make.

NUTRITIONAL INFORMATION

Calories 259	Sugars 0g
Protein 9g	Fat 16g
Carbohydrate ...20g	Saturates 10g

15 MINS   30 MINS

SERVES 4

I N G R E D I E N T S

425 ml/³⁄₄ pint/1¹⁄₄ cups vegetable stock

100 g/3¹⁄₂ oz semolina

1 tbsp thyme, stalks removed

1 egg, beaten

50 g/1³⁄₄ oz Parmesan cheese, grated

50 g/1³⁄₄ oz/3 tbsp butter

2 garlic cloves, crushed

salt and pepper

1 Place the stock in a large saucepan and bring to the boil. Add the semolina in a steady trickle, stirring continuously. Keep stirring for 3–4 minutes until the mixture is thick enough to hold a spoon upright. Set aside and leave to cool slightly.

VARIATION

Try adding ¹⁄₂ tablespoon of sun-dried tomato paste or 50 g/1³⁄₄ oz finely chopped mushrooms, fried in butter, to the semolina mixture in step 2. Follow the same cooking method.

2 Add the thyme, egg and half of the cheese to the semolina mixture, and season to taste with salt and pepper.

3 Spread the semolina mixture on to a board to about 12 mm/¹⁄₂ inch thick. Set aside to cool and set.

4 When the semolina is cold, cut it into 2.5 cm/1 inch squares, reserving any offcuts.

5 Grease an ovenproof dish, placing the reserved offcuts in the bottom. Arrange the semolina squares on top and sprinkle with the remaining cheese.

6 Melt the butter in a pan, add the garlic and season with pepper to taste. Pour the butter mixture over the gnocchi. Bake in a preheated oven, at 220°C/425°F/Gas Mark 7, for 15–20 minutes until puffed up and golden. Serve hot.

Potato Noodles

Potatoes are used to make a 'pasta' dough which is cut into thin noodles and boiled. The noodles are served with a bacon and mushroom sauce.

NUTRITIONAL INFORMATION

Calories 810   Sugars 5g
Protein . . . . .21g   Fat 47g
Carbohydrate . . .81g   Saturates 26g

 30 MINS   25 MINS

SERVES 4

INGREDIENTS

450 g/1 lb floury (mealy) potatoes, diced

225 g/8 oz/2 cups plain (all-purpose) flour

1 egg, beaten

1 tbsp milk

salt and pepper

parsley sprig, to garnish

SAUCE

1 tbsp vegetable oil

1 onion, chopped

1 garlic clove, crushed

125 g/4½ oz open-capped
    mushrooms, sliced

3 smoked bacon slices, chopped

50 g/1¾ oz Parmesan cheese, grated

300 ml/½ pint/1¼ cups double
    (heavy) cream

2 tbsp chopped fresh parsley

1 Cook the diced potatoes in a saucepan of boiling water for 10 minutes or until cooked through. Drain well. Mash the potatoes until smooth, then beat in the flour, egg and milk. Season with salt and pepper to taste and bring together to form a stiff paste.

2 On a lightly floured surface, roll out the paste to form a thin sausage shape. Cut the sausage into 2.5 cm/1 inch lengths. Bring a large pan of salted water to the boil, drop in the dough pieces and cook for 3-4 minutes. They will rise to the surface when cooked.

3 To make the sauce, heat the oil in a pan and sauté the onion and garlic for 2 minutes. Add the mushrooms and bacon and cook for 5 minutes. Stir in the cheese, cream and parsley, and season.

4 Drain the noodles and transfer to a warm pasta bowl. Spoon the sauce over the top and toss to mix. Garnish with a parsley sprig and serve.

COOK'S TIP

Make the dough in advance, then wrap and store the noodles in the refrigerator for up to 24 hours.

Puddings &Desserts

For many people the favourite part of any meal is the desserts and puddings. The recipes that have been selected here will be a treat for all palettes. Whether you are a chocolate-lover or are even on a diet, in this chapter there is a recipe to tempt you. Choose from a light summer delicacy or a hearty hot winter treat, you will find desserts to indulge in all year round. If you are looking for a chilled sweet, choose the rich Vanilla Ice Cream, or if a warm pudding takes your fancy, Crispy-Topped Fruit Bake will do the trick.

Carrot & Ginger Cake

This melt-in-the-mouth version of a favourite cake has a fraction of the fat of the traditional cake.

NUTRITIONAL INFORMATION

Calories 249	Sugars 28g
Protein 7g	Fat 6g
Carbohydrate ...46g	Saturates 1g

15 MINS   1¼ HOURS

SERVES 10

INGREDIENTS

225 g/8 oz plain (all-purpose) flour

1 tsp baking powder

1 tsp bicarbonate of soda

2 tsp ground ginger

½ tsp salt

175 g/6 oz light muscovado sugar

225 g/8 oz carrots, grated

2 pieces stem ginger in syrup, drained and chopped

25 g/1 oz root (fresh) ginger, grated

60 g/2 oz seedless raisins

2 medium eggs, beaten

3 tbsp corn oil

juice of 1 medium orange

FROSTING

225 g/8 oz low-fat soft cheese

4 tbsp icing (confectioners') sugar

1 tsp vanilla essence (extract)

TO DECORATE

grated carrot

stem (fresh) ginger

ground ginger

1 Preheat the oven to 180°C/350°F/ Gas Mark 4. Grease and line a 20.5 cm/8 inch round cake tin with baking parchment.

2 Sift the flour, baking powder, bicarbonate of soda, ground ginger and salt into a bowl. Stir in the sugar, carrots, stem ginger, root (fresh) ginger and raisins. Beat together the eggs, oil and orange juice, then pour into the bowl. Mix the ingredients together well.

3 Spoon the mixture into the tin and bake in the oven for 1–1¼ hours until firm to the touch, or until a skewer inserted into the centre of the cake comes out clean.

4 To make the frosting, place the soft cheese in a bowl and beat to soften. Sift in the icing (confectioners') sugar and add the vanilla essence (extract). Mix well.

5 Remove the cake from the tin (pan) and smooth the frosting over the top. Decorate the cake and serve.

Crispy-Topped Fruit Bake

The sugar cubes give a lovely crunchy tasted to this easy-to-make pudding.

NUTRITIONAL INFORMATION

Calories 227	Sugars 30g	
Protein 5g	Fat 1g	
Carbohydrate . . .53g	Saturates 0.2g	

15 MINS   1 HOUR

SERVES 10

INGREDIENTS

350 g/12 oz cooking apples

3 tbsp lemon juice

300 g/10½ oz self-raising wholemeal (whole wheat) flour

½ tsp baking powder

1 tsp ground cinnamon, plus extra for dusting

175 g/6 oz prepared blackberries, thawed if frozen, plus extra to decorate

175 g/6 oz light muscovado sugar

1 medium egg, beaten

200 ml/7 fl oz/¾ cup low-fat natural fromage frais (unsweetened yogurt)

60 g/2 oz white or brown sugar cubes, lightly crushed

sliced eating (dessert) apple, to decorate

VARIATION

Try replacing the blackberries with blueberries. Use the canned or frozen variety if fresh blueberries are unavailable.

1 Preheat the oven to 190°C/375°F/Gas Mark 5. Grease and line a 900 g/2 lb loaf tin (pan). Core, peel and finely dice the apples. Place them in a saucepan with the lemon juice, bring to the boil, cover and simmer for 10 minutes until soft and pulpy. Beat well and set aside to cool.

2 Sift the flour, baking powder and 1 tsp cinnamon into a bowl, adding any husks that remain in the sieve. Stir in 115 g/4 oz blackberries and the sugar.

3 Make a well in the centre of the ingredients and add the egg, fromage frais (unsweetened yogurt) and cooled apple purée. Mix well to incorporate thoroughly. Spoon the mixture into the prepared loaf tin (pan) and smooth over the top.

4 Sprinkle with the remaining blackberries, pressing them down into the cake mixture, and top with the crushed sugar lumps. Bake for 40–45 minutes. Leave to cool in the tin (pan).

5 Remove the cake from the tin (pan) and peel away the lining paper. Serve dusted with cinnamon and decorated with extra blackberries and apple slices.

Banana & Lime Cake

A substantial cake that is ideal served for tea. The mashed bananas help to keep the cake moist, and the lime icing gives it extra zing and zest.

NUTRITIONAL INFORMATION

Calories	235	Sugars	........31g
Protein	.........5g	Fat	...........1g
Carbohydrate	...55g	Saturates	.....0.3g

  35 MINS   45 MINS

SERVES 10

INGREDIENTS

300 g/10½ oz plain (all-purpose) flour

1 tsp salt

1½ tsp baking powder

175 g/6 oz light muscovado sugar

1 tsp lime rind, grated

1 medium egg, beaten

1 medium banana, mashed with 1 tbsp lime juice

150 ml/5 fl oz/⅔ cup low-fat natural fromage frais (unsweetened yogurt)

115 g/4 oz sultanas

banana chips, to decorate

lime rind, finely grated, to decorate

TOPPING

115 g/4 oz icing (confectioners') sugar

1–2 tsp lime juice

½ tsp lime rind, finely grated

1 Preheat the oven to 180°C/350°F/Gas Mark 4. Grease and line a deep 18 cm/7 inch round cake tin with baking parchment.

2 Sift the flour, salt and baking powder into a mixing bowl and stir in the sugar and lime rind.

3 Make a well in the centre of the dry ingredients and add the egg, banana, fromage frais (unsweetened yogurt) and sultanas. Mix well until thoroughly incorporated.

4 Spoon the mixture into the tin and smooth the surface. Bake for 40–45 minutes until firm to the touch or until a skewer inserted in the centre comes out clean. Leave to cool for 10 minutes, then turn out on to a wire rack.

5 To make the topping, sift the icing (confectioners') sugar into a small bowl and mix with the lime juice to form a soft, but not too runny, icing. Stir in the grated lime rind. Drizzle the icing over the cake, letting it run down the sides.

6 Decorate the cake with banana chips and lime rind. Let the cake stand for 15 minutes so that the icing sets.

VARIATION

For a delicious alternative, replace the lime rind and juice with orange and the sultanas with chopped apricots.

Potato & Nutmeg Scones

Making these scones with mashed potato gives them a slightly different texture from traditional scones, but they are just as delicious.

NUTRITIONAL INFORMATION

Calories	178	Sugars	.........8g
Protein	.........4g	Fat	...........5g
Carbohydrate	...30g	Saturates	.......3g

15 MINS   30 MINS

MAKES 6

INGREDIENTS

250 g/8 oz floury (mealy) potatoes, diced

125 g/4½ oz/1 cup plain (all-purpose) flour

1½ tsp baking powder

½ tsp grated nutmeg

50 g/1¾ oz/⅓ cup sultanas (golden raisins)

1 egg, beaten

50 ml/2 fl oz/¼ cup double (heavy) cream

2 tsp light brown sugar

1 Line and lightly grease a baking tray (cookie sheet).

2 Cook the diced potatoes in a saucepan of boiling water for 10 minutes, or until soft. Drain thoroughly and mash the potatoes.

3 Transfer the mashed potatoes to a large mixing bowl and stir in the flour, baking powder and grated nutmeg, mixing well to combine.

4 Stir in the sultanas (golden raisins), beaten egg and cream and then beat the mixture thoroughly with a spoon until completely smooth.

5 Shape the mixture into 8 rounds 2 cm/¾ inch thick and put on the baking tray (cookie sheet).

6 Cook in a preheated oven, 200°C/400°F/Gas Mark 6, for about 15 minutes or until the scones have risen and are golden. Sprinkle with sugar and serve warm and spread with butter.

COOK'S TIP

For extra convenience, make a batch of scones in advance and open-freeze them. Thaw thoroughly and warm in a moderate oven when ready to serve.

Panforte di Siena

This famous Tuscan honey and nut cake is a Christmas speciality. In Italy it is sold in pretty boxes, and served in very thin slices.

NUTRITIONAL INFORMATION

Calories 257   Sugars 29g
Protein ....5g   Fat 13g
Carbohydrate ...33g   Saturates 1g

10 MINS   1¼ HOURS

SERVES 12

INGREDIENTS

125 g/4½ oz/1 cup split whole almonds

125 g/4½ oz/¾ cup hazelnuts

90 g/3 oz/½ cup cut mixed peel

60 g/2 oz/⅓ cup no-soak dried apricots

60 g/2 oz glacé or crystallized pineapple

grated rind of 1 large orange

60 g/2 oz/½ cup plain (all-purpose) flour

2 tbsp cocoa powder

2 tsp ground cinnamon

125 g/4½ oz/½ cup caster (superfine) sugar

175 g/6 oz/½ cup honey

icing (confectioners') sugar, for dredging

1 Toast the almonds under the grill (broiler) until lightly browned and place in a bowl.

2 Toast the hazelnuts until the skins split. Place on a dry tea towel (dish cloth) and rub off the skins. Roughly chop the hazelnuts and add to the almonds with the mixed peel.

3 Chop the apricots and pineapple fairly finely, add to the nuts with the orange rind and mix well.

4 Sift the flour with the cocoa and cinnamon, add to the nut mixture; mix.

5 Line a round 20 cm/8 inch cake tin or deep loose-based flan tin (pan) with baking parchment.

6 Put the sugar and honey into a saucepan and heat until the sugar dissolves, then boil gently for about 5 minutes or until the mixture thickens and begins to turn a deeper shade of brown. Quickly add to the nut mixture and mix evenly. Turn into the prepared tin (pan) and level the top using the back of a damp spoon.

7 Cook in a preheated oven, at 150°C/ 300°F/Gas Mark 2, for 1 hour. Remove from the oven and leave in the tin (pan) until cold. Take out of the tin (pan) and carefully peel off the paper. Before serving, dredge the cake heavily with sifted icing (confectioners') sugar. Serve in very thin slices.

Tuscan Pudding

These baked mini-ricotta puddings are delicious served warm or chilled and will keep in the refrigerator for 3–4 days.

NUTRITIONAL INFORMATION

Calories	293	Sugars	........28g
Protein	.........9g	Fat	..........17g
Carbohydrate	...28g	Saturates	.......9g

 20 MINS   15 MINS

SERVES 4

I N G R E D I E N T S

15 g/½ oz/1 tbsp butter

75 g/2¾ oz mixed dried fruit

250 g/9 oz ricotta cheese

3 egg yolks

50 g/1¾ oz caster (superfine) sugar

1 tsp cinnamon

finely grated rind of 1 orange,
   plus extra to decorate

crème fraîche (soured cream), to serve

1 Lightly grease 4 mini pudding basins or ramekin dishes with the butter.

2 Put the dried fruit in a bowl and cover with warm water. Leave to soak for 10 minutes.

COOK'S TIP

Crème fraîche (soured cream) has a slightly sour, nutty taste and is very thick. It is suitable for cooking, but has the same fat content as double (heavy) cream. It can be made by stirring cultured buttermilk into double (heavy) cream and refrigerating overnight.

3 Beat the ricotta cheese with the egg yolks in a bowl. Stir in the caster (superfine) sugar, cinnamon and orange rind and mix to combine.

4 Drain the dried fruit in a sieve set over a bowl. Mix the drained fruit with the ricotta cheese mixture.

5 Spoon the mixture into the basins or ramekin dishes.

6 Bake in a preheated oven, at 180°C/350°F/Gas Mark 4, for 15 minutes. The tops should be firm to the touch but not brown.

7 Decorate the puddings with grated orange rind. Serve warm or chilled with a dollop of crème fraîche (soured cream), if liked.

Pear & Ginger Cake

This deliciously buttery pear and ginger cake is ideal for tea-time or you can serve it with cream for a delicious dessert.

NUTRITIONAL INFORMATION

Calories 531	Sugars 41g	
Protein 6g	Fat 30g	
Carbohydrate . . .62g	Saturates 19g	

15 MINS   40 MINS

SERVES 6

INGREDIENTS

200 g/7 oz/14 tbsp unsalted butter, softened

175 g/6 oz caster (superfine) sugar

175 g/6 oz self-raising flour, sifted

3 tsp ginger

3 eggs, beaten

450 g/1 lb dessert (eating) pears, peeled, cored and thinly sliced

1 tbsp soft brown sugar

1 Lightly grease and line the base of a deep 20.5 cm/8 inch cake tin (pan).

2 Using a whisk, combine 175 g/6 oz of the butter with the sugar, flour, ginger and eggs and mix to form a smooth consistency.

3 Spoon the cake mixture into the prepared tin (pan), levelling out the surface.

4 Arrange the pear slices over the cake mixture. Sprinkle with the brown sugar and dot with the remaining butter.

5 Bake in a preheated oven, at 180°C/350°F/Gas Mark 4, for 35–40 minutes or until the cake is golden and feels springy to the touch.

6 Serve the pear and ginger cake warm, with ice cream or cream, if you wish.

COOK'S TIP

Soft, brown sugar is often known as Barbados sugar. It is a darker form of light brown soft sugar.

Zabaglione

This well-known dish is really a light but rich egg mousse flavoured with Marsala.

NUTRITIONAL INFORMATION

Calories ....158 Sugars 29g
Protein ....1g Fat 1g
Carbohydrate ...29g Saturates 0.2g

5 MINS   15 MINS

SERVES 4

I N G R E D I E N T S

5 egg yolks

100 g/3½ oz caster (superfine) sugar

150 ml/¼ pint/⅔ cup Marsala or
  sweet sherry

amaretti biscuits (cookies), to serve
  (optional)

1 Place the egg yolks in a large mixing bowl.

2 Add the caster (superfine) sugar to the egg yolks and whisk until the mixture is thick and very pale and has doubled in volume.

3 Place the bowl containing the egg yolk and sugar mixture over a saucepan of gently simmering water.

4 Add the Marsala or sherry to the egg yolk and sugar mixture and continue whisking until the foam mixture becomes warm. This process may take as long as 10 minutes.

5 Pour the mixture, which should be frothy and light, into 4 wine glasses.

6 Serve the zabaglione warm with fresh fruit or amaretti biscuits (cookies), if you wish.

Mascarpone Cheesecake

The mascarpone gives this baked cheesecake a wonderfully tangy flavour. Ricotta cheese could be used as an alternative.

NUTRITIONAL INFORMATION

Calories ....327 Sugars 25g
Protein ....9g Fat 18g
Carbohydrate ...33g Saturates 11g

 15 MINS   50 MINS

SERVES 8

I N G R E D I E N T S

50 g/1¾ oz/1½ tbsp unsalted butter

150 g/5½ oz ginger biscuits
(cookies), crushed

25 g/1 oz stem ginger (candied), chopped

500 g/1 lb 2 oz mascarpone cheese

finely grated rind and juice of 2 lemons

100 g/3½ oz caster (superfine) sugar

2 large eggs, separated

fruit coulis (see Cook's Tip), to serve

1 Grease and line the base of a 25 cm/10 inch spring-form cake tin (pan) or loose-bottomed tin (pan).

2 Melt the butter in a pan and stir in the crushed biscuits (cookies) and chopped ginger. Use the mixture to line the tin (pan), pressing the mixture about 6 mm/¼ inch up the sides.

COOK'S TIP

Fruit coulis can be made by cooking 400 g/14 oz fruit, such as blueberries, for 5 minutes with 2 tablespoons of water. Sieve the mixture, then stir in 1 tablespoon (or more to taste) of sifted icing (confectioners') sugar. Leave to cool before serving.

3 Beat together the cheese, lemon rind and juice, sugar and egg yolks until quite smooth.

4 Whisk the egg whites until they are stiff and fold into the cheese and lemon mixture.

5 Pour the mixture into the tin (pan) and bake in a preheated oven, at 180°C/350°F/Gas Mark 4, for 35–45 minutes until just set. Don't worry if it cracks or sinks – this is quite normal.

6 Leave the cheesecake in the tin (pan) to cool. Serve with fruit coulis (see Cook's Tip).

Chocolate Zabaglione

As this recipe only uses a little chocolate, choose one with a minimum of 70 per cent cocoa solids for a good flavour.

NUTRITIONAL INFORMATION

Calories 224   Sugars 23g
Protein . . . . .4g   Fat 10g
Carbohydrate . . .23g   Saturates 4g

10 MINS   5 MINS

SERVES 4

INGREDIENTS

4 egg yolks

50 g/1¾ oz/4 tbsp caster (superfine) sugar

50 g/1¾ oz dark chocolate

125 ml/4 fl oz/1 cup Marsala wine

cocoa powder, to dust

1 In a large glass mixing bowl, whisk together the egg yolks and caster (superfine) sugar until you have a very pale mixture, using electric beaters.

2 Grate the chocolate finely and fold into the egg mixture.

3 Fold the Marsala wine into the chocolate mixture.

4 Place the mixing bowl over a saucepan of gently simmering water and set the beaters on the lowest speed or swop to a balloon whisk. Cook gently, whisking continuously until the mixture thickens; take care not to overcook or the mixture will curdle.

5 Spoon the hot mixture into warmed individual glass dishes or coffe cups (as here) and dust with cocoa powder. Serve the zabaglione as soon as possible so that it is warm, light and fluffy.

COOK'S TIP

Make the dessert just before serving as it will separate if left to stand. If it begins to curdle, remove it from the heat immediately and place it in a bowl of cold water to stop the cooking. Whisk furiously until the mixture comes together.

Honey & Nut Nests

Pistachio nuts and honey are combined with crisp cooked angel-hair pasta in this unusual dessert.

10 MINS   1 HOUR

SERVES 4

I N G R E D I E N T S

225 g/8 oz angel-hair pasta

115 g/4 oz/8 tbsp butter

175 g/6 oz/1½ cups shelled pistachio nuts, chopped

115 g/4 oz/½ cup sugar

115 g/4 oz/⅓ cup clear honey

150 ml/¼ pint/⅔ cup water

2 tsp lemon juice

salt

Greek-style yogurt, to serve

1 Bring a large saucepan of lightly salted water to the boil. Add the angel hair pasta and cook for 8–10 minutes or until tender, but still firm to the bite. Drain the pasta and return to the pan. Add the butter and toss to coat the pasta thoroughly. Set aside to cool.

2 Arrange 4 small flan or poaching rings on a baking tray (cookie sheet). Divide the angel hair pasta into 8 equal quantities and spoon 4 of them into the rings. Press down lightly. Top the pasta with half of the nuts, then add the remaining pasta.

3 Bake in a preheated oven, at 180°C/350°F/Gas Mark 4, for 45 minutes, or until golden brown.

4 Meanwhile, put the sugar, honey and water in a saucepan and bring to the boil over a low heat, stirring constantly until the sugar has dissolved completely. Simmer for 10 minutes, add the lemon juice and simmer for 5 minutes.

5 Using a palette knife (spatula), carefully transfer the angel hair nests to a serving dish. Pour over the honey syrup, sprinkle over the remaining nuts and set aside to cool completely before serving. Serve the Greek-style yogurt separately.

COOK'S TIP

Angel-hair pasta is also known as *capelli d'angelo*. Long and very fine, it is usually sold in small bunches that already resemble nests.

Quick Tiramisu

This quick version of one of the most popular Italian desserts is ready in minutes.

NUTRITIONAL INFORMATION

Calories 387	Sugars 17g	
Protein 9g	Fat 28g	
Carbohydrate ...22g	Saturates 15g	

15 MINS   0 MINS

SERVES 4

INGREDIENTS

225 g/8 oz/1 cup mascarpone or full-fat
   soft cheese

1 egg, separated

2 tbsp natural yogurt

2 tbsp caster (superfine) sugar

2 tbsp dark rum

2 tbsp strong black coffee

8 sponge fingers (lady-fingers)

2 tbsp grated dark chocolate

1 Put the cheese in a large bowl, add the egg yolk and yogurt and beat until smooth.

2 Whisk the egg white until stiff but not dry, then whisk in the sugar and carefully fold into the cheese mixture.

COOK'S TIP

Mascarpone is an Italian soft cream cheese made from cow's milk. It has a rich, silky smooth texture and a deliciously creamy flavour. It can be eaten as it is with fresh fruits or flavoured with coffee or chocolate.

3 Spoon half of the mixture into 4 sundae glasses.

4 Mix together the rum and coffee in a shallow dish. Dip the sponge fingers (lady-fingers) into the rum mixture, break them in half, or into smaller pieces if necessary, and divide among the glasses.

5 Stir any remaining coffee mixture into the remaining cheese and spoon over the top.

6 Sprinkle with grated chocolate. Serve immediately or chill until required.

Raspberry Fusilli

This is the ultimate in self-indulgence – a truly delicious dessert that tastes every bit as good as it looks.

NUTRITIONAL INFORMATION

Calories ....235 Sugars 20g
Protein ....7g Fat 7g
Carbohydrate ...36g Saturates 1g

5 MINS   20 MINS

SERVES 4

INGREDIENTS

175 g/6 oz/½ cup fusilli

700 g/1 lb 9 oz/4 cups raspberries

2 tbsp caster (superfine) sugar

1 tbsp lemon juice

4 tbsp flaked (slivered) almonds

3 tbsp raspberry liqueur

1 Bring a large saucepan of lightly salted water to the boil. Add the fusilli and cook for 8–10 minutes until tender, but still firm to the bite. Drain the fusilli thoroughly, return to the pan and set aside to cool.

2 Using a spoon, firmly press 225 g/8 oz/1⅓ cups of the raspberries through a sieve (strainer) set over a large mixing bowl to form a smooth purée (paste).

3 Put the raspberry purée (paste) and sugar in a small saucepan and simmer over a low heat, stirring occasionally, for 5 minutes.

4 Stir in the lemon juice and set the sauce aside until required.

5 Add the remaining raspberries to the fusilli in the pan and mix together well. Transfer the raspberry and fusilli mixture to a serving dish.

6 Spread the almonds out on a baking tray (cookie sheet) and toast under the grill (broiler) until golden brown. Remove and set aside to cool slightly.

7 Stir the raspberry liqueur into the reserved raspberry sauce and mix together well until very smooth. Pour the raspberry sauce over the fusilli, sprinkle over the toasted almonds and serve.

VARIATION

You could use any sweet, ripe berry for making this dessert. Strawberries and blackberries are especially suitable, combined with the correspondingly flavoured liqueur. Alternatively, you could use a different berry mixed with the fusilli, but still pour over raspberry sauce.

Peaches & Mascarpone

If you prepare these in advance, all you have to do is pop the peaches on the barbecue (grill) when you are ready to serve them.

NUTRITIONAL INFORMATION

Calories	301	Sugars	....24g
Protein	....6g	Fat	....20g
Carbohydrate	...24g	Saturates	....9g

 10 MINS   10 MINS

SERVES 4

I N G R E D I E N T S

4 peaches

175 g/6 oz mascarpone cheese

40 g/1½ oz pecan or walnuts, chopped

1 tsp sunflower oil

4 tbsp maple syrup

1 Cut the peaches in half and remove the stones. If you are preparing this recipe in advance, press the peach halves together again and wrap them in cling film (plastic wrap) until required.

2 Mix the mascarpone and pecan or walnuts together in a small bowl until well combined. Leave to chill in the refrigerator until required.

VARIATION

You can use nectarines instead of peaches for this recipe. Remember to choose ripe but firm fruit which won't go soft and mushy when it is barbecued (grilled). Prepare the nectarines in the same way as the peaches and barbecue (grill) for 5–10 minutes.

3 To serve, brush the peaches with a little oil and place on a rack set over medium hot coals. Barbecue (grill) for 5–10 minutes, turning once, until hot.

4 Transfer the peaches to a serving dish and top with the mascarpone mixture.

5 Drizzle the maple syrup over the peaches and mascarpone filling and serve at once.

Vanilla Ice Cream

This home-made version of real vanilla ice cream is absolutely delicious and so easy to make. A tutti-frutti variation is also provided.

NUTRITIONAL INFORMATION

Calories 626	Sugars 33g
Protein 7g	Fat 53g
Carbohydrate ...33g	Saturates 31g

5 MINS   15 MINS

SERVES 6

INGREDIENTS

600 ml/1 pint/2½ cups double
  (heavy) cream

1 vanilla pod

pared rind of 1 lemon

4 eggs, beaten

2 egg yolks

175 g/6 oz caster (superfine) sugar

1 Place the cream in a heavy-based saucepan and heat gently, whisking.

2 Add the vanilla pod, lemon rind, eggs and egg yolks to the pan and heat until the mixture reaches just below boiling point.

3 Reduce the heat and cook for 8–10 minutes, whisking the mixture continuously, until thickened.

VARIATION

For tutti frutti ice cream, soak 100 g/3½ oz mixed dried fruit in 2 tbsp Marsala or sweet sherry for 20 minutes. Follow the method for vanilla ice cream, omitting the vanilla pod, and stir in the Marsala or sherry-soaked fruit in step 6, just before freezing.

4 Stir the sugar into the cream mixture, set aside and leave to cool.

5 Strain the cream mixture through a sieve (strainer).

6 Slit open the vanilla pod, scoop out the tiny black seeds and stir them into the cream.

7 Pour the mixture into a shallow freezing container with a lid and freeze overnight until set. Serve the ice cream when required.

Florentines

These luxury biscuits (cookies) will be popular at any time of the year, but make a particularly wonderful treat at Christmas.

NUTRITIONAL INFORMATION

Calories 186	Sugars 19g
Protein 2g	Fat 11g
Carbohydrate ...22g	Saturates 5g

🍰 20 MINS   🕐 15 MINS

MAKES 10

I N G R E D I E N T S

50 g/1¾ oz/ 10 tsp butter

50 g/1¾ oz/¼ cup caster (superfine) sugar

25 g/1 oz/¼ cup plain (all-purpose) flour, sieved (strained)

50 g/1¾ oz/⅓ cup almonds, chopped

50 g/1¾ oz/⅓ cup chopped mixed peel

25 g/1 oz/¼ cup raisins, chopped

25 g/1 oz/2 tbsp glacé (candied) cherries, chopped

finely grated rind of ½ lemon

125 g/4½ oz dark chocolate, melted

1 Line 2 large baking trays (cookie sheets) with baking parchment.

2 Heat the butter and caster (superfine) sugar in a small saucepan until the butter has just melted and the sugar dissolved. Remove the pan from the heat.

3 Stir in the flour and mix well. Stir in the chopped almonds, mixed peel, raisins, cherries and lemon rind. Place teaspoonfuls of the mixture well apart on the baking trays (cookie sheets).

4 Bake in a preheated oven, at 180°C/ 350°F/Gas Mark 4, for 10 minutes or until lightly golden.

5 As soon as the florentines are removed from the oven, press the edges into neat shapes while still on the baking trays (cookie sheets), using a biscuit (cookie) cutter. Leave to cool on the baking trays (cookie sheets) until firm, then transfer to a wire rack to cool completely.

6 Spread the melted chocolate over the smooth side of each florentine. As the chocolate begins to set, mark wavy lines in it with a fork. Leave the florentines until set, chocolate side up.

VARIATION

Replace the dark chocolate with white chocolate or, for a dramatic effect, cover half of the florentines in dark chocolate and half in white.

Summer Puddings

A wonderful mixture of summer fruits encased in slices of white bread which soak up all the deep red, flavoursome juices.

NUTRITIONAL INFORMATION

Calories 250	Sugars 41g	
Protein 4g	Fat 4g	
Carbohydrate . . .53g	Saturates 2g	

 10 MINS   10 MINS

SERVES 6

I N G R E D I E N T S

vegetable oil or butter, for greasing

6–8 thin slices white bread, crusts removed

175 g/6 oz/¾ cup caster (superfine) sugar

300 ml/½ pint/1¼ cups water

225 g/8 oz/2 cups strawberries

500 g/1 lb 2 oz/2½ cups raspberries

175 g/6 oz/1¼ cups black-
  and/or redcurrants

175 g/6 oz/¾ cup blackberries
  or loganberries

mint sprigs, to decorate

pouring cream, to serve

1 Grease six 150 ml/¼ pint/⅔ cup moulds (molds) with butter or oil.

2 Line the moulds (molds) with the bread, cutting it so it fits snugly.

3 Place the sugar in a saucepan with the water and heat gently, stirring frequently until dissolved, then bring to the boil and boil for 2 minutes.

4 Reserve 6 large strawberries for decoration. Add half the raspberries and the rest of the fruits to the syrup, cutting the strawberries in half if large, and simmer gently for a few minutes, until beginning to soften but still retaining their shape.

5 Spoon the fruits and some of the liquid into moulds (molds). Cover with more slices of bread. Spoon a little juice around the sides of the moulds (molds) so the bread is well soaked. Cover with a saucer and a heavy weight, leave to cool, then chill thoroughly, preferably overnight.

6 Process the remaining raspberries in a food processor or blender, or press through a non-metallic strainer. Add enough of the liquid from the fruits to give a coating consistency.

7 Turn on to serving plates and spoon the raspberry sauce over. Decorate with the mint sprigs and reserved strawberries and serve with cream.

Chocolate Cheesecake

This cheesecake takes a little time to prepare and cook but is well worth the effort. It is quite rich and is good served with a little fresh fruit.

NUTRITIONAL INFORMATION

Calories . . . . .471 Sugars 20g
Protein . . . . .10g Fat 33g
Carbohydrate . . .28g Saturates 5g

15 MINS   1¼ HOURS

SERVES 12

I N G R E D I E N T S

100 g/3½ oz/¾ cup plain (all-purpose) flour

100 g/3½ oz/¾ cup ground almonds

200 g/7 oz/¾ cup demerara
    (brown crystal) sugar

150 g/5½ oz/11 tbsp margarine

675 g/1½ lb firm tofu (bean curd)

175 ml/6 fl oz/¾ cup vegetable oil

125 ml/4 fl oz/½ cup orange juice

175 ml/6 fl oz/¾ cup brandy

50 g/1¾ oz/6 tbsp cocoa powder,
    (unsweetened cocoa), plus extra
    to decorate

2 tsp almond essence (extract)

icing (confectioners') sugar
    and Cape gooseberries (ground cherries),
    to decorate

COOK'S TIP

Cape gooseberries (ground cherries) make an attractive decoration for many desserts. Peel open the papery husks to expose the bright orange fruits.

1 Put the flour, ground almonds and 1 tablespoon of the sugar in a bowl and mix well. Rub the margarine into the mixture to form a dough.

2 Lightly grease and line the base of a 23 cm/9 inch springform tin (pan). Press the dough into the base of the tin (pan) to cover, pushing the dough right up to the edge of the tin (pan).

3 Roughly chop the tofu (bean curd) and put in a food processor with the vegetable oil, orange juice, brandy, cocoa powder (unsweetened cocoa) almond essence and remaining sugar and process until smooth and creamy. Pour over the base in the tin (pan) and cook in a preheated oven, 160°C/325°F/ Gas Mark 3, for 1–1¼ hours, or until set.

4 Leave to cool in the tin (pan) for 5 minutes, then remove from the tin (pan) and chill in the refrigerator. Dust with icing (confectioners') sugar and cocoa powder (unsweetened cocoa). Decorate with Cape gooseberries (ground cherries) and serve.

Char-Cooked Pineapple

Fresh pineapple slices are cooked on the barbecue (grill), and brushed with a buttery fresh ginger and brown sugar baste.

NUTRITIONAL INFORMATION

Calories 461	Sugars 44g	
Protein 5g	Fat 30g	
Carbohydrate . . .45g	Saturates 20g	

10 MINS   10 MINS

SERVES 4

I N G R E D I E N T S

1 fresh pineapple

B U T T E R

125 g/4½ oz/½ cup butter

90 g/3 oz/½ cup light muscovado sugar

1 tsp finely grated root ginger

T O P P I N G

225 g/8 oz/1 cup natural fromage frais

½ tsp ground cinnamon

1 tbsp light muscovado sugar

1 Prepare the fresh pineapple by cutting off the spiky top. Peel the pineapple with a sharp knife, remove the 'eyes' and cut the flesh into thick slices.

2 To make the ginger-flavoured butter, put the butter, sugar and ginger into a small saucepan and heat gently until melted. Transfer to a heatproof bowl and keep warm at the side of the barbecue (grill), ready for basting the fruit.

3 To prepare the topping, mix together the fromage frais, cinnamon and sugar. Cover and chill until ready to serve.

4 Barbecue (grill) the pineapple slices for about 2 minutes on each side, brushing them well with the ginger butter baste.

5 Serve the charcooked pineapple with a little extra ginger butter sauce poured over. Top with a spoonful of the spiced fromage frais.

VARIATION

If you prefer, substitute ½ teaspoon ground ginger for the grated root ginger. Light muscovado sugar gives the best flavour, but you can use ordinary soft brown sugar instead. You can make this dessert indoors by cooking the pineapple under a hot grill (broiler).

Italian Chocolate Truffles

These are flavoured with almonds and chocolate, and are simplicity itself to make. Served with coffee, they are the perfect end to a meal.

NUTRITIONAL INFORMATION

Calories 82	Sugars 7g
Protein 1g	Fat 5g
Carbohydrate 8g	Saturates 3g

 5 MINS   5 MINS

MAKES 24

I N G R E D I E N T S

175 g/6 oz dark chocolate

2 tbsp almond-flavoured liqueur (amaretto)
  or orange-flavoured liqueur

40 g/1½ oz/3 tbsp unsalted butter

50 g/1¾ oz icing (confectioners') sugar

50 g/1¾ oz/½ cup ground almonds

50 g/1¾ oz grated milk chocolate

1 Melt the dark chocolate with the liqueur in a bowl set over a saucepan of hot water, stirring until well combined.

2 Add the butter and stir until it has melted. Stir in the icing (confectioners') sugar and the ground almonds.

3 Leave the mixture in a cool place until firm enough to roll into 24 balls.

4 Place the grated chocolate on a plate and roll the truffles in the chocolate to coat them.

5 Place the truffles in paper sweet (candy) cases and chill.

Index